SILENT HEROES

FINAL FLIGHTS OF THE MIGHTY EIGHTH

James Clements, Editor
John W. Gumpper, Illustrator
William Ellis, Computer Coordinator
Stephen Heasley, A.P. European History Instructor

"Those who have long enjoyed such privileges as we enjoy forget in time that men have died to win them."
Franklin D. Roosevelt

Cover Lithograph by

Gregg Thompson

P.O. Box 2341

Mission Viejo, CA 92690

Prints of cover lithograph are available by contacting Mr. Thompson at the above address.

(About the Front Cover)

"The Piggy-Back Flight"

Gregg M. Thompson, Artist

31 Dec. 1944. While returning from a bombing raid over Hamburg, Germany, two B-17s from the "Bloody 100th" bomb group collided in mid air. The two stuck together as machine guns and propellers punctured the aluminum skins of the two aircraft. Glenn Rojohn, the pilot of the upper aircraft, and his copilot, William Leek, continued to fly both aircraft long enough for 12 men to bail out of the two planes. Rojohn and Leek crash landed the two planes in a field in Germany and walked away from the wreckage.

Mr. Rojohn's actual narrative can be found on page 139 of this book.

New Horizon Publishing

129 W. Neshannock Ave.

New Wilmington, PA 16142

1-800-995-7746

ISBN #1-884687-07-5

Library of Congress #97-066097

THE GOLDEN TORNADO FOUNDATION

This book was made possible by a grant from The Golden Tornado Foundation, Inc. Proceeds from its sale will go to the Foundation.

Founded in 1990, The Golden Tornado Foundation, Inc. is a nonprofit publicly supported organization whose activities span a wide range of cultural, educational, and recreational projects. The Foundation supports the Butler Area School District in improvement projects which foster an enhanced quality of life for area students, residents, and visitors. Examples of these improvement projects include: a student loan fund, mini-grants for educators, support of the Butler Senior High Stadium and the new Stadium Annex. Each year The Golden Tornado Foundation initiates programs to generate private gifts to support such projects. The Foundation is recognized and approved by the Bureau of Charitable Organizations.

Additional copies of *Silent Heroes Among Us* may be purchased by contacting the:

Harriger Educational Services Center
167 New Castle Road
Butler, PA 16001
(412) 287-8721

Special Thanks To:

Todd Ellis
Computer Technical Director

Kevin Tritch
Assistant Computer Technical Director

Student Typists:

Shannon Crawford, Donald Crimbchin, Chas Dumbaugh, Jonathan Eichner, Jenn Geibel, Mike George, Theresa Henry, Rachel Hinterlang, Dave Hoovler, Steve Hornyak, Scott MacMaster, Eric McKinnis, Steve Mekis, Matthew Slater, Patty Thalhofer, Kris Toft

Table of Contents

Flight Crew Members and Authors

Ground Crew and Support Personnel and Authors

PREFACE

What makes a hero? Recently 128 persons reached across two generations and found the answer. In doing so they captured something precious which would have soon been lost. The result is what you are holding - a book about living, love, devotion, honor, and patriotism told by those who lived it and interpreted and transcribed from the unique vantage point of those two generations removed.

(The Beginning)

It began with a phone call. I teach high-school English, and was a bit surprised several summers ago when "Hap" Nicholas, a neighbor of mine, called. "I'd like your input on something," he said. "Can you come over this afternoon?" I was busy at the time and almost put off his invitation, but there was something in the vagueness of his request and the tone of his voice...

Later in his living room "Hap" told me a part of his past - a past of which I was completely unaware. He said, "I was a navigator on a B-24 in the waning days of World War II." He and the other nine members of his crew had flown twenty-one missions. "Hap" also revealed that he was the co-founder of the Western Pennsylvania Wing of the Eighth Air Force Historical Society. He concluded by saying, "Our ranks are thinning. I thought you might have an idea or two for some sort of memorial - something we could leave for future generations."

I really didn't know what to say. I was younger than "Hap", and admitted that I had never heard of the Eighth Air Force.

"Well..." he finally said in obvious disappointment, "then you really don't have any idea for a memorial."

While groping for an answer, I asked him to explain what a navigator on a bomber did.

"Hap" mulled this over for several moments and then slowly began. As he continued, his voice became animated, and his words flowed more easily. During his explanation he recalled an event which illustrated one duty, then another, and another. For the next twenty minutes Hap actually was back on his B-24 as a twenty-year-old navigator. His face glowed with excitement as the names of long-ago places, friends, and events poured forth.

I didn't notice the time slip by. When he was done I realized I had been mesmerized. I now saw "Hap" as an entirely different person - a man who had faced death for his country. I thought of the many others like "Hap" who had never related to anyone what they had done.

"You know," I finally said, "I don't think a memorial in stone or metal could convey or capture what you and your fellow crewmen did. It needs to be documented... How about a book as a memorial? A book's message will last as long as someone somewhere keeps a copy. Lots of books last hundreds of years."

There was a long silence. "Who would write it?" "Hap" asked.

"My students would." There was another long pause.

"Hap" looked hard at me. "Do you really think they could?"

I looked steadily back at him. "I not only think they could; I know they could."

And they did!

(The Project)

It's taken us two years, a lot of searching, trial, and error. While other books of reminiscences have been written concerning World War II, this one is very different.

There have been numerous positive experiences for the students, parents, and the veterans involved.

First, it gave my students something meaningful to write about. Literature is basically the passing on of events, feelings and emotions from one person and/or time to another. From the beginning the students knew that in a relatively short period this material would be lost forever, and that they had the skills to document and preserve it. We called the project *"Operation Immortality."*

Secondly, the project bridged generations. The veterans met some very fine young persons. They found that the hopes, emotions, and desires of these young people were much the same as those to which they once aspired.

Students also formed closer ties with their parents who in many cases unselfishly took hours to help drive hundreds of miles over the Western Pennsylvania area in order to obtain first-hand accounts. Sometimes they even sat in on the interviews and came away with as much of a new appreciation of history and patriotism as their sons or daughters.

And finally, and most importantly, it gave these young people the opportunity to meet some real heroes - those who put their lives on the line for our country, and never said much about those experiences for over fifty years. When the material had been collected, when the stories were all told, the students agreed that the title was obvious because these men and women truly have been - **Silent Heroes Among Us.**

(Acknowledgements)

When my friend and noted illustrator John Gumpper learned of the project, he asked if he could be of any assistance. I jumped at his offer. John's beautiful renderings of the planes of the period enhance part of the cover and the section-divider pages. For John this was a labor of love. He had been trained to fly P-51 Mustang fighters and was on his way to the Pacific when Japan surrendered. (The rumor was the Japanese gave up when they heard he was coming.)

I would like to thank "Hap" Nicholas and the members of the Western Pennsylvania Wing of the Eighth Air Force Historical Society and their wives for their cooperation and hospitality. They opened their homes and their hearts to these young people and made this all possible. In some cases veterans shared not only their memories but refreshments and meals. Students also returned from some interviews with souvenirs such as: .50 caliber shells, models, silk survival maps, insignia patches, personal papers, and most remarkably photos. When these pictures began to turn up, we realized that they would be wonderful additions to the stories. As a result the book contains over one hundred never-before published photos from various veterans' collections. *(Special thanks to Tom Brown for the use of his extensive album.)*

I would also like to give special thanks to the following: The Golden Tornado Foundation, Inc. of Butler for underwriting the cost of the book; Dr. Michael Strutt and Mike Kelly for their support; my wife Charlotte who helped proofread and put up with my cantankerous moods as the book progressed; Dick Steinlechner and the folks at Globe Printing for their technical expertise and encouragement; Stephen Heasley for allowing the members of his A.P. European History class to participate in this project; William Ellis for his computer expertise; the members of the A.P. physics class for their time and talent on the computers and especially three students - Todd Ellis, Kevin Tritch, and David Hoovler; and to all the students' parents for their support and encouragement.

Lastly I'd like to thank the students who participated this year and last in *"Operation Immortality."* They had enough faith in themselves and the project to see it through. To them I say, *"Congratulations - a work well done! Mission completed."*

James Clements, Editor

FLIGHT CREW MEMBERS

© John Gumpper

"The Allied Air Force achieved the impossible."

General Dwight Eisenhower,

Supreme Allied Commander in Europe.

Leroy Bloom

448th Bomb Group (H)
712th Squadron
Radio Operator

by
Rachel Crider

Leroy Bloom was a shoe salesman at Gimbles before enlisting with a friend in the Army. He had refused to enlist until the Army promised to allow him to join the Air Corps, not realizing that after he joined they could send him anywhere they wanted to. The next day he and his friend quit Gimbles. The company treated them well when it learned they had joined the Army. They were given their pay for the rest of the week, the next week, and all the paid vacation they had. This was on a Monday. He and his friend remained together through a good part of their training until Leroy went to radio school and his friend went to armory school. The greatest experience Leroy had in training was flying with movie star Jimmy Stewart.

We went to Keil, Germany. When we came back I developed a toothache. Now they have a rule in the Air Force that if you have a toothache, no fillings - pull the tooth because if they fill it wrong and you're up in high attitudes, you can develop an abscess. You would be in so much pain the pilot would have to turn the plane around and return to base. So I was sent into the hospital to have the tooth pulled.

While I was in the hospital another man took my place as radio operator. They were to go on a mission the next morning. In the morning I heard the planes getting ready. I ran down to the field, but my crew had already taken off. So I went with another crew whose radio officer had gotten sick. I saw my plane flying away from the formation. I didn't know why it was flying away but we never heard from it again.

Now I had no plane crew to fly with. About four or five days later some new people arrived. I was in the Operations' Office. This lieutenant was told they would have to find a crew for him. I liked his looks, so I went to him and volunteered to be his radio man. An engineer, a navigator, two waist gunners, and a combination ball-turret tail gunner volunteered also. Now we had a seven-member crew. After about six missions we were made a deputy lead. We flew to the right of the lead ship. After about ten missions we became a lead ship. After about fifteen to seventeen missions we became a group and wing leader.

The engineer on the plane had a first cousin who lived in London. About six weeks after he disappeared, when we did not receive word from the Swedish Embassy, I gathered some of his clothing we had already turned in and got a pass and went to London. I found the address (of the cousin) and went there.

About eight or nine months later, I saw a picture in "Stars and Stripes." I looked at it closely, got a magnifying glass, and it was my former ball-turret gunner. It said, "U.S. Crew Coming Off A Plane." I took it into the Operations' officer. They put it under big glasses and determined it was our missing crew. Apparently they had reported in, but the American Embassy had messed up and never reported it to Eighth Air Force Headquarters.

In November of 1944 the maintenance crew came to us in late evening and told us they were stripping our plane of all our guns, and we were going on a mission without guns. The pilot told us we were going to Sweden to pick up a crew. They kept it quiet.

We flew into Stockholm in the middle of the night, no lights, no guns, nothing.

That was Swedish rules - come in without guns. We landed and picked up two crews, one of which was my old crew. We brought them back. After we got them to the bunk house, they told me all kinds of wild stories of how good life was in Sweden. Then my pilot came in and told them I only had one more mission to reach thirty and be able to go home. But they were here for the duration. I returned home by December 8,1944 after completing one more mission.

On December 31, 1944, Leroy Bloom was married to his long-time sweetheart. He returned to Gimbles, where he became a radio/television salesman. Eventually he moved to Chicago for a time to work in the radio and television industry. He and his wife raised and put through college three children, all of whom are successful in their chosen fields. His most memorable experience, once he retired, was being allowed to fly in a B-24 Liberator for free. Leroy is very active in veterans' groups. He loves law and is the only judge advocate on the state level and one of three on the local level in the history of the Jewish War Veterans Association of the U.S.A. who is not a member of the bar. He presently serves on the Association's National Executive Committee. He is also a member of the board of directors of the National Museum of Jewish Military History in Washington, D.C. and a vice-chairman of the Allegheny County Commissioners Veterans' Advisory Council.

P-51 Mustang with M.P. Quonset huts in the background at Fowlmere Airbase.
(Photo courtesy Tom Brown)

Arden Bomeli

487th Bomb Group
837th Squadron
Pilot

by
Joe Sobieralski

On a brisk day in early November, in a beautiful home in Pittsburgh, a bespectacled World War II veteran sat down to discuss memories of his tour of duty. It was evident that it was the first formal interview he had experienced on the subject; he constantly glanced at the model planes which were strewn across the dining room table. As the interview progressed the former B-17 "Flying Fortress" pilot became more at ease, but only after the tape recorder was turned off was he able to truly relax. The candid and insightful way he spoke made the chill of the autumn breeze dissipate into a feeling of warmth. He told the story of his third mission.

It was February 3, 1945. I was hoping for a milk run, but we were up a bit early that morning; so we could assume it was going to be a long day and an eastern target. Sure enough, when we walked into the auditorium for briefing, and I had taken a seat, I looked up at the ceiling to a map of Germany. There it was, a trip to Berlin. Nice!

We were a green crew. Too dumb and numb to be completely frightened, and so we listened to the colonel and his aides. Finally the colonel gave us his parting shot. "I want every bomb in Berlin." I think we had the third best bomb record in our division, but I have been known to be wrong. Anyhow, we were on to the truck to the hardstand where "My Gal Ellen," my plane, was waiting for us. No matter what happened, they always had that plane ready to fly. I remember when we were assigned to "My Gal." The head of the ground crew said to us, "I've never lost a plane or crew. Don't mess up my plane." We all "Yes sired" him. I had always felt good that they had never lost a plane or crew.

Anyhow, we were finally all in the plane, two in the nose, myself and my navigator in our pilots' seats, five more in the waist until we were airborne; then they would go to the ball, tail, top turret and radio room. We started the engines, and went to the head of the runway, and waited our turn to take off. Then we were in the air, in the formation. Then it was onto group, wing, division and finally the whole Eighth. The mission was a maximum effort of the twenty-two groups that comprised the Eighth Air Force. That day, our group, the 487th, was to be the sixteenth group into the target. We thought, "Maybe that would be good [because] the Germans might run out of ammunition for their anti-aircrafters. No such luck.

Finally after one-and-a-half hours we left the coast of England. We went across the North Sea and to the narrow opening of the Zeidder-Zee that the Germans allowed the bombers flak free. I never understood why they allowed these so-called corridors, but they did. Everything was going along smoothly.

We were far enough east into Germany that we could've gone back, dropped our bombs in the North Sea, and still got credit for a completed mission. But we didn't. The colonel said at the briefing that he wanted all bombs on Berlin. Remember, I said earlier that we were a green crew, dumb and numb. That we were, and perhaps stupid, too. With the colonel's admonition, I polled the crew, reminding all that we could go on or turn back and still get credit for a completed mission. Well, no one wanted to admit that we were chicken, so we all agreed to go on.

We were having trouble keeping up with our group. We were dropping back and losing altitude to boot. But we were getting closer to Berlin. Finally we were with the last of the twenty-two groups, the square D, also known as the 100th Group, the German's favorite target. It was the 100th who fired on the Me 109s, when in trouble with their gear down. As was known on both sides, when an American bomber was in the trouble and lowered the landing gear, the German fighters would escort the bomber to a German airfield, rather than complete the shooting down of the crippled plane. The 100th violated the trust, and they became the target of the German Luftwaffe.

We had reached the I.P. and opened our bomb bay door. At that point the bombers decided to hit the northwest corner of Berlin. I corrected our path to the left. In the meantime the 100th went to the heart of Berlin. We crossed the lake on the western approach to Berlin. Bombs were dropped. After a minute and approximately twenty seconds we saw the bombs hit the northwest residential area of Berlin.

After bombs away, I went to the rally point, up to twenty-six thousand feet. At the rally point we met the 100th coming away from the target and started our journey back to home base. Now relieved of the bomb load and the spent gas, the three engines did not labor as hard or use the additional fuel that it would when four engines operate smoothly. Still, the three engines guzzled more fuel than normal. But there we were flying "tail-end Charley" with the 100th Group. Nothing

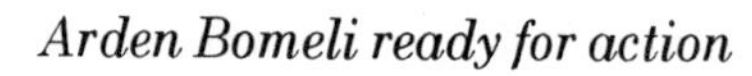

Arden Bomeli ready for action

(Photo Courtesy Arden Bomeli)

unusual was happening. We were on course. A watch was kept for fighters.

We were a little over halfway out of Germany when the 100th turned left, away from course. At that point we were alone and on our own. As time passed we wanted to be sure of our location in Germany and decided to fly directly toward a flak area. I was called and told that as soon as I saw flak in five to seven minutes to take a zero heading for five minutes and then resume a course westerly with a two-degree correction to the left of our present course. Sure enough, in five minutes there was the flak as I had expected. We then knew our location in Germany. After five minutes we resumed our westerly course with the two-degree correction which would ultimately take us out of Germany - just below Denmark, between Denmark and Helogalund Island for our exit across the North Sea to England.

At this point we were feeling quite good about the mission, although this feeling was not going to the last that long. Time went on. We were perhaps thirty to forty miles from the coast when I noticed we were running low on fuel. We were perhaps seventy or eighty miles from England, but only forty from Sweden. If we stopped in Sweden the crew's war would be over. We needed to get to England. To take the strain off the three engines, we decided to cut some power and glide to England. We lost five hundred feet per minute in altitude, and when we reached the coast of England we were flying at four thousand feet. We landed at the first air field for gas. As it was, where we picked up the gas, we were only six miles from base. When we landed we had seventy-five gallons of gas left. We also got a chewing out by our operations officer!

After the war Mr. Bomeli became a dentist and later opened a practice. He has since retired, but volunteers for a number of groups in the Pittsburgh area. In his spare time he considers himself a "computer hobbyist," and recently he and his wife enrolled in a computer course at a local college. He is a very gracious and young-hearted man.

(Photo Courtesy Arden Bomeli)

Charles H. Booth, Jr.

458th Bomb Group (H)
Pilot

by
Todd Madden

On April 21, 1996 I set out to meet Charles H. Booth Jr., a retired colonel of the United States Air Force. Around two o' clock a rather tall, strong-looking man walked through the doors of King's Restaurant. He and his wife sat down at a table close by me. A few minutes later the same man walked over and said, "Todd Madden? Hello, I'm Charles Booth." I couldn't help but notice the radiance and excitement that shown in his eyes.

As a kid I always wanted to be a pilot, so when I was sixteen I set out to and received my pilot's license. I used to do all sorts of crazy things [in the air] back then because there weren't very many people in the air or that had pilot's licenses. I would fly under bridges and do rolls and lots of other things. When Germany invaded Poland, I knew that soon we would be involved. Anyways, I decided that I was going to enlist in the Canadian Air Force. When my father heard this, he said, "You dumb S.O.B. why don't you enlist in the United States Army Air Force." That's what it was called back then, "The Army Air Force," not just "The Air Force." In July, 1941 I went down, got my physical, and enlisted in the United States Army Air Force. I was called to active duty as a Flying Cadet in December, 1941. I wanted to be a fighter pilot just like everyone else. So I went through a school, training in PTs, BTs, and ATs. When we finished the training, last names A-H became bomber pilots, and the rest became fighter pilots. That's pretty democratic huh? (Laughs softly.)

When I was sent overseas, I was stationed at Horsham Saint Faith. It is in Norwich, England, about one hundred miles north of London. We were under the command of James H. Isabell, a West Point graduate who acted as a father-figure to many of us, although he was not much older than most of the guys. We couldn't have been more fortunate. The base we were stationed at was a permanent base, meaning it was like a hotel. We had assigned rooms and didn't have to travel from base to base. To get to the luxurious base that we were at, we had to fly B-24 Liberators to Africa. Instead of flying directly over the North Atlantic, we had to take the long route due to terrible weather conditions over the Atlantic.

While being stationed in Norwich, I met mostly English people. Every mission you went on, you knew that you were supposed to drop bombs, and they would inevitably explode and kill someone. But this was our job, so we did it. We couldn't wait to get back to the base. In our early missions, the fighter planes could only escort us so far [due to small fuel tanks], so we used to say that the Luftwaffe would escort us the rest of the way to our target. While on these missions, I learned to become tremendously God fearing. Every time we were up in the air I'd be praying that I'd never swear, drink, smoke, or chase girls if He'd only get me through my mission safely. On most of my missions, the targets were either in France or Germany. The average mission was usually about six hours long. My longest mission was to Munich which was about nine hours and fifteen minutes long. Bomb runs took between twenty to thirty minutes.

On one of my missions to Cologne, we had an indicated airspeed of 155 miles per hour, but we had a headwind of one hundred miles per hour. This meant that we had a ground speed of fifty-five miles per hour, and to the enemy it probably seemed like we weren't even moving. The flak gunners loved this. Although this was pretty frightening, on my second mission, March 8, 1944, our bomber was shot up by a German plane and heavy flak. They shot holes through the wing and body of our plane. I was also hit by the flak in the right hand and leg.

All of my combat missions were memorable, however, my thirtieth and last stands out, even though I was wounded on my second mission to Berlin, March 8, 1944. One always is a little edgy the first mission and more so on the last mission. I flew all of my missions as a "Command Pilot" with a "lead crew." "Lead crews" were the premier crews in a group. The "Command Pilots" were supposed to "see all and know all" and be in charge ("leading") of a squadron, group, wing division or air force.

Before my final mission, I had evidently eaten some bad food as I possessed a very squeamish stomach! Our target was not that bad - a bridge in an area with predicted light flak and a low possibility of fighter opposition.

A leader is supposed to lead, and wars do not stop for the soldiers to take care of their personal hygienic problems. To shorten the story, I "messed" my pants - turned my electrically heated suit thermostat as high as it would go. After seven hours, we returned to home base. The base C.O. came in his staff car to our revetment to congratulate me for the completion of my final and thirtieth mission. After one look at me, he made me put on my gloves before he would shake hands. Then he held up the mission critique until I could shower and change clothes.

I always thought that if for some reason, I would have had to "bail out" that day, the Germans would have said, "We're not shooting too many down, but we are scaring the s— out of them!"

After a mission like this you cannot wait to get out of your clothes. Being that it is minus-sixty degrees Fahrenheit up there, you had to be dressed properly. We usually wore long underwear, uniform pants, electric pants, an alpaca suit, throat mile, electric gloves, silk gloves, an oxygen mask, Mae West, parachute, and a flak vest. After we took all this off and were finished showering, we would go to an assembly, be given a shot of whiskey, and have the critique on how we did with our mission.

After completion of our thirtieth mission, we were sent home and the war ended shortly afterwards. I went back to working for my father at Burrell Construction and Supply, and took over the family-owned business. The company is now called Burrell Group Inc., and a few of the things we own include: Burrell Mining International, Burrell Mining Australia, Burrell Mining Utah, Omega Transworld Ltd., and Continental Development Company. When The Korean War started, I was recalled to one week of active duty. I had a choice of staying home or going to war because I had five dependents. I chose to stay at home with my family, "but if the big one comes" I told them I'd go. In March of 1979, I retired from the Air Reserves.

Although many of the men who did survive received medals and all sorts of honors, I think that they'll agree with me that we were just trying to stay alive over there. We were very fortunate that the American public was behind us one hundred percent. I learned a lot from my experiences in the Air Force, and am glad to have served my country proudly. Over the past five years I have been making a movie from photos and movie footage I have from the war. I'm making the movie in tribute to the families and friends of those of the 458th Bomb Group who died in combat. We're (survivors of the war) not the heroes. The real heroes of the war are all dead...

Chester Brewer

452nd Bomb Group
729th Squadron
Tail Gunner

by
Suzanne Kile

Chester Brewer's home in Sewickley, PA is adorned with memorabilia of his bombing days in WWII. Numerous books of the Eighth Air Force are proudly displayed on shelves along with encasements of medals and maps of his bomb runs. Mr. Brewer proudly recalls every experience from the day he was sworn into the Air Force up to the day he was discharged.

Chester Brewer has led an amazing and eventful life. He is twice a widower, father of nine, and a grandfather of thirteen. The stories and events he relayed were told with such enthusiasm that the listeners found themselves in awe over the fact that so many tragic and wonderful things could happen in one man's lifetime. Concerning this interview, Mr. Brewer states to one of his children that "maybe he was going to get someone to listen to him." The interviewer gladly listened with a sense of respect and wonderment.

Chester Brewer graduated in 1941 from the Manhattan High School of Aviation Trades in New York City. At this time there was a great demand for skilled labor because the war was beginning and the production of war goods became a necessity. Corporations and businesses came to the high school to recruit the graduates according to their skills. Mr. Brewer began to work for Sperry Gyroscope. The company made the Univac, the first real computer. The Univac was designed specifically for the U.S. Navy in order to control the guns upon battleships.

As the war began to heat up, Mr. Brewer and his buddies decided they "didn't want to miss out." At age twenty Chester Brewer went to Grand Central Station and was sworn into the U.S. Air Force.

He was not required to attend basic training because during the summers at the high school, he had attended military training in Fort Dix, New Jersey. He was placed on the flight line as a second-class mechanic in Odessa, Texas. When he was transferred to the Rio Grande Valley, he saw men being trained for bombardiers. As he saw the young fellows going up into these planes, he realized that, "My God, if they can do that, we can do that." It was then that he applied for aviation cadet training. He attended nine weeks of pre-flight, then went to primary training where classifications of pilot, bombardier, and navigator were assigned. He was eventually assigned to bombarding school. He was at the school for almost six weeks when positions for aerial gunners opened up, and he volunteered for the position. He was shipped to Salt Lake City where all the pilots, navigators, radio controllers, and so on were assigned crews. Mr. Brewer, now a tail gunner, was assigned to his crew and began training with them. The training was complete. Mr. Brewer and his crew of ten were ready for European embarkment. They sailed on the Queen Elizabeth with fourteen thousand other servicemen to Norwich, England. This was in March of 1944.

He was stationed in Deopham Green, England, and assigned to the 452nd Bomb Group. Before his crew was able to fly their own missions, the pilot had to orient himself to combat. He was placed with an experienced crew and prepared to fly a mission. Mr. Brewer recalls going down to the flight line to wish the pilot luck. During this mission, the plane that carried Mr. Brewer's pilot was shot down above

Abbeyville, France. The crew bailed out over the English Channel. Of the ten men, only four were rescued, one of whom was Mr. Brewer's pilot. "That's when the reality struck us, what this is all about." The twenty-year old pilot was sent to Scotland for rest and recuperation.

Mr. Brewer's navigator had given him a map of Europe upon which Mr. Brewer had marked every mission he flew, the target, and the time the mission took. He had a code with his parents because he could not tell them directly how many missions he had flown. His middle name was Ward, so after each mission he would write home saying, "Congratulate "Ward" on his third birthday," replacing the three with the number of missions he had just completed. His parents then would then know when their son would be home. Mr. Brewer recalls the worst mission he flew. The target was Brunn, Czechoslovakia. His bomb group sent out twenty planes for this mission; nineteen of them actually made it to the target, and only five of them made it back to the base. The Eighth Air Force lost seventy-four bombers that day.

When each new crew started, they were placed in the Purple Heart Squadron. This was the place in the flight formation where it is easiest to get picked off by enemy planes. As a crew survived mission after mission, they were moved up in the formation to the second line and eventually to the lead squadron. Mr. Brewer and his crew made it to the lead squadron. On his crew's 27th mission, which would have been Mr. Brewer's last mission because he flew one extra than his crew, a Major pilot from the 15th Air Force was brought in from Italy to train as a command pilot. This pilot took Mr. Brewer's place in the tail of his plane. Mr. Brewer was left out of the 27th mission. His crew felt that it was for the best because then Mr. Brewer wouldn't finish the tour of twenty-eight before them. It was on this mission that Mr. Brewer lost his crew. They were flying over Leipzig, Germany when two planes of their group collided. Two men from the crew survived the collision. One lost his leg and the other later died of alcoholism.

(Photo Courtesy Charles Sujantek)

After his crew was lost, the Air Force was going to send Mr. Brewer home. However, he had only flown twenty-seven missions, and in order to get the Distinguished Flying Cross (DFC), he had to fly twenty-eight. He was not going home until he flew the 28th. "That's how funny things are, and you wonder why you do things like that." Mr. Brewer's 28th mission was to give troop support to the invasion forces as they were approaching Paris. During the flight, an anti-aircraft shell directly hit his plane right in between the gas tanks and the wing. It "ate a hole that damn big (expressing the size with his hands)." This was the first time Mr. Brewer had ever been in a plane that had a direct hit. Fortunately, the plane made it back to the base. "Another ironic thing, I got back and the ground crew was all around and said, 'Boy, how lucky you were,' and this and that, and then somebody said 'This is the 13th.' The 13th - that was my birthday - August 13th I flew my last mission." He said he never gave it a thought because he was "so mixed up losing the crew and everything." Mr. Brewer turned twenty-one the day of his last mission, completing his tour and acquiring the Distinguished Flying Cross, which he now proudly displays in his home.

Mr. Brewer returned home where he was decorated with the DFC, and given two weeks of rest and recuperation. The Air Force then gave him a choice of what line of work he wanted to pursue. He chose aircraft mechanics because he graduated from a vocational high school with those skills. In Amarillo, Texas he took a B-17 mechanics' course and was sent to Chanute Field, Illinois. Chanute Field was where training on B-29 engines was held. Mr. Brewer and his buddies did not know this until they reached their destination. Training on B-29 engines meant that they would be going back to the war in the Pacific. "We don't want to go back overseas. Why should we have to go?" When school formation was called, Mr. Brewer and his buddies stayed in the barracks. There was no way they were being sent back overseas. The first sergeant was sent to get them for formation, but they refused to go. After the refusal, the Air Force posted a court-martial for them. Four days later, the Air Force changed their orders and they were shipped to Madison, Wisconsin. Before they got there Mr. Brewer and his buddies steamed open their orders to make sure they weren't going to get in a fix like they had in Texas. By that time they didn't care if they got in trouble for it. In Madison, Wisconsin they worked on the flight line; they didn't have to return to the war.

It was at this time that the government came out with the point system to determine discharge eligibility. A person received a certain number of points for the years they served, the time they spent overseas, and other aspects of military life. Mr. Brewer had acquired enough points that he was shipped to Fort Lewis, Washington. It was there that Mr. Brewer trained to fight forest fires. He stayed in old Civilian Conservation Corps (CCC) camps and fought forest fires. The day came when a list of men eligible for discharge was read. Mr. Brewer remembers it vividly. "They started reading, and they got to my name, and I threw up. I can remember it so well; I had an emotional upset." After two years and 353 days of service to his country, Chester Brewer was discharged from the United States Air Force at Walla Walla, Washington's general hospital. Ironically, after all that Mr. Brewer had done in the war effort, the twenty-eight missions he flew, and the tragedies he had faced, his discharge paper reads "Fire Fighting Engineer," not "United States Air Force." Mr. Brewer feels he could "care less now."

Mr. Brewer returned home and lived off the "52/20" club. This was when the Government supplied war vets with twenty dollars a week for fifty-two weeks or until employed. He worked at different corporations until he had three months to reclaim his old job because of seniority. He moved back to New York to work at Sperry Gyroscope, and he began to court the girl who had lived on his block before the war. Sperry Gyroscope ran out of work and Mr. Brewer was forced to move to Pittsburgh, where his parents lived, to work odd jobs. He then returned to New York to get married. After this Mr. Brewer and his family moved all over the U.S., but he finally settled in Pittsburgh where he worked for Pittsburgh Coke and Chemical for fourteen years. Mr. Brewer's children now live all over the United States, but he still goes to visit them, and plans to buy a fax machine to make communication easier.

Chester Brewer is quite a remarkable man. One could only show the utmost respect for a man who did so much in support of his country. His pride of the WWII days is evident when one steps into his house, but when one sits and talks to him, he is able to draw the listener into the suspense and tragedy of his bombing days. When the stories are all told and the memorabilia is shown, there is a sense of wonderment. Mr. Brewer brushed with death on more than one occasion, was shipped all over the United States, and flew all over Europe, but is still able to remember every detail of the two years and 353 days he proudly served the United States of America.

Charles Brewick

91st Bomb Group
323rd Squadron Navigator

by
Kristen Newell

Mr. Charles Brewick is an extremely brave and proud, yet completely humble and modest man. He is thankful for his safe return from the war, and considers it a continuation of his duty to share and discuss his stories. It is his pleasure and to our benefit that he relates his experiences before, during and after his service with the Eighth Air Force.

I was eighteen when I was drafted into the Armed Forces. I went to basic training in Louisiana. I then enlisted in the Air Force...No it was the "Army Air Corps" back then. I had to take a bunch of tests and then mark my preference... the preferences were pilot, navigator, or bombardier. I picked navigator because I liked mathematics, and I figured I had more chance there than I would as a pilot. My navigation training was in Texas, and then we took crew training inside the B-17s in Oklahoma. Then I went overseas by convoy to England. The people were real nice then, but are even nicer now that there are not as many of us there. (Laughs.)

I flew thirty five missions (that was the required number) with the same group but different planes. The famous "Memphis Belle" came from the same group as me but was in a different squadron. I believe it was in the 324th, while I was in the 323rd. It flew twenty-five missions (by the time I got there, they had upped the number to thirty-five). I flew eleven missions in the "Nine-O-Nine." It was famous for flying 140 missions without ever turning back because of mechanical failure, and no one was ever injured while flying in it.

My first mission was in the last part of November, 1944. It was kind of interesting, being the navigator and sitting in the nose of the plane. I was just following along, and I looked off to my right and saw a whole bunch of flak flying past. I said, "Boy, I'm glad we're not going there," and then all of a sudden the group turned...and that's where we went. (Laughs.) So, that was the first mission.

My second mission was the most exciting and dangerous one. It was in a plane called the "Round Trip Topsy." We got hit by fighters, and our plane caught on fire. I think the fire was in the number two engine. An oil line was burning. They told us to get out of formation. I think our bomb bay doors had been shot out or something. We tried to jettison the bombs because of the fire. However, because of the malfunction in the bomb bay doors one of the bombs got jammed in the opening. Either the pilot or bombardier had to go out on the catwalk and try to jimmy it loose. So, we left formation and flew back by ourselves. It took us about three and a half hours. We landed on the coast of England. When we landed, we somehow got off the path of the runway. We hit two concrete mixers and a truck before we got stopped. We all got out, and then the whole plane burst into flames. There was next to nothing left of the plane. Like I said, we were lucky and everyone survived, but the pilot was later shot down. He was a training pilot though, not the one we normally flew with. So, that was the second mission.

After that it all kind of went down hill. There wasn't anything really exciting. I did take part in the thousand plane raids though. After the second mission, I flew again the next day. I had flown three days in a row for my first three missions. That was kind of new and interesting.

I also flew on December 24th in support of the "Battle of the Bulge" which was taking place on the ground. This was an unusual mission because during that battle, we flew at an elevation of 10,000 feet instead of the normal 25,000 feet. This was due to conditions in the weather - especially fog.

My longest mission was probably eleven hours. We ended up bombing Prague in Czechoslovakia that time. That was kind of a mistake though, because we were supposed to bomb Dresden! It just so happened that on that particular day, there was a lot of cloud cover. I wasn't the lead navigator for that mission. I was just following someone, so don't blame that on me! [Laughs.]

My last mission was with a make-up squadron. This was the day they flew across the Rhine. Boy did it feel good to touch the wheels onto the runway after that one - it being my last.

I would have to say that I was pretty much a fatalist while I was over there [Europe]. Actually, you didn't have too much time to think about why things happened the way they did. You just did what you were told and were proud to be fighting for the good guys. My morale never failed me because I was young and full of energy. The few trips to Scotland to play golf didn't hurt either. My buddies and me used to pass the time that way. (I still do.)

Since I've been back from Europe I have returned there for vacations, anniversaries,

Charles Brewick (top second from left) and crew.
(Photo courtesy Charles Brewick)

"Round-Trip Topsy" just after second mission.
(Photo courtesy Charles Brewick)

and reunions. My most recent trip back to England was in 1992. This was the 50th Anniversary of when my group got started. (I joined two years later, in 1944). There was a young man there named Clive Stevens who is a sort of "groupie" for the Eighth Air Force, and I think mainly the 91st Bomb Group. We met him while in England, and then he followed us to our reunion in Arizona. He is a wonderful young man with a passion for information concerning the war and its survivors. He collected all of the pieces for a complete uniform and modeled it for our group. Also, he has restored an old army truck, and talks of restoring a jeep. He says that he wants to start a museum. He recently sent me a large package of his projects and whereabouts and has asked us to keep in touch. We have also been to other reunions. At one of these I saw a member of my old crew.

The best time I had during my service was definitely the day I came back from my thirty-fifth and final mission. After that I was released and went home. So, I was already home when the war ended, but I was still happy to hear the news on the radio. Would I ever fight for my country again? No, I'm too old. (Laughs.)

After Mr. Brewick returned to the United States, his college attendance was made possible through the G.I. Bill. He went to Iowa State University, and was then employed by U.S. Steel. He is now retired and enjoys spending his free time on the golf course. He has a wonderful family that includes a wife and two sons.

Although Mr. Brewick claims that most of his stories are "not too exciting," it is clear that he is a hero and excellent role model, and the United States was lucky to have him on their side. Obviously most memories and recollections of the war are less than pleasant for Mr. Brewick. However, it is encouraging and notable that in every picture taken of him during his service, he is beaming a warm and proud victory smile.

Lawrence Brown

452nd Bomb Group
731 Squadron
Flight Engineer and Gunner

by
Amanda C. Holmes

Lawrence Brown is a man who is proud of what he did for our country years ago and how the military shaped him as a person. He has a pleasant demeanor and is quite patient with those who lack the knowledge of his past that he holds so dear. Mr. Brown has shared his experiences of the Air Force with us as I interviewed him at his home.

I joined in April 1941 when I was twenty-one - one day before my draft card came. For nine months I served in a chemical warfare band at Edgewood Arsenal, Maryland when the Japanese bombed Pearl Harbor. They asked us all if we could play an instrument, I played the trumpet, but they never asked if we could play well. Three of my buddies and I were not very popular with the master sergeant of the band who was trying to develop a dance orchestra out of it. We were definitely not boogie woogie dance musicians. We were involved with the band until we found out that the requirements for aviation cadets were lowered because the demand for air crews was so very high. The four of us passed the written test and also the physical exam. We were now Air Force. This training took nine months to complete and all four of us were classified for pilot training. It was divided into four categories. First preflight, then primary, basic and finally advanced. Even as a young boy my dream was to become a pilot.

To make a long story short, I accumulated about two hundred hours of flying time and had reached the last stage of my training in advanced at Yuma, Arizona. I had been flying AT-17s and AT-9s alternating every day. They were twin aircraft. The AT-17 was very slow, but on the other hand the AT-9 was a speed demon.

While my classmates were purchasing their officers' uniforms and getting ready to graduate, I was suddenly put up for a check ride. They gave me one with a heavy-set major. He created a forced landing for me by shutting down one engine. I landed at an emergency field making all the turns into the good engine. He seemed satisfied with my ability to fly. But I was called before the washout board and eliminated from further training. My whole world collapsed. It was during this period that my parents were having domestic problems. The psychiatrist at the board meeting in privacy asked me if I had any personal problems. As a brainwashed cadet my answer was, "No excuse sir." All that training and rigorous military hazing for nothing. To this day fifty-three years later, I cannot forget it, and never will. The commanding officer (CO) sent my parents a letter praising me, but informing them that I lacked the inherent ability to fly. He did not say I lacked the killer instinct of a fighter pilot they claimed I had.

I was reclassified and sent to a aircraft mechanic school in Texas. After graduation, I was sent to a machine-gun training at Tyndall Field, Florida. I, a non-killer, was now going to man two .50 caliber machine guns.

We formed our B-17 crew in Lincoln, Nebraska for more training and then departed for England flying in a new B-17 along the northern route. This bomber was then flown to a field near Belfast, Ireland for combat modifications. We came back to England on a small channel boat and traveled by truck to our new home, the

German fighter pilot bailing out of an Me 109.
(Photo courtesy Tom Brown)

452nd Bomb Group. We arrived at dusk when the group was returning from a mission. That is when I found out what the red flares meant. They had wounded aboard and had priority landing.

Before each mission we would get up at three o' clock AM and have breakfast. We ate really good. We could have as much eggs and bacon as we wanted. I often felt bad because others in the military had rations. The whole time we were in England they never served us milk to drink. We would then have a briefing concerning our task for that mission. The instructors always told us that when you are flying you have to block all your thoughts out of your mind and stay focused on your job. Because of the long period of time we stayed up in the air, they always kept candy aboard to keep us awake. Then, after we completed the mission, we all received brandy to calm us down. Those on the ground worked so hard for us. We called each other by our first names. It did not matter if you were ground crew or a pilot. We were all the same when we worked. The planes that I was a gunner on were the B-17s which were also called the Flying Fortresses

On our first mission we failed to blend into our group as they were forming above the field. We then headed for France with the idea of catching up to them at the coast line. We never found them and were headed for Germany. We knew something was wrong when we came under attack with antiaircraft fire. The pilots, navigator, and radio operator all admitted we were lost and had no communication. We turned around and headed home but flew south of England above the Atlantic Ocean and were headed for the United States of America. The Air Sea Rescue gave us a correct compass heading after we radioed for help. That got us back to England.

We completed our thirty-five missions in three months. Some were milk runs. Some were hectic, and others were branded in our memories. We faced bad weather conditions, aircraft fire, and at times bad luck. On the planes I was on we never lost any men, plus our plane never got damaged too severely. It did not matter what time of day or night it was, you could always hear the ground crew working on the planes. They did great work because there was not one mission out of all thirty-five that we had to turn around due to any malfunctions. To be sure that our plane always stayed functional in the air, it was my responsibility to check various systems, such as electrical and mechanical. To this day I still have my logbook that has all my missions recorded in it.

After we completed our term in England, they told my crew that we would be going home. We were on our way back to the U.S.A. aboard the French liner, Ile' de France. But even at that time the German subs still patrolled the ocean. We docked in New York and were greeted by a handful of Red Cross girls who gave us cartons of milk to drink. We didn't get any greetings like the convoys did - no whistlers, no bands, just a carton of milk.

A week later the war was over in Europe. On my second day at home I put on prewar clothes so I could go to Pittsburgh and buy some new ones. Two elderly ladies saw me when I got off the streetcar. One of them remarked loudly so I could hear, "Look at that young fellow. He should be in the service." I spent four years and one month in the service, and that was my reward!

I found a job in a Gulf Oil warehouse. Shortly afterwards I was driving gasoline trucks. As the years rolled by, the size of the tankers increased. My safety record was outstanding with thirty-three years of accident-free driving. We traveled throughout West Virginia, Ohio, and Pennsylvania.

I am now retired with a wonderful wife, a daughter, son-in-law, and two grandchildren, a boy and a girl.

Lawrence Brown's crew flew 35 missions without getting a single wound. Their B-17 took all the damage. Kneeling - first row, left to right - Van Drury, Wraga, Dave Fletcher, Carl Swick. Standing - second row, left to right - Lawrence Brown, Bob Schroeder, John Dunn, Sam Webster, George Cartwright, Frank Glass.
(Photo courtesy Lawrence Brown)

Hilton Buzard

25th Bomb Group
652nd Squadron
Weather Reconnaissance

by
David L. Hoovler

"There is a Flying Fortress outfit somewhere in England that has never fired a shot at an enemy plane and probably never will. Yet the work of this particular unit may determine whether a thousand warplanes are dispatched against the Reich." So reads a U.S. press release from 1944. The outfit spoken of was the 652nd Bomber Squadron, and the work done by that squadron was, indeed, crucial to the Allied cause. What follows are the words Hilton Buzard, of the 25th Bomber Group, used to describe his squadron's work and his very "unconventional" pilot.

We were one hundred percent reconnaissance, and the squadron that I was in, the 652nd, was Heavy Weather. I think the unique thing about our squadron was that the shortest flight I was on during the war was over fifteen hours, and we didn't even have a chair to sit on. If you wanted to sit down, you just sat down in the waist of the plane or in the radio room. There were no facilities for us whatsoever. We did happen to have windows in the waist, unlike the B-17s that actually went on bomb runs, where you just shot out of holes in the side of the plane.

We didn't carry any bomb load, any guns, or armament. The reason for that was that we flew into the Azores Islands, and it was a neutral country, so we weren't allowed any armament whatsoever on our airplanes: no guns, no ammunition, nothing. The other thing is that we flew just as a lone aircraft. The Germans could have come out and shot us out of the air real easy - and they knew it. They knew what we were, we were sitting ducks, but they also intercepted our messages so that they got the weather reports the same as our people. I think we made sure, probably, that they got those, so that they wouldn't be out shooting us up. On two occasions, we had seen German aircraft. One time there were two Me 109s that came out and flew on either side of our wings, and they could have just taken us out any time they wanted to 'cause we had nothing. One time they strafed the runway at Watton right ahead of us - they knew our take-off time.

The other thing that was unique about our squadron was that we flew four flights a day and we never missed a flight. We kept a B-17 over the North Atlantic all the time, and we kept one over the South Atlantic all the time, gathering weather information; we carried a meteorologist. We flew south of Ireland, and we went down to Lands End, England, and that was our last contact with land on two flights a day. We went around south of Ireland towards Iceland, and we went out and back. We would be out over the water twelve or thirteen hours. Our station, our base, was up northeast of London, which was a long ways away. That's what accounted for us being out fifteen, sixteen hours. On the other flight, a plane went down to the Azores every day and landed, and it stayed overnight, while the one that went down yesterday came back. The flight from England would get there about noon; and the other was ready to come back, so we kept a B-17 over the South Atlantic all the time.

We flew a lot of missions. In a bomb group, where they were bombing, they had to fly twenty-five missions; that made a tour of duty. Well, for us, we had to fly five hundred combat hours; that was a tour of duty.

I can never remember for sure. We either had fifteen crews and sixteen aircraft or vice versa, and keeping four in the air every day was a real problem for our ground crews. We weren't attached to an airplane. Whatever was available, whatever was fit to fly when our flight came up, that's the one we flew. So in the bomb groups, you heard people [say] they had an aircraft that was theirs, and they had their nose art and everything . Well, that didn't work in our outfit.

We had a lot of dead time - I'll explain a little bit of how they took readings. We took our first reading fifty feet off the water. Then we'd go five hundred feet increments, and we'd get to twenty-eight thousand feet. Every five hundred feet they'd level off and take meteorology readings. One of the things I did as a gunner - in the bottom of the waist of a B-17 there's what they call the camera hatch; you could lift a panel out of there and that's where you'd mount a camera to take an aerial photograph - and the meteorologist had to get wind-drift readings. So he told the pilot what headings he wanted. He would fly a triangle or something - I'm not sure just what we'd do. But in the daytime, we had bombs that were about eighteen inches long and about three inches in diameter. In the daytime, you'd pull a cork out of that bomb, and he'd tell you when to drop it, and that bomb would submerge in the water and come back up. It would get some water in there, and that would give smoke off. A series of those: five or six, I forget. My job was, when he told me over the intercom to drop that bomb [out of the camera hatch]. Then he would read that smoke, as the wind drifted, and he would get the wind readings. At night, we had a different type of bomb with about the same configuration, but when it submerged and got water in it, it broke out in a flame, so he could read the flame at night on it. That was part of the duties I had. But we would have some dead time when the pilot would say, "Anybody want to fly, come up." Or the copilot. The copilot would want to go take a rest or something - lay down someplace. So they allowed us to ride the clouds and so forth, because it was just dead flying time, so I think that was a morale booster. The only two people who could do it was the two gunners. We only had two gunners - the rest of them all had a position in the plane and a duty to do, so we got to fly, and that was a fun thing, a morale booster.

There were no guns on any of our planes. We never carried them. Well, I asked at the reunions, and a couple of people say we did have guns, but ninety percent of us say we had never seen them - a gun on a B-17. A little confusion, but I'm sure we didn't have guns. So, I did the cooking - we had a little electric hot plate, and so forth, and whatever they give us that had to be heated up for the crew, I'd do that - and drop the bombs, the other gunner and I. Yeah, "gunner" was a misnomer as far as that was concerned.

My pilot had one hang-up. In our crew I was responsible for getting the special equipment when we were flying. We flew an eight-man crew, and I had to get the parachutes. Well, my pilot didn't want a parachute for himself. That was the last thing before take-off he'd be on the intercom system saying, "How many parachutes on, Buzz?" I said, "Seven, and you're not riding down with me." I made sure that he didn't have one. Those were things you heard about over there: a pilot carried a baby shoe with him or something like that, and he forgot it, and he didn't come back. I'm not superstitious, but I made sure there was one parachute short every flight.

My pilot - he was different. We had lots of funny stories. He was a total alcoholic, a young man. Well, to begin with, when we got to our outfit in England I was put off of my crew - the one I trained with here in the States - and then this man made up a crew over there, within in the organization, so I didn't even know my pilot. I flew with him about three flights until I realized that he was drunk. Then I made up my mind that if he ever came out, and I thought he was sober, I wouldn't fly with him, 'cause I knew then that he could fly drunk, but I didn't know if he could fly sober or not.

We were going to the Azores on a flight one day, and you'd get briefed before you'd go - the whole crew would get briefed. They said that at a certain time that day we would meet a hundred-ship convoy coming out of North Africa to England. At the right time, there it was. It was a beautiful, sunny day out, I recall; I can still see all these ships. It was a square box ten ships wide and ten deep. Out on each corner - and I'm not sure if it was all four corners - there was baby flattops, aircraft carriers - they had baby, small ones; they weren't great big like they are now. But there were at least two and there might have been four with this convoy.

Well my pilot was a nut. His name was Donnegan, and he was Irish, and my navigator's name was DeLorme, and he was Italian. They were always bantering back and forth on the intercom, calling each other a "dumb Wop" and "pig-shit Irish," or whatever, and so Donnegan, when he saw that flattop, he couldn't resist. He said, "We'll make a pass, and we'll put our gear down, and we'll act like we're going to land on that baby flattop." Now, to tell you the truth, the landing deck on that wouldn't be any wider than half of a B-17. So we go back, and he drops the landing gear, and he's coming in, and we're right there just off to the side of the darned ship. Well he's giggling and laughing and so forth, and we're looking and the sailors on there, they're waving all kinds of flags that they can't receive us and one thing and another. (Laughs.) Donnegan thought that was great, so he came around and made the second attempt at it. DeLorme yelled at him, "We're getting out of here. There'll be a submarine out on the horizon, and he'll know we're messing around with something!" If they were watching us, because of the Earth's curvature, they wouldn't see the convoy, but they'd see us. So we got out of there, but I always thought that was a funny story.

One Sunday morning we were coming in from an "Allah" flight, that was a North

Hilton Buzard in front of "Woodpeckers' Delight" an English Mosquito Bomber constructed of wood with Rolls-Royce engines.
(Photo courtesy Edward Jones)

Atlantic flight, and at the southern tip of Ireland was a lighthouse that was out on a little rock island, just solid rock. We had to stay south of that. Most people don't know it, but Southern Ireland was not an ally of ours. They were friendly to the Germans, and we were not allowed to fly over Ireland. That was a no-no. Of course, Donnegan being Irish, DeLorme being Italian, when we come in this Sunday morning we got up to this lighthouse, and Donnegan just said, "I'll just show you a beautiful country" - talking to DeLorme. And he - (laughs) - he brings that B-17 down over Southern Ireland at about two hundred feet; we're going up and down like this. (Gestures.) People were going to church; I can still see them, and they - Southern Ireland was a backward country - they were going with two-wheeled basket-like carts that I associate with the Philippine Islands. Those people were on their way to church and they were jumping out of those things and into ditches, and the cows were jumping the fences and everything else. Well, of course the word got back to our base, that they had an unidentified aircraft, a B-17, over Southern Ireland. Of course everybody knew who it was, so whenever we got back to the base a bunch of wheels were there to take Donnegan and give him the devil.

There wasn't anything he wouldn't do. He was a nut. We were flying an "Allah" flight on V-E Day, May 7, 1945. We took off about ten o'clock AM and knew the big announcement was due at any time. We were somewhere out over the North Atlantic that afternoon when we got the big news that the war in Europe was over. Needless to say, we had to finish our flight.

I had flown over England on many night flights before, and due to the total blackout we couldn't tell whether we were over land or water. When we came back that night and made our first ground contact at Lands End, we had a wonderful surprise waiting for us. England was ablaze...At this point you must remember that England had had a total blackout for over six years, which meant that no one could burn brush piles, hay stacks, garbage dumps, or anything else that would not burn out in a few hours. Well, that day everyone set fire to everything that had accumulated for six years. We were probably one of the few crews that were airborne and privileged to view the extravaganza. Not only were there fires, but every light in England was turned on. What a wonderful night it was, lights and fire for as far as one could see.

...As we progressed north east from Lands End to Watton, Donnegan became more and more thrilled and curious, so we started to fly lower and lower, against all regulations, over more towns and cities. We had that B-17 down to house-top level. We could see people dancing on the streets, climbing poles and anything else that people do when they are celebrating. I am not sure of the city, but I think it was Westminster. He had us down so low that we looked straight out the windows and saw the great stained glass windows of some great cathedral. At this point he was so proud of himself that he announced we would tour London and see what Buckingham Palace looked like at night. Believe me, we did just that. It was a sight that I can recall to my mind at will - absolutely beautiful. We flew right over the Palace, which was totally lit with big flood lights, and I am sure that we were below one thousand feet. While flying over the Palace, we heard on the radio that there was an unidentified plane over London, and they were considering shooting it down. I think that the last part of this story can be documented.

They were waiting for us at the strip when we landed that night. They threatened Donnegan with a court-martial, but I don't know what the outcome was.

Those were a couple outstanding instances that I remember. That kept your morale up a little bit; just flying with him was sort of a fun thing to do.

Mr. Buzard returned home on September 22nd, 1945 to his wife, Nora, and two children. Since the war, in addition to raising his daughter and two sons, he has worked in the construction and ready-mix cement business, and is still a partner and manager of a ready-mix cement plant near Clarion, Pennsylvania. While his children have spread across the U.S. (to Ohio, Washington, D.C., and California), he and Nora continue to live just a stone's throw from where he was born.

William Clark

458th Bomb Group
754th Squadron
Bombardier

by
Jennifer M. Nelson

Few people today make a career out of their enlisting in the Armed Forces. Lieutenant Colonel William Clark was one of those few, proud, and brave. He dedicated his life and a majority of its works to his country. They are acts that he never regrets, and he would never take back.

I did my bombardier training in Texas at Houston and at Big Spring. I finished that in October, 1943. That was when I got married to Maxine Nelson. After that I went off to Salt Lake City. The program there was to organize into a crew. They had all different types there like pilots, navigators, bombardiers, and gunners. There, they pulled names out of a hat, I think. They put ten people together and called it a crew. From there we went by train from Salt Lake City to El Paso. We went the long way. We went from Salt Lake City to the coast of California near San Francisco. Then we went down the coast and over to Texas. We stayed there three to four months. The idea there was to learn and practice dropping bombs and shooting guns out of the airplane. This was preparation to make us all "combat ready," and so that we knew more than the enemy. But, I had no idea what combat was about, until actual combat. In February of '44 they moved us to Topeka, Kansas. The Air Force, the Army, and the U.S. Government came up with a brand new B-24 airplane. It was a four-engine bomber. The name of it was the "Liberator."

The eighth of March we got on a plane and went to West Palm Beach, Florida where we spent three days. Then we went down to take the southern route to England. We went to Puerto Rico, Trinidad, British Guiana, Natal in South America, Robert's Field in Freetown which is in Africa, Algeria, to the Valley of Wales in Ireland, and then to England. There we spent a month learning how to use safety equipment and to fly around Britain which was pretty crowded.

There were quite a few colorful characters in the Air Force. For some it was the way they flew, the way they slept, or the way they partied. Some people didn't seem to sleep at all, and they always seemed to do a good job. Other people, like me, couldn't get enough sleep, but we tried to do a good job. Also, I think I was the only one on our crew who wasn't from Texas.

As far as the missions were concerned, some of them were worse than others. Generally speaking, you would have to get up in the middle of the night just to prepare for a mission. It was usually about two or three o'clock in the morning when it was still dark. We would eat breakfast, then have a mission briefing to determine how many bombs we were going to drop and to make sure we had enough ammunition. Most of the time we had a great number of airplanes flying. Because of this, we had to follow a certain procedure for climbing out, circling, and getting ready to go out in a big formation. Often there were a thousand planes flying over Germany all together, so you had to be careful you didn't run into the other guy, and that they didn't run into you. Everybody had to do a pretty good job. Our plane was quite frequently in the front of the formation. The very first airplane that took off shot flares. You could tell which plane to follow by the color of the flare. That was probably one of the most dangerous parts of the whole mission - just getting into formation and getting together to fly over the English Channel to German occupied territory. When you have that number of planes, its likely that some of them would get confused and go the wrong way which was really bad.

Every mission you were exposed to antiaircraft guns. You could look down, and you would see the flames comin' out of the gun. Pretty soon there would be a black puff of smoke somewhere in the area. Each puff gave off flak from the shell exploding. That was probably the scariest part of a mission. It was my job to make sure the bombs were dropped and that they hit their targets. When I wasn't doing that, I was shooting a fifty-caliber machine gun at enemy planes. I did that just about every mission. It's like shooting pheasants - only a little more dangerous. Weather also caused a lot of problems. I was in D-Day. I flew two missions. We barely got any sleep at all. One was flown early in the morning. You could look in any direction, and it seemed like the sky was full of airplanes. It was scary, interesting, exciting, all of that. Because of maintenance, most planes were only flown by the same group five or six times. If one group was ready to go and their plane wasn't available, they would just swipe another one and vice versa.

William Clark and crew - William Clark kneeling on far right.
(Photo courtesy William Clark)

Watching our own planes getting shot down was probably the worst part of the whole thing [the war] . Sometimes you'd be looking out the window during a flight and a piece of flak would hit the plane you were looking at, and it would almost disappear out of sight. That's the reason why we tried not to get too acquainted with the people that weren't on our crew. It's very sad when you lose a good friend. A lot of it seemed like good luck. If you have fifty planes in formation, all within a hundred feet of each other, you can look around and two or three are missing. It makes you wonder, "Why not me?" It was what everyone thought, I think. I always had the feeling that I was going to make it, so I never really worried. I had a great faith in my religion that took over for me while I was there. The Twenty-third Psalm was kind of what I tried to live by. Every airplane we ever flew was supposed to be a "bad one." There was always someone saying that - The "Doomsday Boys," you see? We might be getting ready for a mission and this guy would say, "Oh, you'll never make it. That's a bad one!" But most of the guys weren't very superstitious about stuff like that though.

On the night before a mission we would frequently write letters, just in case - last letter home. It went pretty fast though. We did about thirty-two missions in two months. We didn't really have a lot of free time except for the week off for R&R in London. It was nice to get away from the bombing for a while. The rest of the time we were ready to be called up on the base.

I came back from Europe in 1944. I went back to pilot training at that time. In November of '45 I became a pilot in the Air Force. I stayed in the Air Force until I finally retired in 1964.

I don't really think people have forgotten too much since the war, but it certainly is different between being here [the U.S.] and there [England] - between reading or hearing it and doing it. It has widened my view on the world enough to help me. I got educated. It turned me from a small country boy into someone who knew something. I'm sure of that. I enjoyed it, and I would definitely do it again.

A definite sense of pride and patriotism is present in Mr. Clark's words and actions. Because of these qualities he has earned the Distinguished Flying Cross along with an Air Medal and Air Commendation awards with three Oak Leaves.

William Clark continues his love of flying in Temple Hills, Maryland through his personal hobbies, and he shares his knowledge through flying instruction that he gives in his spare time.

The cathedral at Cologne miraculously still standing after heavy Allied bombing in the area.
(Photo courtesy Gene Hinchberger)

Stanford Cohen

385th Bomb Group
54th Squadron
Tail Gunner

by
Heather Perkins

At an age when most young men are playing sports and thinking about girls, Stanford Cohen was longing to join all his older friends in enlisting in the Army. He hated school, and it did not help that everywhere he looked there was major propaganda urging young men to fight for their country. Cohen's father was against him joining, but finally, two years later, at the age of sixteen, he convinced his father to allow him to enlist. He even had to lie about his age to get accepted, but he did not care. He started out going for another job but eventually volunteered to be a gunner.

After spending three weeks in basic training and three weeks in gunnery school, he was amazed to see the tail gunner seat was only as big as a bicycle seat, and he had two manual guns. The young men were trained to hate the Japanese. When they would practice shooting, instead of a bullseye there would be a tiny Japanese cartoon figure for them to aim at. It was drilled into their heads that Hitler was evil.

When he started, all those in the Air Force had to get special pictures taken. The men had to hold up a blue long-sleeved shirt to themselves and get a strip of three pictures taken. If a crew's plane went down, they were supposed to go to a church, and a nun would take one of the pictures and make them fake identification so they could survive.

Cohen thought it would be a good idea to keep a journal of each mission he went on, but he stopped writing after his seventh mission. On his first mission the seriousness of war had not sunk in, and he felt like he was in a roller coaster. By his third mission, however, he had seen enough flak for the rest of the war. Upon inspecting the plane after one mission, the crew saw three large holes.

His parents wanted him to write letters home, so when he had free time he would write ten generic letters he could stuff into envelopes every week. All letters sent home were shrunk so they would take up less space on the plane and was called "V-Mail." Parts would be blacked out on letters if they gave away information that could be used by the "enemy."

Cohen knew a man who seriously wounded his arm during the war. When he came back from the infirmary everyone was silent because they felt badly for him. The young man, however, was laughing and poking fun at the others because he was going home and the rest of them had to stay and fight. Even though he would probably never regain use of his arm, he was ecstatic to be going home. At that moment the men were having a hard time feeling sorry for him because they were envious.

At one point during the war, Germany occupied Holland. The Germans had stopped all trade in and out of the country, and the people of Holland were starving. A truce was called so that American troops could fly food and drop it into Holland. Cohen's crew was one that went on the food runs. He could see little dots of people down on the ground, waiting for them. He felt good knowing he did more than fight from a plane during the war.

After his fifteenth mission, Cohen was in the top ten percent of the point class and was allowed to go home on a furlough. He was enjoying his time at home and dreaded returning, but knew he would inevitably have to return. On the last day of his furlough, he heard on the radio the United

A B-24 cut into by an Me 262's thirty millimeter cannon fire.
(Photo courtesy Frank De Cola)

States had dropped a nuclear bomb on Japan. He was saved from returning.

For a while he did not know what he wanted to do with his life and worked numerous jobs. When he first got out of the war, his Army pay was eighty-five dollars and was taken up to ninety dollars when he got married. At the birth of his child, he was paid 105 dollars. Times were very hard for the Cohen family. Money was always short, but Mr. Cohen was the kind of man who, when a man selling things door-to-door came to his house, gave the man his last five dollars. He finally took a test and got into college. In college, his English teacher was wonderful, and inspired Cohen to do something with his life, and so he became a teacher.

In 1963 he returned to his old base in England. He wanted to go to one of the pubs he and his buddies used to frequent, so he went out and bought an English raincoat to try and blend in. He went into the pub talking with an English accent and felt he was doing a good job at blending in. Soon the pub filled up, and he was curious as to the reason for the sudden business. Then a man came up to him and asked him if he was "the Yank in town". Then he learned the gossip wire had been buzzing with the news of his arrival, and everyone had come out to see him.

When he was visiting in Germany, he went to a railroad station they had once bombed. The station had been rebuilt and was nicer than any that were in the United

States at the time. He could remember how they had been explicitly told at the time they had to be one hundred percent accurate on the bombing so they would not hit the Catholic Church that sat next to it. He was glad to see it was still standing.

Today, Cohen is a teacher of pharmacy at the University of Pittsburgh. He is a reserved man who lives in Squirrel Hill with his wife of forty-seven years. He has owned four pharmacies and a restaurant, all of which he ended up selling to his daughters. He has led a fascinating life. He can recall being at Martin Luther King Jr.'s "I Have a Dream" speech, right up close. He hardly ever talks about the war and his experience. He only started thinking about the war after he and his wife met a couple on the Pennsylvania Turnpike who told him about the Eighth Air Force Historical Society, to which he now belongs.

In a study in his basement, amid a computer and numerous books, pictures of planes hang on the wall. He has a medal and also a certificate given to him after his sixth mission inducting him into the "Lucky Bastard Club." He says they were just trying to relieve some tension with a little humor when he received the certificate.

He believes people today have forgotten too much. Not many of his students are aware he was in the war. On one Veteran's Day, he went to class and told his students it was strange, but no one had thanked him for their freedom that day. Despite it all, Stanford Cohen says he would fight for his country again.

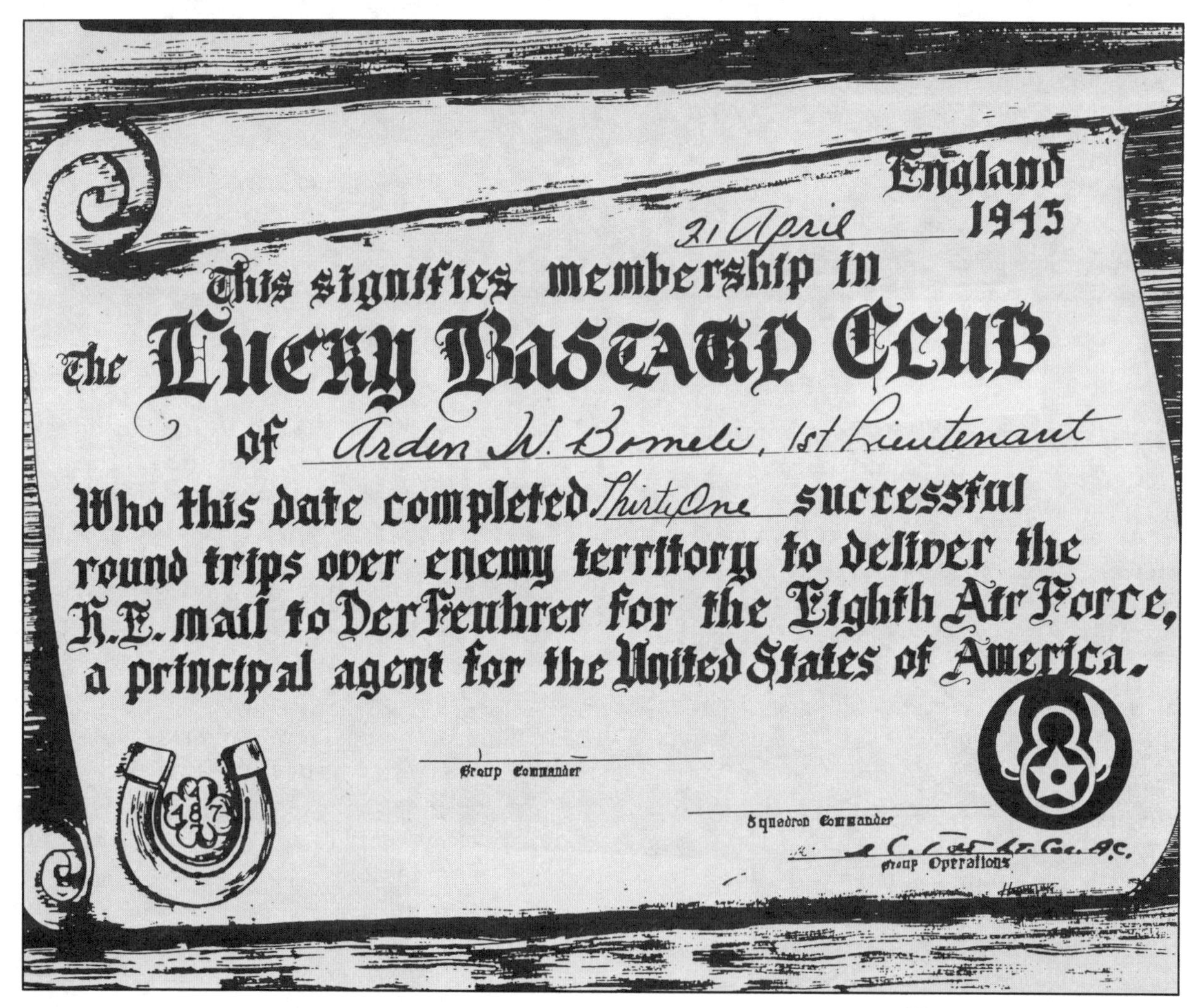

England
21 April 1945

This signifies membership in
the Lucky Bastard Club
of Arden W. Bomeli, 1st Lieutenant
Who this date completed Thirty One successful
round trips over enemy territory to deliver the
H.E. mail to Der Feuhrer for the Eighth Air Force,
a principal agent for the United States of America.

487

Group Commander

Squadron Commander

Group Operations

(Courtesy Arden Bomeli)

John Connors

482nd Bomb Group
813th Squadron
Waist Gunner

by
Amy Stewart

Driving up a country road, there is a farm with a house on top of a hill. This house belongs to a young looking World War II veteran named John Connors. Connors was a waist gunner and a flight engineer in a special division of the Eighth Air Force known as the Pathfinders.

Propaganda was abundant in 1942, when John Connors enlisted in the Air Force. This was the day after his eighteenth birthday. He remembers hearing that, "Hitler was going to take over the world." if they didn't fight. So, he enlisted to help the cause. Miami Beach was his basic training site. At this time, they only had one month of basic training because of the need for men in combat. He then was transferred to Fort Myers for five weeks of gunnery school. There they would go up in planes and shoot at a streamer that was flying alongside of them attached to another plane. The better shot you were, the better job you would get in combat. Connors was known as a "flexible gunner," meaning he could be anywhere in the plane because he was a good shot. After his training, Connors came down with appendicitis and was on convalescent leave for a while. On May 1, 1942, John Connors went to war.

Connors was stationed at Alconbury in England. He was part of the very specialized group known as the Pathfinders 482nd Bomb Group. They only called this outfit to fly very important missions. Connors flew fourteen missions with the Pathfinders. His outfit was then transferred to the Royal Air Force for six photography missions, then to the 401st Air Force for their last five. "Our outfit was really something special," he says. There was no ball turret on their bomber known as "My Melancholy Baby" because of specialized radar equipment that was in its place. "Germans could tell that it was our plane because there was no gun sticking out," Connors points out. This made things even more dangerous than they already were. The Germans had an easier time shooting at them because of their lack of a ball-turret gunner. The Germans could come up from underneath and attack without the threat of this gunner.

Connors remembers his scariest moment in combat was on a mission in 1944. He said, "They sent out three airplanes, and there were thirty men and we lost twenty-one. The other two were shot down. Our airplane was the only one of the three that came back. That was a big hole in our village. In our barracks, we were close together, and we all knew each other. When we lost twenty-one men, that was the worst. It was February 4, 1944. After we got back and found out twenty-one of our friends were killed, that's when it set in, and it was scary. But, we didn't know until we got back that they were shot down. We never heard of any survivors out of the twenty-one, no prisoners-of-war or anything. We never heard about any of them."

No one from Connors' airplane was ever killed in combat, but there were some unfortunate accidents other places. Connors lost many friends during the war. He remembers, "The one that hit me the most was my best friend "Bottle" Newman. We called him "Bottle" because he was a little bigger on the bottom than he was across the shoulders. Him and I were riding in the tailgate of a truck, and it was snowing. When you're riding along, and the snow's blowing one way, and your going the other way, you don't know which way you're going. And when the truck came to a stop, and he realized it came to a stop, he jumped out, but the driver backed up and killed him. Nobody knew he was under the truck but me because it was snowing so bad you couldn't even see. I climbed under the truck to see where he was, and he was crushed to death. So, that's the biggest tragedy in my military career."

Connors came close to tragedy a few times himself during his years in the war. During one especially cold mission, Connors actually got hurt. This was the only injury for their crew the entire war. During combat, while confronting an enemy plane, he got the heel of his foot hit with a bullet. Then on top of the wound, he got frostbite. "It got down to sixty-three below [zero] up there." When they landed at the base, he went to the doctor. The doctor could not tell if the injury on Connors' foot was from the bullet or from the frostbite. "But, I didn't care much and he didn't either. He was too busy with other serious things." Connors said chuckling. Another brush with fate was not during combat at all. It was during a "whiskey run." He recalls, "[The airplane] went to Scotland, and the high-ranking officers in the group were going up for the weekend; so they wanted a radio operator on the plane and a flight engineer which I was qualified for. So the sergeant told me they were ready to take off, and they needed a flight engineer right away. He said to get out there as soon as possible because they were not going to wait. Well, everybody wanted to go to Scotland for the weekend so I got on my bicycle and rode about a mile out there. They were warming up at the end of the runway, and I just skidded my bicycle into the bushes, and got on the plane. I no sooner got on, shut the door, and we taxied up, then there was a fellow riding alongside the airplane in a jeep. We stopped, and I opened the door. He said he was lieutenant so-and-so and he was going on the flight because he found out they needed a flight engineer. He bumped me so I had to get off. He told me to take his jeep back to the barracks, and he got on the airplane. Shortly after, about an hour, they hit a mountain and were all killed. That's scary, real scary! That's as

Frank De Cola at gunnery school - Wendover, Utah
(Photo courtesy Frank De Cola)

close as I came to getting killed."

Times were not all bad. Actually, bad times were rare. Connors was at Alconbury for twenty-seven months, a long time for flying only twenty-five missions. This left lots of time for having fun, and they had a lot. "You never would have thought there was a war going on 'til you had to fly. We spent the rest of the time enjoying ourselves. We'd go to dances and go fishing. That two years and three months we were over there, we had a good time." There was lots of entertainment in town. At the dances, the female-to-male ratio was fifty to ten, so there was always a new girl to dance with every night. Connors says, "We went to dances two nights a week. The dances were Wednesday and Saturday nights. We always had a lot of night life." Connors knew his unit was very relaxed. They could do as they pleased, most of the time, as long as they did not have to fly. He remembers, "We had regular hours. In the morning, we'd wake up and go to the sergeant's office to see if our name was posted to fly. If it wasn't posted to fly, we were on our own. It was amazing. I was in town all the time. Then I'd call back up there to see if my name was on the bulletin board. If it wasn't on the bulletin board to fly, I didn't even have to come back. So, it was a big picnic for the Air Force, but not for the infantry. There were other outfits that were real strict, but ours was real relaxed." In a group picture of his flight crew, all of the men are in different uniforms. This showed how relaxed his unit was.

While fighting for his country Connors met many famous people. One special memory was meeting Jimmy Stewart. This was special because Stewart was his commanding officer, and he came to brief the crew. Another interesting person he met was Jimmy Cagney. Connors recalls this meeting vividly. "He came and entertained the troops at the base. And in the evening, after the show was over, he went up to the officer's club. A friend of mine invited me up there. I got a real kick out of him [Jim Cagney] because he was drinking a lot of beer, and he was dancing. It was amazing; he didn't have any props or anything, just tables in the dining room, and he was dancing on top of them! He entertained us for three or four hours." Winston Churchill wrote a letter to the pilot of Connors's plane. He had a copy of it, but someone stole it out of his locker before he came home. Some other famous people Connors met overseas were; Clark Gable, Robert Preston, and Bob Hope. Connors really enjoyed most of his time overseas.

On April 25, 1945 Connors flew his last mission. This was not last because of injury or completing enough missions to go home; that number was thirty-five. It was the last mission because it was the last mission of the entire war. The war was over. Connors remembers, "I was anxious to get back, but as soon as I got back I was anxious to get back over there." The Air Force did ask Connors if he wanted to reenlist, but he respectfully declined their offer. He was discharged in September, 1945. He was twenty-one years old. When he came back home, he started driving motorcoach buses. He did this for nine months. Then he worked for Duquesne Light for a short period of time. After that, for eleven years, he worked on the Pittsburgh Railway. His next, and final job was as a tractor-trailer truck driver. He then retired and started to farm full-time the land he owned. Connors was married forty-seven years and had one daughter.

A few years ago, Connors and a friend of his from the war went back to England to see the base and to be guests at a "hanger dance" in their honor. This dance was actually held in an airplane hanger on Alconbury Base. Connors was surprised at the changes on the base since he had served there. When he was there seven thousand people lived at the base. It was just an airstrip in a cornfield then. Now there are three schools, a Burger King, and other nonmilitary places. The town near the base was also quite different from fifty years ago. In 1944 there was not enough room for two buses to go down the main street at the same time. Nor were there any freezers, so there wasn't any ice either. Connors enjoyed this trip to Europe. Which brought back many memories.

World War II left a deep impression in many people's minds that they will never forget. John Connors will remember the people he knew and the things he did in World War II. Some memories will be good, like the dances, and some very sad, like the loss of his friend "Bottle" Newman. But these times will be with him forever. The good and bad experiences of the war are what shaped these veterans' lives and minds. They are all heroes. Lest we not forget.

John Connors and crew January 15, 1944. Top row, left to right - Robert Norton (Alimony Joe), Richard Koch (Baron), Capt. Thewaiter (Sportie), Lt. Tellboum (Time Bomb), Sgt. Hatfield, Major Bird (Uncle Clem). Bottom row, left to right - E.A. Newman (Bottle), C.T. Foster (The Snowman), J.N. Connors (Henry Aldrich), K.L. Higgins (The Old Gentleman).

(Photo courtesy John Connors)

John Cotter

445th and 489th Bombardment Groups
703rd Squadron
Tail Gunner

by
Laurie Kristufek

John Cotter is an extremely intelligent man who appears much younger than he really is, with sparkling blue eyes and a real zest for life. He chooses his words carefully and seems to enjoy sharing his experiences.

I was a college student - St. Vincent College. I was only there one year. I just finished my freshman year, and then I enlisted in the Eighth Air Force. You had to enlist to get into the Air Force. Otherwise, you could be drafted into the infantry. I enlisted in what they call Aviation Cadets, where first of all you had to take qualification tests. You had to score so much and then you had to take a physical and pass both of those. You had to have an IQ that exceeded 110. It was quite selective at the time. This was all in 1943. I had just turned eighteen. I could have taken an educational deferment, but I didn't want to. A friend of mine that I played ball with - you know how you buddy up - wanted to go too. In fact he talked me into it. When you're seventeen or eighteen, you're quite impressionable. (Laughs.) So we both decided to join. I lived in a little town about thirty miles south of Pittsburgh, called Charleroi. You had to go to Pittsburgh to take these tests. So we took the tests, and we both passed the written tests. After that, you had to go back and take the physical. This friend of mine failed the color-blind test. (Laughs.) Of all things! The color-blind test! They said not to get excited about it - that color-blindness may fade in and out. They said it was important to eat lots of carrots. He went right out and got a big bag of carrots. He was munching on carrots for about three weeks. We took the streetcar back to Pittsburgh so he could retake the test. I told him not to worry about it because I'd stand behind the man giving the test and if he couldn't see the colored numbers, I'd hold up the fingers to show what number it was. So we started, and he was doing pretty good. All of a sudden the guy giving the test started laughing and said, "Why don't you just tell him instead? Get out of here!" So my buddy failed again - didn't eat enough carrots or something, I don't know. So he didn't go, and I went. He was later drafted to the infantry. In fact, he was over there on D-Day. On the first day he got wounded in his leg. He was only in combat one day. He got a pension; he's been living high off the hog ever since. (Laughs.)

The Air Corps is very different than the Army, Navy, the Marines and things like that. It's an altogether different existence. My father had been in World War I, and he had always impressed upon me the importance of serving your country. So I thought I had better hurry up and get overseas before the war's over. So I cut out of Cadets to gunnery school so I could hurry up. Believe it or not, I was a tail gunner. I went overseas to fly my missions. See, you only had to fly so many missions. When I started, you had to fly 25. When I got to about 23, they upped it to 30. (Laughs.) I flew 29 missions. Later, they said if they had checked the records right, I could have gotten away with 25.

I flew missions every two, three, four days or once a week. That would be the standard procedure. On a normal mission you would be up early, two or three in the morning for a briefing and not be back till late afternoon. In the briefing room, they would tell you where you were going, what the target was, such as a factory or railroad, or whatever and how many planes and squadrons were going. They would tell you what to expect as far as flak area. Flak was the bursting German shells. We called it something else too. (Laughs.) They also told you the amount of enemy resistance, what types of planes we would encounter, and where. The Eighth Air Force was what they called heavy bombardment, and the Ninth was our fighters, or our cover. They were to give us protection as far as they could. The only thing is that fighters didn't go as far as bombers. They could only go a short distance into Germany, and then they turned around, and it was "I'll see ya." (Laughs.) Then you were on your own.

Then we would drop the bombs. They blanketed a large area, and targets were missed a lot. You dropped your bomb load so your plane became a little bit lighter, easier to move. You're like a crippled duck in water with that bomb load. There's no flexibility or maneuverability at all. Then you would turn around and head back home. Basically, that was a mission. You flew it and came back home.

D-Day was something else altogether. We had no idea what was really involved there, even in the briefing room. That day there were so many planes in the air you couldn't see the sky - so many ships too, you know, to make the invasion. You could hardly see the water, there were so many ships. With D-Day you only had to fly from England across the Channel, a very short run, so I flew three missions. That was the only time you would fly over one mission in one day. Missions that day were only two or two-and-one-half hours.

As soon as you came back they gave you whiskey to relieve the stress - you know - some guys couldn't handle it. It was to calm the nerves. The stress was quite pronounced. After every six missions they would send you to R and R up in Liverpool for about three days for rest and relaxation.

World War II was different than any war thereafter. The public was so supportive. They couldn't do enough for you.

John Cotter returned to the States in 1944. He finished college at Duquesne University on a G.I. Bill instead of attending Duke University on a full scholarship for football. He later served in the Korean War as an officer in the infantry. He lives in the Garden City section of Monroeville, PA, with his wife Helen.

Waiting for planes to return at Fowlmere control tower. (Photo courtesy Tom Brown)

William E. Craig

493rd Bomb Group
863rd Squadron
Pilot

by
Leanne S. Whitesell

William E. Craig, of Pittsburgh, Pennsylvania, was the pilot of a B-17 Flying Fortress during World War II. Mr. Craig and his bombing crew immediately bonded. Herb Lancaster was his copilot during the war and his best friend throughout life. Mr. Craig served from 1942-1945 and received several honors. He is a gentleman who is quiet and modest.

I was born on July 13, 1920, and the Depression affected my life. I was the oldest of three. At times, I worked when my father didn't work. I gave them the money that I earned from various jobs until I was married. At age sixteen, I worked at Bard's Dairy Store in Pittsburgh. Later, I worked at Duquesne Light Company, as a cable tester. When I started for the Light Com-

William Craig and crew. From left to right. Walt Rutske, Walt P. Burget (Phil), Bill L. Morris (Tex), Pyle W. Mac Rochi (Mac), Bill Craig (Skipper), Herbert Lancaster (Herly), Elliott Peterson (Pete), Glenn E. Henning, George W. Bemis (Pappy), Cecil Imel (Snafu). (Photo courtesy William Craig)

William Craig in a trainer in 1943.
(Photo courtesy William Craig)

pany, I went back to night school [for college] trying to get into engineering. I started at Duquesne Light on August 6, 1941. I worked there for one year and then enlisted in the Air Force as a cadet.

The cadet program lasted about six months. I took two courses on Morse code. My first mission I flew as a copilot with a fellow named Mike Karsada, from Rankin, PA. He taught me the importance of checking the flaps, oxygen and all the other safety procedures. [This was really important. It proved that our crew really cared about each other.] The bonding was so effective, if it worked. If it didn't, they almost had to break up the crew.

It's unbelievable what those young men did. Those fellows were really something. Everyone did their job to the best of their ability. If the men hadn't paid the price, and we had lost the war, we'd all be speaking German.

I took off on a mission and there was something wrong with the fuel. We had fuel, but we were losing fuel for some reason. We were on the mission, and something didn't feel right. It wasn't a mission of any great distance, and we would be back in under five hours. We got through the mission, and on the way back the rain moved in. I told Pete, the navigator, I wanted to head into Woodbridge, an emergency landing field. When we got to Woodbridge, I saw the field, dropped the wheels, and turned. Woodbridge was wide enough for three B-17s to take off on. I left the formation and the rest of the planes headed back to our base at Debach [near Ipswich, England]. [I pulled up to refuel and] I didn't even have one hundred gallons of gas in that plane. (Laughs.) I would have never been able to make it over and back. I made up my mind to do what I did, and it worked out. That's about the way it is; we made a decision and did it.

We only had one fifteenth of a second when we were encountered by [German] fighters. They would come through [the sky] and fly through the formation. Those men were doing their jobs. If the Germans would have had those jets a year or so earlier, it would have been a devastating challenge to encounter. The autobahns, [super highways], in Germany, were used by the German jets. They would come up and go after us. They would make an attack when we were bombing, and then they would 'scoot'. Once, I was in a formation where a Focke-Wulf 190 [a German fighter plane] came

William Craig fifty years later in an AT-6 trainer May 22, 1993 at Custer Airport, Monroe, Michigan (Photo courtesy William Craig)

right down through us. He was a good pilot, but he had a lot of nerve. (Laughs.)

There were lots and lots of things that happened. The time went fast. Once we came off of a mission, we had only three to four hours of flying against the wind to get back. We also had corridors located on a map where there would be minimum flak. Sometimes we weren't so lucky to escape it though. Once, on a mission, a piece of flak lunged into Phil's neck. It didn't break the skin or draw any blood.

The closest I came to a really bad situation was when we were flying to Nuremberg. In Nuremberg, they knew their jobs. They would pick any plane, and they knew the speed and the altitude of our planes. They would [be able to] put a shell in our wing. I looked off to my left and there was no one [positioned] there. I moved from the right out of my position to the empty position on my left. There were two puffs of black air seconds later. They just picked any plane, and I happened to be lucky that day when I moved at the right time.

I flew on twenty-seven bombing missions. I also flew two food missions to Amsterdam when the war was over there. The lowlands were flooded in Amsterdam, and we filled the bomb bay and took cases of food. We went in at fifty feet, and we dropped the cases on a golf course. Once, when we had three cases hung up, we threw them out the back of the plane and they landed in the water.

Herb had an Uncle Joe, who lived in Germany. Every time we made a mission, he yelled, "Look out Uncle Joe, here they come!" We had to have a little chuckle. (Laughs.) He said that every time.

How did you feel about the missions? Were you scared?

Oh yeah, I prayed a lot. I'm a Catholic, and I said the rosary. I still say the rosary. That's just the way it is. We felt like we were doing the right thing. We had a reason to be there. When I looked at the number of men serving in the war, I was no different. I was just doing my job, trying to get back to a better way of life. I did my job, and when I came home, I was happy. I grew up a lot because I saw death. We always had a bed, good food, and great comaraderie.

I loved to dance when I was younger. They used to have dances on the base, and they would have trucks that brought in the girls from the town. The girls would come and dance with us. A lot of the men drank and smoked. I never started smoking or drinking, and I never had to stop. I used to go along as an officer and help escort the girls back to their homes. I also delivered milk while I was over there. They didn't have milk like we had. They had a big container of milk, and people would come out with a pitcher. I was allowed to do it because I wasn't married. If I was married [during the war], I would have had to stay on the base.

I am fortunate to have survived, but so many others that didn't need to have credit as well. My entire crew survived the war. The men in my crew were:

Pyle W. MacRoshi "Mac"- Bomber
Herbert Lancaster "Herby"- Copilot
Cecil H. Imel "Snafu"- Nose Gunner
Elliot H . Peterson "Pete"- Navigator
William E. Craig "Skipper"- Pilot
Walter P. Burget "Phil"- Tail Gunner
George W. Benio "Pappy"- Flight
Engineer Bill L. Morris "Tex"
- Waist Gunner
Glen E. Henning "Glen"- Ball Turret
Gunner Walt Rutske "Walt"
- Radio Operator

On November 10, 1945, William E. Craig was relieved of active duty in the Eighth Air Force. He returned to his home in the South Hills of Pittsburgh and continued to work for Duquesne Light Company for forty-two years before retiring. When he returned home he met and married Kathleen Sonnett on June 22, 1946. They have just recently celebrated their fiftieth wedding anniversary, and they have five children and thirteen grandchildren. They are now living in Avalon, a suburb of Pittsburgh, Pennsylvania.

William Cully
100th Bomb Group (H)
351st Squadron
Pilot

by
Amanda Ross

As we sit in the small office, my attention is drawn to the pictures and models of B-17 Bombers that seem to just flow naturally into the decor and would go unnoticed, except for the purpose of my visit. I settle into my chair and learn how a simple twist of fate can affect a person's entire life. It is the story of Bill Cully.

When Pearl Harbor was bombed Bill Cully was a senior in high school. He had graduated and went to Penn State the next fall. It soon became evident that, as the war escalated, "we would all be involved in the service somehow." Cully had planned to join the Navy, but as is often the case, his plans took a turn in another direction. "I had a cousin who was in the Air Force studying to be a pilot at the time I was enlisting in the service. My aunt, his mother, was always talking about him and saying, 'The Air Force this, and the Air Force that.' - You know how parents are. Well, my mother got it into her head that I should go into the Air Force too. I had already taken all of the physicals necessary and was to be sworn into the Navy in two days when my mother called me and said, 'Why don't you give the Air Force a try?' So I did."

After he was sworn in, Cully returned to Penn State to finish out the semester, but before long the inevitable occurred. "In February of 1943 I got called to serve. I went to basic training at Miami Beach. From Miami, I went to what they called a College Training Detachment, and was there for three months. It was there that we had ten hours of flying time in a Piper Cub, which is a little two-seater plane. My only flying experience prior to this was a two-dollar ride I took once at a fair. After we got our three months in, we went to Santa Anna, California, for classification. We were there for another three months for our preflight training. Primary training gave you eighty hours of flying time. My advanced training was in a two-engine plane. From there, I was sent to gunnery school where I graduated from cadets and flew in a B-17. We had crew assignment in Lincoln, Nebraska. After we were assigned to a crew, we went to overseas training.

"The best time I had in the military was during my overseas training. We were stationed in Tennessee, about ninety miles north of Memphis. We would fly in the morning and then we were free from lunchtime until the evening of the following day. Three of us - my bombardier, another fellow, and myself - would get on a bus and ride into Memphis. Once we got into Memphis, we would rent a car and drive around. The three of us ended up meeting three girls on one of our trips into the city, and every time we went there, we would meet up with these three girls. Sometimes, we would take them to dinner. After dinner, we took them to the Peabody, which was a big hotel in Memphis where we all danced on the roof. Then we took the girls home and headed back to our base. I was nineteen years old, at that time and I didn't miss a beat. Those were the fun times."

But the fun times didn't last forever. Cully was sent to England in August of 1943. It was there that he became a pilot in one of the most notorious bomb groups of World War II - "The Bloody 100th." "There was a story that had to do with how our group came to be called 'The Bloody 100th.' Supposedly there was a group coming back from a mission, and one of the

Vapor trails at 20,000 feet over Germany.
(Photo courtesy Frank De Cola)

squadrons got separated from the group. Each group was made up of four squadrons. Anyway, the squadron that got separated was attacked by German fighters. The story goes that our squadron let their wheels down, which was the signal that they had given up. At that point, the Germans moved in to escort the squadron to the nearest German landing area. Well, as the Germans moved in, our squadron started shooting at them. They shot down every German fighter that had been after them. So that's why my group was called 'The Bloody 100th.' Of course, I haven't been able to find anyone to verify that story as either true or false, but it's the only one I've ever heard to explain that nickname." So the legend of "The Bloody 100th" lives on.

"We had a nice barracks; there were only ten people sharing it. We played cards, and some of the guys went to the Officers' Club. One bad thing about our base, though, was that there was no heat in the lavatories. The only heat came from the hot water, and the steam that it would give off. Needless to say, we probably weren't the cleanest guys during the winter. We really only cleaned up to go into London.

"We did have a fellow in our barracks who worked for Operations. He was assigned to go around at about three in the morning to wake crews up before a mission. Usually, you didn't even know if you would be flying a mission the next day, but this guy would give us a hint if he knew we were assigned. He'd tell us that we might want to get to bed early because we could have a busy day ahead of us. So we knew we would probably be flying a mission the next day.

"Briefings consisted of everyone who would be flying a mission assembling in a big room. There was a stage in the front of the room with a curtain drawn across it. When everyone sat down the curtain would be drawn, and there in front of you was a map with the day's mission laid out in thread. They knew flak, or antiaircraft locations, and they mapped out corridors, taking you right through it.

"On my first mission, I really didn't know what to expect - no one had warned me. We had what they called flak-suits, which were sheets of metal covered in canvas. Since I had no idea what I was heading into, I had taken as many pieces of that flak material as I could. I had it lying all around the ground by my seat - anywhere I could put it and still be able to move. There is nothing that can ever replace your first mission for the uncertainty that you face. You hear stories, and you watch movies, but until you live through it, you never really know what it's like.

"It really didn't bother you until you started to see the flak and you realized that you all had to fly through it - turning back was not an option. At the altitude at which we flew, it was easy for the antiaircraft guns on the ground to pick us up on clear days. We were luckier on cloudy days. When it wasn't sunny, we used a material that was like tinsel for a Christmas tree. We would throw it out the doors, and it would cause the radar on the ground to get jammed so they couldn't locate us. A mission on an overcast day is what I would call a milk-run.

"The second time we were forced to land, we lost an engine. When an engine went out, you were supposed to stop the propeller from turning by what was called feathering the prop. That meant that you had to turn the propeller so that it was perpendicular to the wind. That way, when you shut it down, there was no chance of rotation. Well, when our engine went out, we didn't get the prop feathered in time, and as a result a cylinder head blew through. This caused tremendous vibration in the airplane, and the only way to control the vibration was to slow the speed of the plane. We were flying at about 120 miles per hour. Even at that speed, the wind caused the propeller to spin, and every time it would spin around a cylinder would pop. We were able to get a fix on an airfield where we could land, so we figured we had better start going down. We were at about ten thousand feet, and we weren't near the airfield yet. There were tanks on the ground, and at the level we were flying, they were able to spot us. As soon as they had us in their sights, they started shooting at us, but luckily they missed. We were finally able to get the plane on the ground in Belgium."

"On one of our missions, to Berlin, our bombs wouldn't release. They were held on by brackets or hooks, and for some reason they got stuck and wouldn't let go of the bombs. Well, we couldn't bomb Berlin, but we had to get rid of the bombs. Our bombardier had to go back into the bomb bay and manually release the bombs. We ended up dropping bombs all over Germany. Whoever caught them, we never knew. That was a tough mission. We went all the way to Berlin and couldn't drop our dang bombs!

"On another mission, we had some kind of plane that no one had ever seen before actually fly right through our formation. No one shot at it because no one knew what it was. We all went back to the base and reported it, and it turned out that it had been a single-engine jet that the Germans had developed. That was the first time any of us had seen a jet aircraft.

When all was said and done, Bill Cully and his crew had made a success out of their war experience, but Cully takes little, if any, credit for this. "It's really just a story of luck. I got through my missions and never got wounded. No one in our plane ever got wounded. We were lucky to survive.

"I flew thirty-four missions - I was sick on one. On V-E Day, I was in Washington D.C. on my way to Miami. I was at home when the Japanese war ended. In those days if you weren't in the service at the time, you didn't dare wear your uniform. Since I was so young and not in uniform, when V-J Day came, people thought I was a civilian, so I didn't get the congratulations and the spontaneous hugs that the other soldiers got.

"When I was finished in the service, I went back to Penn State and was there for about a year and a half. Then I met a young lady, and transferred to Pitt. I was in the Reserve for awhile.

"It's ironic to see the camaraderie between members of the Air Force. I'm closer to some of those guys who I only knew for a brief time than I might be with someone I knew all through grade school and high school. My crew had a great relationship - we all did our part. We shared the worst times of our lives."

The friendships that Bill Cully developed during the war endure to this day. The experiences of this man will live on and touch the lives of future generations.

James E. Doerr

457th Bomb Group
751st Squadron
Flight Engineer and Gunner

by
Erin Hoehn

Mr. James E. Doerr's life was changed dramatically for the better by his service experience in the Eighth Air Force. He thought it was the most maturing experience of his life and undoubtedly has no regrets for his service in World War II. Mr. Doerr vividly recalls the apprehensions and memorable times he experienced as a turret gunner and flight mechanic while stationed in England.

Pearl Harbor made me want to enlist. Up until that time, there was just the draft. I, like the people [of the United States], was very, very upset that Japan would drop a surprise on us like that. I decided to enlist in the Army Air Force after graduating from high school. I was just nineteen, but my family had no reservations about me going. I was trained to fix B-17s and I also went to gunnery school. We left the States here in January of 1944, almost a year after I had enlisted and was trained as a flight mechanic.

We first landed in Europe at a base in Scotland until they decided where we were to be assigned in England. Being young kids and our first time in Europe, we decided to get on a bus and have a look around. I knew that we were at a base in Scotland, but I did not know exactly where. I sat down on the bus beside a Scottish man and I said, "Where are we?" He said, "Ayre." I thought that he didn't hear me. I said, "I asked you, where are we?" He again replied, "Ayre." I said, "I guess you don't understand me, sir." He said, "No, you're at Ayre....A..Y..R..E, that's the name of the city." I always remember that as my first experience in Europe - Ayre, A..Y..R..E.

From Ayre, we were sent to Peterborough, England, where I remained stationed. It was in the middle of England, where there was a lot of farmland and the people were really hard up for food. We gave them many of our supplies, all of our extras we could spare. If our parents would send us things, we would usually give it to the English kids - even old newspapers; kids had never gotten anything like that before.

Well, we were really nervous our first mission. Every mission you would pray that you would come back alive. The missions always began at four or five o'clock in the morning with a briefing. They told you where you would be going and what targets you were expected to hit. When the crew all got into the plane to leave, we would turn on the radio and Axis Sally would tell us where to go. She would reaffirm our mission from what we were told at the briefing. I will always remember hearing Axis Sally before missions.

We would take off at sunrise. That would be the most beautiful thing to take off in that airplane and look right at that sun rising up, and then fly right up over it. That would really be beautiful. It's things like that a person remembers.

My area in the B-17 was very small. I was between the pilot and copilot. The pilot would be sitting and I would be standing, but we were on the same level. The space was just big enough for me to slide into. About a year ago there was a B-17 at Harrisburg, and I took my grandson to see it. I had a really hard time fitting in that space and walking up through. You see, I was considerably smaller back then.

Even if you didn't see any flak or enemy fighters, there was still danger that your plane would go down over water. A

James Doerr and crew Top row, left to right - Second Lt. Cahelo (Bombardier), Second Lt. Carson (Navigator), First Lt. Graf (Navigator), Major Hosler (Copilot), First Lt. Godfrey (Pilot), Second Lt. Grimes (Tail Gunner), Bottom row, left to right - Calhoon (Top-Turret Gunner), Rubbie (Ball-Turret Gunner), Hiebert (Waist Gunner), Blackwell (Radio Operator), Jim Doerr (Waist Gunner).

(Photo courtesy James Doerr)

mission, for me, would run anywhere from four to twelve hours. We went to Berlin and Munich many times. These were our longest missions and the hardest because the targets were deep into German territory. Sometimes I would even go on two missions a day.

In the Air Force you were up in an airplane, you were at thirty-two thousand feet and all your missions were to factories, rail centers, and places like that. You were never told that you were going to kill any people. If anyone on the ground got killed, you looked at it as an accident, you had to. Most of our missions were early in the morning and they [the Germans] had air-raid warnings. There was really no reason that people had to be there. War is a terrible, terrible thing. I have seen pictures of some of the German cities that were heavily bombed. It's tragic. The pictures were used to judge if we hit our target.

Going to Munich was pretty scary. It was a long run and it was a well-defended city. I went there five times. Munich is pretty far into Germany and there was a ball-bearing factory there that we would bomb. It was a very dangerous business, but after you do it time after time it is just like a job, and you hope that you get back safely.

I thought my pilot was a great man, a fine gentleman. When he was killed they broke up our crew. He was hit by flak. It hit the center of the airplane, in a crucial place, right where all of the fuel is. I was on the mission, but not in the same plane. It was the first time I was not in his crew. He was trying to become a group leader and was leading the entire group of planes. This was to raise his rank. He was a captain trying to become a major. I witnessed the plane go down. It was his twenty-forth mission. His name was Jerome Godfred, a very, very fine gentleman.

It was really sad to see an American plane not come back. Every day, when you went out, you did not know who wasn't coming back. I was really lucky not to lose anyone really close to me except for my pilot. I never thought I was going to get hit, I always kept a positive attitude. Whenever you are nineteen, you think you can beat the whole world.

One time we were hit in the front of the plane with some flak, which flew back and hit me in the knee. It made an awful gash, but it was so cold that it stopped bleeding.

A lot of people think that it was common to get hit or shot down. Actually, a very minute amount of planes were shot down considering the number that flew missions.

We never had any major problems in the air. Sometimes the bombs, whenever they would be released, well, it would be so cold that they would not automatically release like they were supposed to. I would have to go into the bomb bay and kick the bombs, so they could release. This was one of my jobs as the flight mechanic. I couldn't really fix anything while the plane was in the air except maybe the radio. If something malfunctioned, we would just pray that we would make it back to base safely. I would then report what was wrong to the ground crew.

My family thought that the service was the best thing that ever happened to me. I used to be very, very shy before I went over. My aunts used to tell me I would go hide in the corner and I wouldn't talk to anyone. I guess being in the service and the war changed me. I think that the fact that I got home safely and virtually uninjured was a great accomplishment. For me it was a great experience. I think today, the best thing that could happen to this country would be if they took every boy, after he graduated from high school, and put him in the service for two years. That would be a wake-up call and would teach them some discipline. I think the service does make you grow up and find new responsibility. I have no regrets whatsoever.

Mr. James Doerr flew in thirty-five successful mission to targets in Europe, mostly Germany. He reached his maximum flight missions, allowing him to return to the *United States. However that was not the end of his military service. The end of World War II found Mr. Doerr at Iwo Jima as a flight engineer. He volunteered to return to service where he was part of a crew that searched for and rescued American planes that went down in the Pacific.*

Today, Mr. Doerr is retired from the United States Postal Service and lives with his wife of forty-eight years. He has four children and, so far, five grandchildren. In his free time he enjoys woodworking and attending many reunions for the Army Air Force around the country. In fact, he still keeps in touch with a fellow crewman living in San Diego, California.

P-51 "Mary Queen of Scotts"

(Photo courtesy Tom Brown)

Charles Fisher

384th Bomb Group
544th Squadron
Flight Engineer and Gunner

by
Kerri Pakutz

Charles Fisher, worked on the railroad as a machinist apprentice at the time of the bombing of Pearl Harbor. After the war, he was a pre-med student, swimming director, Y.M.C.A. boys' work secretary and eventually retired from the Bell Telephone Company after thirty-five years of service.

I enlisted in Pittsburgh in 1942 because I felt that it was my patriotic duty, and to avoid the draft. I wanted to be able to pick what part of the military I wanted to join, which was the Air Force.

I went to Bell Aircraft Specialist School in Niagara Falls to study special engine mechanics. I signed up for aerial gunnery, and through that school they sent me to Tampa, Florida. In Tampa, I flew with the B-26 bomber crews as a flight engineer. At that time, they were doing a lot of bombing over Europe. My next step was to go to Walla Walla, Washington, on the west coast. I was assigned to a B-17 bomb crew. It was then we were assigned to the Eighth Air Force in England, and I began bombing missions in Germany on a B-17 Flying Fortress as a flight engineer / gunner.

My first mission was tough. Our plane position was "tail-end Charlie", and if you know anything about that, it was the worst position to be placed in, because of all the flak and fighter planes you received from the Germans. I must say that it was the first time that I ever experienced the Holy Spirit. When we first got up there with the Germans, my knees were knocking, and I was just shaking all over. I said a little prayer, and all of a sudden a calmness overcame me, and for the rest of my missions I felt at peace.

At that time in the war the average number of missions you had to fly were twenty-five, but as the war grew on, the numbers increased. It was the worst time in the air war when I began with the Mighty Eighth. Many planes went out, but few came back.

Our second mission was just like our first. The plane we had was named, "Slightly Dangerous." Both during the first mission as well as the second, it was shot up pretty bad. All I had to do was pray, and the calmness returned, and I felt God's presence once again.

Our third and final mission was probably the scariest out of all three put together. Our mission was to bomb Stuttgart, Germany, which was an aircraft electrical plant that we were told to wipe out. Before takeoff, the crew was informed that there might not be enough fuel to get back to the base. Our instructions were to fly over our target, bomb the target, and return to the base. But a problem arose. As we flew over our target, we encountered a thick cloud cover which prevented us from seeing the target. A second pass was attempted, and after destroying the target, we began our journey home. Our informants were right - we ran out of fuel. The pilot and crew of the plane decided that instead of parachuting, he and the rest of us were going to stick it out with the plane and crash-land. We all gathered ourselves into the radio room and sat huddled together. We braced ourselves when we crashed. No one was hurt, and we were all thankful. The navigator told us that we were in enemy-occupied France approximately fifty miles north of Paris. So in order to avoid getting caught, the crew decided to start scattering. After we set fire to the plane, the ball-turret gunner, whose name was Jim Wagner, and myself started to walk along the tree line of the woods. Our goal at that moment was to get as far away from the plane as we possibly could. Jim and I came to a high wall after walking a while. I boosted him up to see what it was on the other side and if it was safe for us to hide in. It was an old garden overgrown with weeds. I turned to Jim and said, "Let's get over there and see what we're gonna do." So, we jumped over the wall and hid among the weeds.

We weren't there too long when we heard voices on the road. It was a German search party. They just peeked inside the gate and didn't even bother coming in to check it out. Jim and I were scared half to death. We decided to stay there for the rest of the day and relax. When the sun began to set, and it grew colder, Jim and I decided that we'd better start looking for a place to stay through the night. Over in the field was a Frenchman tending to his windmill, so we decided to approach him. It was dusk when we reached him, and in our best French explained that we were Americans whose plane had just crashed and that we needed a place to sleep. The Frenchman understood us but motioned for us to stay down because there were Germans all around. He left for a moment and returned with a young boy who led us into a French village. The boy took us into a house, and the man of the house said, "You'll be safe in my house today because they're (the Germans) searching the haystacks. But, tomorrow, they'll begin searching houses." He told us that his family had no connections with the French Underground, but his son-in-law went into Paris often, and could look for someone to make contact with.

We slept there, and early the next morning. While it was still dark the Frenchman gave us civilian clothes to wear, fed us, and put us in a haystack out in the country where we spent four days. These kind people brought us food and wine, and on

B-17 Flying Fortress

(Photo courtesy Tom Brown)

the fifth day they brought us back to a house that was next to the farmhouse. Jim and I then had the first chance to shave that day since our plane crash. The farmer couldn't speak much English, so he indicated for us to stay away from the windows. A little later, they brought in a young woman who was a teacher that could speak English somewhat better. She also told us to stay away from the windows because if the children saw either of us they would run back to school and tell someone. The teacher went on to explain that the French Underground had been contacted but hadn't responded back yet. To be safe Jim and I spent the night in the house. In the morning we saw a car outside in which two men got out of and proceeded into the farmhouse. These two men drove us towards Paris, and on the way we passed the garden where Jim and I sought refuge, as well as our plane. By then the only things left were the engine and wings.

As we arrived near Paris the two Frenchmen drove into a courtyard of a house where Jim and I spent a good portion of the day. He and I were given cheese and wine in the house and were eventually led into a room where there were two more Frenchmen. Amongst the Frenchmen, there, was a priest who could speak little English and was extremely hard to understand. He began asking questions to Jim and I. Every once in a while he'd ask us, "Compris?" That meant "Do you understand?", and we said, "Yeah." Then a little later he said, "Compris?" Once again we replied, "Yeah." He then pointed at us and said, "You German. Americans say 'Yes.' Germans say 'Yah.'" Jim and I later discovered that when a plane crashed, just as ours did, the Germans would dress up in the American uniforms, and would attempt to get into the French Underground. If they succeeded and got through, then those Frenchmen and whatever soldiers found there were killed. But if the Frenchmen found out that you were German, you were killed.

What these two Frenchmen and the other man were doing was a test to see if we were really who we said we were. Jim and I finally convinced them we were American. They left, and another man came in to drive us into Paris in his truck. The truck had two compartments for hiding; one in the cab roof, and one under the seat. We stayed there overnight, and in the morning the man went to load his truck. When he returned his wife's cousin said that she wanted to go into Paris, so Jim and I hopped in the back of the truck. The Frenchman dropped off his wife's cousin, and the rest of us proceeded towards the outskirts of Paris. As we approached the area German sentries stopped the Frenchman to inspect his truck and its contents. Jim and I had been hiding among the boxes and were mighty lucky that the Germans didn't inspect thoroughly. Not being discovered, we moved on.

The truck driver took us to an apartment, and in the basement of that apartment, we stayed until he finished unloading his truck. The driver then led us to another apartment, which belonged to a married couple who had two small children. Jim and I stayed there for three days. The man who lived there was a travel agent and could speak English fairly well. He told us that we were the first airmen that he had hid. One night, the phone rang and the Frenchman got up to answer it. He said something to his wife in French and she immediately started to cry. He turned to us and said that his contact with the French Underground had been captured by the Gestapo, and didn't know how much information they might get from him - so he'd have to get us out of his house. Jim and I followed him to his abandoned office on the second floor. He and Jim and I spent the night there. The Frenchman left that morning to go to work, but left instructions not to answer the door or go near the windows. He returned later with two Frenchmen who were going to take us to our next destination. The two men asked us if we had our ID papers, and our reply was, "No." They let us get washed up and shaved, and told us that we were going to stop along the way to get identification. After our identification papers were made, the men drove us to another home belonging to two women who were living together. The one woman had a daughter who was fifteen or sixteen at the time, and the other woman had two children. Jim and I stayed there for at least four or five weeks. After this short period, Jim and I were told that it was time to move again. We headed for the train station, and one of the women we stayed with told us to follow a certain man on the train, but not to get too close to him, or we'd surely be captured. The man's name was Claude. The train was crossing the Line of Demarcation, and it was required of everyone to have paperwork explaining your reasons for crossing over. Claude, Jim, and I were sitting in the dining car while our papers were being inspected, and a German officer came to me and began asking me questions. He left me and returned to his fellow officers to talk with them. The Germans then left the car, the papers, and the three of us alone. I asked Claude what was the matter, and he told me that the German officer wasn't familiar with the form I had, and thought that it should have been bigger. Claude went on to say that the German had asked me the question in German - which I didn't have to answer, but if it had been French - I'd have been in trouble.

When we had finally arrived in southern France, the three of us went to a tavern. On the second floor fifteen Frenchmen had joined us. A guide came into the room who was to lead us through the mountains, and he instructed us to leave the tavern by twos every three minutes. Our entire party boarded a five-coach train which was headed towards the Pyrenees Mountains. Claude, Jim, the guide, two Frenchmen, and I were all sitting in the last coach. The train stopped and the guide got off. We started up a mountain trail, and when we looked back no one else had gotten off the train. For two hours we walked up the mountain. The guide told us to stop there and wait while he checked about the border. It seemed forever while we waited. At midnight we quit waiting and assumed that the guide had gotten scared that the Germans had inspected the other coaches and captured the other escape members.

We went back into town and rode the train back to the first station, where we had tea and wine in the tavern. One of the Frenchmen that were still with us said that he knew a smuggler during peacetime who smuggled things between France and Spain. If he could somehow get in touch with him, then he could lead us through the mountains. In the meantime, Claude said that he wasn't going to go any further with us, but back to Paris. The Frenchman that knew the smuggler returned and told us that he had made contact with him. So the four of us: the two Frenchman (who, by the way, were named Vic and Renee), Jim, and I got onto a bus.

We arrived at a mountain village, and all got off the bus. Vic went to make his contacts again and returned to explain that his friend had agreed to take us up the mountain. Vic also said that there was an escape party being organized and that it would be ready in a day or so. The four of us stayed at the smuggler's home for three days. When the escape party was complete, there were fifteen Frenchmen, two Jewish couples, and the guide's teenage son. The entire group started up the mountain, passed the first peak, and then proceeded down into the valley. While we rested, we noticed a solitary figure standing at the peak, slowly descending. Other figures began to appear. We were afraid that it was a German search party, so we hid. It turned out to be another escape party. We joined forces, and now together we had about thirty people traveling with us. All day we walked, and that night we slept in a sheep herder's shack, and walked the entire next day. Finally the search party came to a ravine which was close to the border. By this time we were all soaked to the bone, cold, and our shoes were falling apart.

In the ravine the guide said that someone could build a fire to dry our clothes and warm ourselves. That night we crossed a creek, and on the other side was a path. The path led to the central guard and we were told to keep our guide in sight. The instructions were to keep moving because it would soon be dark. The Jewish couple had begun their walk up in front of the group, but as everyone kept moving, they fell behind with the guide's son. At this time, a car drove up the path and turned on heavy searchlights. We climbed up the path just to get away from the area, and that's when we reached the top of the mountain. Someone took a head count, and discovered that the Jewish couples' and guide's son weren't with us. So, a guide volunteered to go back and look for them. He told us to move on. After walking for what seemed an eternity, we arrived at a little country all by itself up in the Pyrenees Mountains. A decision was made to stop at the tavern there, but an innkeeper came to us saying that it was unsafe for us to be there because there was a German search party nearby, and they could offer no protection for us. We kept on going - we were now in Spain. We found an inn in which we checked in, and sat down to have some wine. The innkeeper came over to us there, and by that time, we felt that there was nothing else that could go wrong because everything else had somewhat ended that way. He said that there were two men in our room wanting to speak with us. Jim and I went to the room and the men began asking us questions.

Jim and I told them that we didn't have to explain anything - but little did we know-they were members from the British Embassy. They explained that two of their men were being held for ransom in the area, and that he had heard about Jim and myself, thinking that we might be the men they were looking for. The British and American embassies had made a special pact that if either finds a soldier in trouble, they would be cared for until they could be returned home. We became English citizens that day, complete with English identification. The two men then drove us to Barcelona and then to the British Embassy. A woman began to ask to interview us there, but asked to hold off on the interview until we had washed up and shaved because it had been so long since either of us had bathed. We showered and shaved, then returned to finish the interview. We were given our identification papers and then were taken to Madrid where we spent three weeks. During that time we enjoyed ourselves going to nightclubs and restaurants. It was really strange to see Germans all around you, even though Spain was a neutral country. When we left Madrid our next stop was the Rock of Gibraltar. Jim and I were turned over to the Colonel stationed there, and he took us through the supply line. He gave us clean uniforms, and told us to stand against the wall, then strip out of our clothes. After doing so he then told us to put on our uniforms. The Colonel said, "You're back in the army now." Jim and I were flown back to England and spent three weeks there for debriefing. Jim and I had to recount everything we did, everything we saw, and everything we heard. After spending fifty-three days in Europe, we could go back home to the States - just in time for Christmas.

Later, when I married, we returned to France to visit with a few of the kind people who cared for Jim and me. I was given the Air Medal and I correspond frequently with my partner, Jim, and a few of the people who took us in.

Mr. Fisher felt it was his patriotic duty to enlist at the age of twenty. He was asked that if he ever had the opportunity would he fight for his country again, and his response was "Yes."

George P. Fisher

306th Bomb Group
368th Squadron
Ball-Turret Gunner

by
Nikki Watterson

As a young man of seventeen, I went to work at the Pittsburgh Post Gazette as an apprentice pressman.

I worked for one year before Pearl Harbor was bombed in December 1940. At this time, most young men were either drafted or enlisted into the service, there weren't many fellows around then. I first tried to get in the Marines, but was not accepted because I am color-blind. Although the Air Force doesn't accept color-blind people either, I enlisted in the U. S. Air Force on August 21, 1941 and was accepted. Instead of giving me color charts, which I can't read, they quizzed me with a yarn test, which I passed. - They had red and blue, I can read those, but don't mix me up with green, I get lost! - At this point in time I was then tested, by shots and aptitude tests, to determine into which school I would be qualified and trained. My tests indicated "Radio School". I saw a big sign that said, "Be A Gunner," I wanted to fly. While being questioned, I indicated my interest in becoming a ball-turret gunner. The guy told me the survival rate was very bad, but I said I wanted to go to Gunnery School anyhow. All gunners at this time were volunteers. Since there was such a drastic need for gunners, they pulled me out of basic training after four weeks, and I was sent to gunnery school.

(Photo courtesy Lawrence Brown)

My first six weeks of training were spent in Texas, where I graduated on October 21, 1942 as a sergeant. Later, I joined a crew at Salt Lake City, Utah as a ball turret gunner. I also attended Radio School and graduated as a staff sergeant. From this point I went through phase training which prepared us for all types of combat conditions we might encounter. I then received further training at Walla Walla Washington, Redmond, Oregon, and Pierre, South Dakota where I trained for cross-country trips. On March 28, 1942 we flew overseas to our destination, stopping in Puerto Rico, Trinidad, Brazil, the Ascension Islands, and French Morocco, to check out the planes and refuel. On the trip overseas we lost four or five planes because of things like engine trouble. Next, the planes stopped at the Shannon Airport, Ireland, where we transferred to a school for aircraft identification and more extensive gunnery training. After two weeks we were shipped by train to our permanent base, Thurleigh, England, near Bedford. We were issued a plane and replaced crews that were lost, destroyed, or taken prisoners. We were assigned to 306th Bombing Group, 368th Squadron of the U. S. 8th Air Force.

Our first plane was never named. May 13 was our first mission. We flew to Meulte, France. You don't know what to expect when you go off for the first time. They get you up at three or four o'clock in the morning and you go to the mess hall and get breakfast, then you go to a meeting hall . . . a briefing, they tell you were you're going to go and what to expect. They tell you escape plans; if you're shot down, and what you should do. After the briefing, you go out and prepare your turret or guns. Mine loaded up from the inside, it held 1150 rounds of ammunition. The usual start-up time is around daybreak. On the first mission, you're scared, you don't know what to expect or anticipate. I imagine most of us were scared at one time or another. There were four squadrons in our group: 367th, 368th, 369th, and 423rd. Each group has six planes, and they all get together and fly their mission; and all the other groups are all over the sky. You fly over the English Channel and test your guns, and then fly to your target. This was a short one. It wasn't too bad. We only ran into a few fighters. We dropped our bombs, and didn't have any losses on that mission. After you get back, they go through interrogation; they asked you what you saw, and where they hit. They used to show us pictures; and we'd pick out where the bombs hit, to see if we hit the targets. After the interrogation you're on your own again . . . until the next one. The first mission lasted five hours and fifteen minutes. Our second mission was a long one. It lasted six hours and twenty-five minutes.

While on our third mission to Wilhelmshaven, Germany, we lost our two outboard engines. Our plane was so damaged that the tail gunner bailed out thinking we were going down. With our aircraft so badly damaged we managed to get to the English coast and made an emergency landing in a beautiful field of buttercups. It was because of this test that we named our next plane "Buttercup."

Our sixteenth mission was on August 17, 1943 to Schweinfurt, Germany. Schweinfurt was one of the worst missions flown. The 8th Air Force lost sixty aircraft, that's six hundred men, on just that one trip.

I flew my last mission, the twenty-fifth, with a new crew on a new plane called "Eager Beaver." That was October 9, 1943. I was a ball-turret gunner replacement for this crew. After my twenty-fifth mission I was awarded the Distinguished Flying Cross. I already had the Air Medal and four Oak Leaf Clusters. At this time those of us lucky to be alive were given the option of staying in England and receiving a commission as second lieutenant, or, if we chose, return to the U.S. I chose to return home. After a short leave, I was sent to Laredo, Texas for training to become a gunnery instructor. My job was to train and instruct men who were being sent into combat from Drew Field, Florida.

On July 15, 1944 while instructing a class on a training mission over the Everglades, another B-17 crossing under us flew too close and hit our plane underneath. The plane was damaged, and it was my duty, as instructor, to get the crew to bail out. After we landed, some were hurt. One landed in a tree, and others were emotionally distraught. I got them together, administered morphine shots, and waited for help. The pilot stayed with the plane and landed it. He was hurt, but alive. Because I had to bail out to save my life, I automatically became a member of the Caterpillar Club, which is still active. After the collision and bail out, I was put in a service hospital in St. Petersburg, Florida. I was sent to Athletics Instructions, where I chose to become a life guard. I was discharged October 22,

1945, after 2 years, 5 months and 18 days in the U.S., 8 months, 13 days (25 missions) in foreign countries, and 145 hours and 25 minutes of actual combat-time (flying).

It's hard for people to sit down and think about war. You have to be in it to experience it. I just hope that people realize what was sacrificed. You almost have to put yourself in the situation, which is very difficult. It's hard to do that today. In fact, even during the war, people in the United States didn't realize what most of the people went through overseas. Soldiers, sailors, Marines, Air Force, no matter what, they all had their own things to face. I hope there's never any wars, because I don't want to see anyone go to war. War isn't a pleasant experience. I'd do it again; I wouldn't hesitate. Everyone says, "How could you become a ball-turret gunner? Nobody would become a ball-turret gunner," but I liked it.

All of our group have reunions annually, and I attend many. From my crew, the only three still living are former Lt. Robinson of Texas (pilot), Beverly Lamb from Virginia (bombardier), and myself. We still keep in touch. There was a book written, First Over Germany, by Russel A. Strong. It's the history of the 306th Bombardment Group. It tells all, and somewhere in the book my name is mentioned for shooting so many German planes. No one is ever sure of just how many planes any one gunner shot down because of all the activity, but I'm sure I did more than my share.

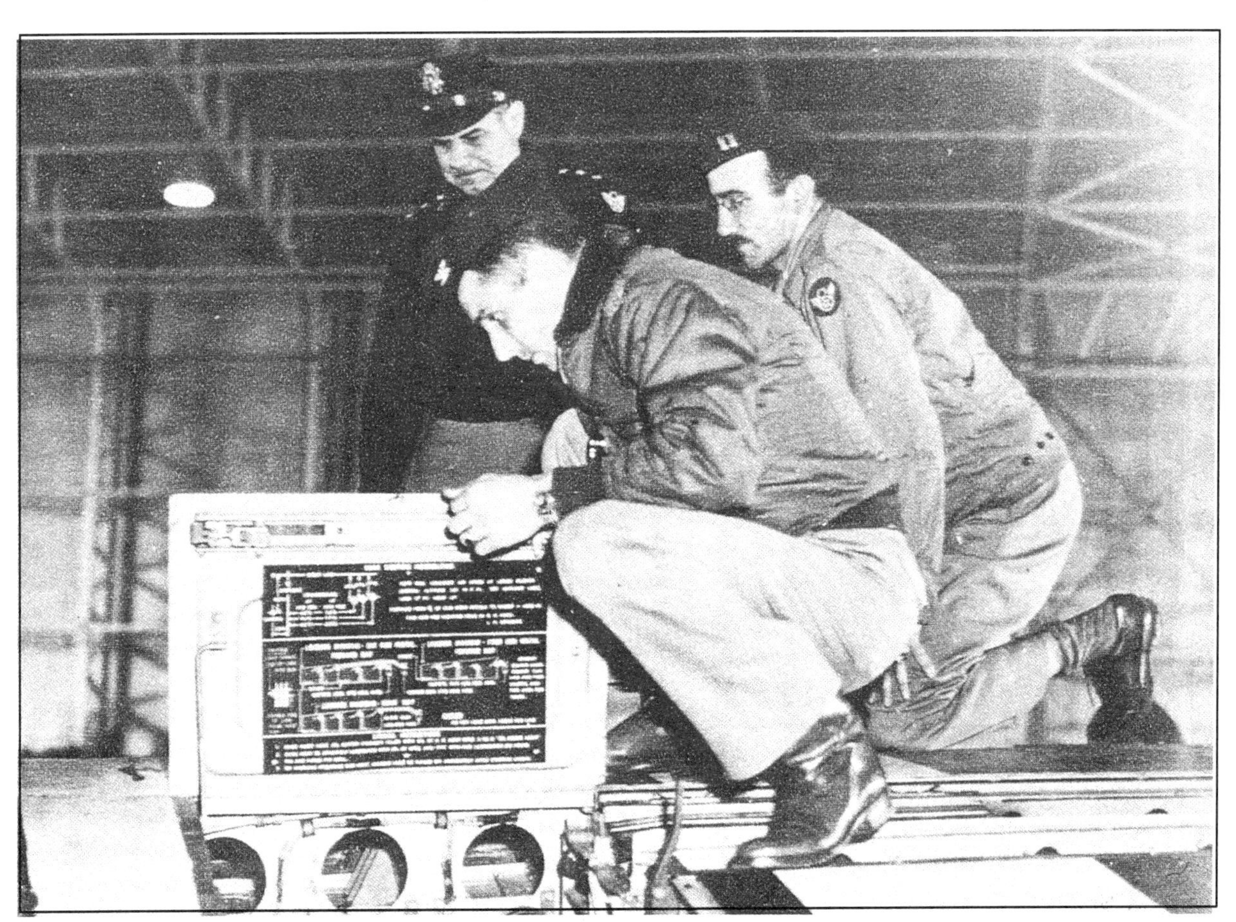

Gen. James Doolittle (far left) with Col. Henry and an unidentified officer checking out a P-51.
(Photo courtesy Tom Brown)

Norman Foss

95th Bomb Group
412th Squadron
Waist Gunner

by

Lori Robinson

The afternoon glow of the sun floods the living room of Norman Foss, casting his gentle features into the soft light. He is a small man with twinkling blue eyes and a head of white hair. His grandfatherly features contrast with his lively personality and enthusiastic smile. He is a matter-of-fact man who prefers to focus on the present and future rather than the past. However, a haunted look shadows his eyes as he reminisces about his days in the Army and his short career as an aerial gunfighter in the Eighth Air Force.

After the spring term of the River Fall's Teacher's College came to a close in the spring of 1942, things were getting very uneasy around town. The war effort was in full swing, and the United States was fully committed. Many of my friends were enlisted in one branch or another during the spring term and were now gone. So, I decided to go.

Soon after being sworn in, a bunch of guys and I were on a train headed for Fort Sheridan, Illinois. Upon arrival, I found out darn quick that I no longer had anything to say about my destiny. At Fort Sheridan we were tested for various things to find out what we were adapted to. I was told that all of us were going to be in the Air Force because that was where they needed men.

So, we were transferred to Buckley Field. Our barracks were tar-paper buildings, as were all other buildings on the base. The school that we were going to was a Fighter Aircraft Armament School. We learned the 50 caliber machine gun thoroughly. We had to learn the name of all the parts, how to dismantle it, and how to put it back together again. For a final test, we had to do it blindfolded! About the only thing that was of value to me later on was the 50 caliber machine gun because that was what we used in the Flying Fortresses in Europe.

As long as I could not get into the pilot training program, I thought that I would try for the next best thing. They were giving exams for aerial gunners, so I applied for it. The tests must have been easy because I was selected to go to Aerial Gunnery School.

We started our training by shooting B.B. guns at stationary targets. The fun really started when we were introduced to twelve-gauge shotguns. Some of these kids had never seen a shotgun let alone fire one! Those that didn't know about a shotgun got the hell beat out of them! (Laughs.)

Eventually, we went from trap shooting to skeet. On the final day of this part of training, we shot seventy-five rounds. We went around the course three times without stopping. I was the only one in the entire class that hit all seventy-five birds. By the way, the truck traveled at a constant speed of thirty miles per hour.

The day finally came for us to do our air firing. We packed up our belongings and went by truck to Indian Springs, Nevada. We ended up doing most of our firing over Death Valley. My first experience at air firing was almost the end. We flew in AT-6s, which was a two-seater trainer. The pilot was up front, and the gunner was in the rear. The only communication was by prearranged hand signals. We fired at a sleeve target towed by another plane. Our ammo was colored so they could identify the hits and give you credit for them. We were flying in formation with six or seven other planes; and when it was our turn at the target, we pulled out of our formation and went down to fire at the target. When I was done firing, I was supposed to tilt my gun up and down. Well, when I did the waving of the gun, without warning, the pilot put the plane up on a wing, and away we went. I was strapped to a safety belt, or I would have gone right out of the plane! There were times, after I was in the safety of my seat, that I didn't know whether we were upside down or whether the planes were! I really had a ride and was too scared to be sick. There was no proof to this, but it was said that the pilots of these planes were goof-offs and they would not send them into combat! (Laughs.)

Later on we were presented with our Aerial Gunner's Wings and our promotions to buck sergeants. They also announced the top five men of the entire gunnery course, and I happened to be third in total scoring. In a few days we were issued B-4 bags and a parachute bag, which meant that we were going to be assigned to a bomb group. We ended up being sent to England as replacement gunners for the Eighth Air Force. I was sent to the 95th Bomb Group air base, which was located in a little English hamlet called Horam.

My flying career was short-lived. I went on two missions over France. Both of these missions were diversions, as they were called. We would take off without a bomb on board, but we made sure we had all the ammo we could handle. One of these missions, we flew over Abbeville, France where there was a German airfield that we called the "Abbeville Kids". We would flush up their fighters and have them follow us. We would then shoot the living hell out of them! They would follow us until they had to get back because of gasoline. While they were chasing us and trying to shoot us down, another one of our bomb groups would come and bomb their air strips and buildings. So when the German fighters tried to land, there were no landing strips for them to land on! Hopefully, they would crash their planes. It was with these sort of tactics that we were able to weaken the German Air Force and gain air superiority for ourselves.

The next mission that I flew was my last. We were going to Norway to bomb a hydroelectric plant just outside of Oslo, Norway. At briefing we were told that we would gain altitude over England and then fly over the North Sea. We were told not to take our Mae Wests (name of life preserver), because if we were shot down, we would land in the North Sea, and a person could not survive for more than five minutes because the water was so cold. After takeoff we flew over England for about an hour forming up our group and then gaining the altitude where we would fly.

About halfway to Norway, I started to hemorrhage through my nose. I told the captain about it over the intercom. It was suggested that I take my oxygen mask off and see if that would congeal the blood. That worked because it was forty below zero in the plane. I couldn't stay off oxygen too long either, so I kept taking the mask off and putting it back on all the way to the target and home again. About halfway home I was getting weak from the loss of blood.

When we landed, I was taken to my squadron flight surgeon for examination. He had me transferred to an evacuation hospital about thirty miles from our air base. I was given a transfusion and put on bed rest for about a week. I was told I was suffering from acute sinusitis, and that I would not get better as long as I was in the damp climate that England was known for. After much deliberation on the part of the flight surgeon, I was grounded permanently.

I laid around for a while, and then I went to Norwich, England and played golf through the Red Cross. I started playing golf in earnest and got acquainted with a lot of Englishmen. They all talked about how that Yankee sergeant could play. (Laughs.)

I kept this up for a couple of months

95th BOMB
8TH AIR F
HORHAM, E
SEPTEMBER

Norman Foss is in the dark jacket directly below where the wings of the two planes seem to touch.
(Photo courtesy Norman Foss)

when the Army busted me to private. As long as I was not flying in combat, they figured that I couldn't be a gunner anymore. So I was assigned to permanent kitchen police. I was surprised to find out that my commanding officer thought that I didn't deserve that demeaning of a job, so he had me assigned to the base commander's table in the officer's mess. On mornings of a mission only the colonel would be at the table. The rest of the staff ate at the combat mess hall. This was real light duty called "Dog Robbing."

Our 95th Bomb Group was one of the first groups to complete two hundred bomb missions. In celebration of this event Glenn Miller's orchestra played for a dance one night. Girls were brought in, from where, I don't know, but they came by the truckloads! There was about two thousand G.I.'s, so it would take a lot of girls if we danced at the same time. But there were a lot of guys like me who didn't care to dance. We just wanted to drink beer and listen to the finest music ever created.

Soon after Christmas of 1944 the Germans made a breakthrough in Europe that was called the "Bulge." Later, there was a great fight called "The Battle of The Bulge." I was in London on a three-day pass and having too much fun to return to the base at the allotted time. I figured that no one would miss me anyway. I would have been right about not being missed, except in my absence there was a big sweep to round up all the unnecessary personnel and herd them into the infantry. The "Battle of The Bulge" had created a demand for more man power. When I returned to base I was told that I would be leaving for the infantry along with a few hundred others from our bomb group. So that was the end of my short-lived career as an aerial gunfighter.

Norman Foss later went into the infantry. His nickname became "Air Corps," and he later became squad leader and earned the title of corporal. He helped courageously liberate the Buchenwald Concentration Camp.

I still remember the welcome we got when we came home. We sailed up New York Harbor on July 11, 1945. There was no prettier sight than the Statue of Liberty standing out there in the harbor. What a welcome we got! There were fire boats shooting streams of water into the air and whistles blowing. Bands played rousing marches that made the hair on my neck stand straight up. There were throngs of people standing on the pier all blowing horns and whistles of some sort.

Later on at Fort Snelling, I was interviewed by an officer that tried to get me to re-enlist. He told me how I could expect to get a commission in a short time and all that bunk. I said, "Sir, there is really only one thing that I want out of this man's army." He said, "What is that, corporal?" I said, "Me - just give me that discharge so I can get out of here!" (Laughs.)

I never talked about my war years. I figured that I had not accomplished any great feats. I was just one of the millions who were glad to escape unscathed.

Heroically, Norman Foss fought for his country earning the Good Conduct Medal and the Distinguished Unit Badge with an Oak Leaf Cluster during the journey. He and his lovely wife, Lois, reside in an affluent neighborhood near Pittsburgh. Norman spends most of his free time writing and playing golf. He also dedicates much of his time to helping mental patients at the local mental hospital. He is a man with strong familial roots bound in love and faith.

Alexander Ganyu

96th Bomb Group
3rd Division
45th Combat Wing Pilot

by
Patty Thalhofer

Picture a kind, knowledgeable, energetic man. Though there were many trials and tribulations during his time in the 8th Air Force, there were also humorous times. Alexander Ganyu was able to meet all the challenges he was faced with and now tells of both the good and bad.

I remember, even before the war, that I would read everything I could get my hands on about WWI flyers and pilots. I read all those stories about all the aces in WWI, and I used to say, "Yeah, I'm gonna be a pilot." Lo and behold it happened. I was in my second year of school in December of '42, and I went and enlisted in the Air Corps. I thought, "If I wait to be drafted I'm gonna be, ya know, who know's where? I'll be in the ground army, walking, [or in the] infantry. I know that my health is good, so I'll enlist." After passing all the tests and being sworn into the Army Air Corps while still in my second year of college, the Army authorities sent me back to school. Three weeks after enrolling, I was called into service on February 22, 1943 reporting to the Pittsburgh, Pennsylvania induction center.

We finished our combat crew training in September 1944 and were assigned to the 96th Bomb Group, 3rd Division, 45th Combat Wing of the 8th Air Force. We were assigned a new B-17, and it had a picture on it of a girl rolling the dice, and the dice showed two twos on it. That's called "Little Joe," if you're familiar with dice rolling. After numerous meetings which we called "ground school," we were anxious to fly our first mission.

October 17 was the first mission I went on, and it was, "Oh boy! This is great! Charge! We're ready to go!" There we were going to Cologne, and I didn't know anything about Cologne, except that it was a big city in Germany. Well, I found out they shoot at you from the ground. I remember the briefing specifically telling us to avoid bombing the cathedral - the only structure standing and undamaged in that area. On this mission, our bomb doors would not open, even with the salvo switch which flings the doors open and also drops the bombs. We flew the same airplane on our third mission, and the same thing happened. We had to crank the doors open and closed by hand which meant that the engineer had to go back to the bomb bay, stand on the narrow catwalk almost on his head leaning to the side, and crank the doors open. Since we are at high altitude, McNeil [one of the crew members] was using an emergency walk-around oxygen bottle. This was very dangerous because the bottle clips onto the flight suit or parachute harness and easily comes apart with all that movement. In spite of this [bomb bay doors not opening] happening twice, our ground maintenance and our maintenance crews were outstanding.

One of the worst [missions] was the little town of Merseburg where they had a synthetic oil refinery. Oil was important for the war industry. Everything ran off of oil, and therefore they protected it as much as possible. The stories we heard was that Merseburg was as well protected as Berlin was, maybe even more so because Merseburg was more important. We hated to go to Merseburg because it was so well defended. On top of that, there was a large city not too far away, Leipzig. If you weren't careful and you got over Leipzig, then you got shot at even more. One of the strange things that happened was that we couldn't figure out why it took us so long to come back off the target. Well, we dropped our bombs, put our nose down, and speeded up to get out of there as fast as we could because they were shooting at us. Well, on this particular mission, I guess we were blown further away then we thought, because there was a tail wind, and we didn't

P-51 Mustang formation.

(Photo courtesy Tom Brown)

know what this tail wind was. By the time we turned around to come back out of there, we were running into this wind that pushed us away. We had an air speed of say 150 m.p.h. and we had a wind blowing at us at one hundred m.p.h. So that means our ground speed was only fifty m.p.h., and that means they shot at us longer. We were over Leipzig coming back out, and they were shooting at us. We must have been shot at for a half hour. Then, on top of that, the guy that was leading us that day was our own colonel from our own bomb group, and his name was Colonel Warren. He wouldn't let us leave formation, and he wouldn't let down. By the time we got out of Germany and into France, we realized that we were going to run out of gas 'cause this terrific wind was causing our ground speed to be so slow. As it happened, he (Colonel Warren) kept telling us to stay in formation and we'd be all right. Well, he didn't even make it back home. I think he landed on the coast of France or Belgium. There were only eight of us that made it back to our base. I was one of the eight, although the other twenty-eight made it back eventually. When I landed, our crew chief on the ground said we only had twenty gallons of gas left. Twenty gallons of gas is not even enough to put the power back on. So that was a terrible mission that day, even though it's not written up in the book as a terrible mission.

I remember one mission, I think the same thing happened on that "Memphis Belle," an incident when a group of guys on my plane were without oxygen, and they passed out because they didn't have any oxygen. Our regulations called for us to be on oxygen at ten thousand feet on. You could pass out from the lack of oxygen from fifteen thousand feet on, and when you're deprived of oxygen you don't know this because you have a "happy moment." The lack of oxygen makes you goofy, and this makes it dangerous. Anyway, we're flying along, and I looked down in the space that was the separation between me and the copilot, and all of a sudden I see a head there, and the head is not moving. So I reach down while the copilot is flying and shake it, and it's still not moving. So I said something to the engineer. We had walk-around bottles which gave you twenty minutes of oxygen. So he [the engineer] put that on and walked over to help this guy. The next thing you know the both of them are laying there. So somebody else comes up to help, and finally I took my hose apart and clipped a bottle on. I went and I got one guy out of there and got him on oxygen. Then I got somebody else out, and the next thing you know I'm out of oxygen. I didn't realize this until I came to and had this oxygen just rushing at my nose and I'm trying to pull it away while my copilot is there holding it. Well, I finally came to and hooked everything up. Everything was OK. We tried to recreate what happened. Apparently, the guy put his oxygen bottle on and was coming up to do something when a connection came loose. He didn't know it. The engineer went back, and the same thing happened to him. This all took place in about five minutes of time. It ended up that everybody got back on oxygen and was OK. But there was five minutes when four guys passed out. It's funny, when we went to see "Memphis Belle," the movie, I'm telling my wife,"My golly, I can't even claim my story because it's almost similar to what happened there, and somebody would think I lifted it." (Laughs.)

We had foggy, rainy weather a lot, and it was dangerous flying. You could well imagine [what it was like] when you're flying around in soup and you have between one thousand five hundred and two thousand airplanes going to this certain area. I don't know at what point this was, but I think we were at about two thousand feet when a B-17 came at me, and I was flying at him. Why I dumped my stick and he pulled his, I don't know. He could have very easily have pulled his, and I could have pulled mine too. We could have run into each other, but as it turned out, we missed each other. It was close enough that I could look up and see him, just a few feet apart. Well, needless to say, it scared the thunder out of me, and I said, "I'm not staying here. I'm not staying here at two thousand feet anymore. I'm climbing, and if I hit anybody that's the chance I'm taking, but I'm getting out of here as quick as I could." So, I got out of the soup, and I was by myself.

Everybody had a .45 (pistol). We were supposed to take our .45s with us in case we got captured or if we got shot down. You could use this to escape or what have you. Well, Marty [one of Ganyu's fellow pilots] had a .45, and he kept it by the head of his bed and I thought, "This is dangerous. Marty is going to have a nightmare, and he's going to take that gun, and he's going to start shooting." Well, I took the gun, and I unloaded and took the clip out, [but] forgot about the slug that was still in there. I aimed it away, and I pulled the trigger. It shot. Well, Marty checked his gun one day, and the clip was not there. I had put the clip in his bag, but actually, the slug went through his duffel bag and it went through part of the case of his Air Medal. It didn't damage the Air Medal, but it damaged the case. He went over to the orderly room and complained about it. He said, "Those guys shooting rabbits out there better be careful. Look what they did to my Air Medal." But it wasn't those guys out there, it was this guy in here [Ganyu] in his own barracks - one of his buddies that did this. But I never owned up to it, I never owned up to it. (Laughs).

In training we had an interesting [event]. We were in Rapid City, South Dakota and we had a West Point man give us a check ride. He was a captain. He said "Your flight was great, and you had good control of the airplane, but you don't have any control over your crew." And I said, "Why not?" and he says, "They don't salute you. They don't do this. They don't

B-17 contrails.
(Photo courtesy Tom Brown)

do that." You know, as long as they [the crew] do their jobs, they don't have to salute. I'm a civilian officer, I'm not a West Point trained guy. I just went through this training because of the war. So, I got my crew together after he [the captain] left and I said, "Look. When you see somebody strange around, why don't you put on a good act?" From then on, they were "Siring" me to death. (Laughs.) I said, "No, no, no. You just do that when somebody strange is around, so I don't get chewed out because you guys aren't doing what you're supposed to be doing." I had good rapport with my crew.

Another event was when all these Hollywood people like Bob Hope and Glenn Miller went to all these camps and entertained the troops. I was never entertained, I was an officer. It's true. Look at it from my standpoint. I'm on the low end of the officer corps, I'm a second lieutenant. That's the high end of the enlisted men. So, the enlisted men got all the seats up front and all the officers were in the back. Well, I says, "I'm on the low end of the totem pole of the officers. Why don't I get a front seat?" (Laughs). But, they did a wonderful job of entertaining the troops - the USO and the entertainers.

The war came along at the time when I was the right age, and that's the only thing I can say. I'm fortunate to be here and I feel very, very lucky.

Alexander Ganyu returned home on April 1, Easter Sunday, of 1945 after successfully completing thirty-five missions in just six months, an outstanding accomplishment. Eventually, he was married, attained his teaching degree, becoming a shop teacher in Maryland, and raised two children in addition to supporting a foster daughter for a brief period of time. He is now retired and lives in New Castle with his wife, Phyllis, where he enjoys spending time with his grandchildren and his visits to the local donut shop where he "hangs out" with some of his friends.

C. "Red" Graves

398th Bomb Group (H)
602nd Squadron
Radio Operator

by
Joshua Ray

Nestled within the suburbs of Pittsburgh, lies the home of Mr. C. "Red" Graves, a very kind, outgoing gentleman, who spends some of his time recruiting cadets for Virginia Tech University. Seated in his living room one can become captivated by his fascinating stories of a past time. Once inside the world of his stories, the only reminder of the world you just left is the soft chiming of the clock in the living room.

Mr. Graves decided to leave college as a senior and volunteer for the Air Force in August of 1942. After he had enlisted he wasn't called for active duty until April 10, 1943. He then underwent his primary training to be a radio operator in Alexandria, Louisiana. While there, his crew was assembled. After finishing their operational training in August of 1943, they traveled to Lincoln, Nebraska to complete what the Air Force called "staging," which was in essence, to prepare for making the trip overseas by getting the necessary equipment and being assigned a B-17G Flying Fortress. When the "staging" period was over, the crew flew their newly assigned plane from Lincoln, Nebraska to Bangor, Maine. After staying several nights, they flew the North Atlantic route in their journey overseas. During the flight across the Atlantic Ocean, the plane iced up, and the crew nearly crashed into the ocean. When they reached Nuthampstead, England, they were put into the 398th Bombardment Group, 602nd Squadron. The first thing they did in England was to go back to school for training. At combat school they flew some training runs, and later Mr. Graves was sent to radio school. At first he wasn't happy with being a radio operator, since his primary ambition was to be a pilot. Due to his unhappiness he didn't perform up to the best of his abilities at his position. But, once he was faced with the reality of the war, he gave his best effort and was praised by the communications officer as the best radio operator that base had ever trained. The crew, as a whole, was judged the best combat crew on their field. They had a good combat record, until they were shot down on their tenth mission, which was to bomb the railroad marshalling yards at Bingen, Germany, on December 29, 1944.

"That day the Germans had our number. We got shot down pretty much over the lines, and five of us were captured, and three were picked up by the Americans because we were that close to the Allied lines. It depended on where you were when you bailed out of the plane, which was spinning. We got a bad hit and were burning badly, and the plane exploded less than two seconds after we got out.

"The navigator was the only one killed. I don't know what happened to him, they just had his number that day. He was the one that had been hit earlier in the mission, just a flesh wound. Poor fellow, he had just married a girl down in Louisiana while we were in training down there.

"We were picked up right at the line, and a major came running up to me with a Luger, and he shot the pistol at me, and I didn't have one. We were picked up right then. We walked a lot, and they took most of the uniform that I had, and I damn near froze. That was the first thing. I got pneumonia on the march, and we went to an interrogation center. Since we were Air Force prisoners, they had a special place they took us for interrogation. It was called Dulag

Luft, and it was just outside Frankfurt, Germany. We stayed there for several days, and they did all the indoctrination that you get when you go into the P.O.W. system. They interrogated us, which wasn't very pleasant.

"We walked probably three hundred kilometers, which would be about 186 miles. We did ride trains some, but that was no real day at the beach either, because our planes were strafing us all the time. I sat in that Frankfurt station. We had bombed Frankfurt ourselves, and I thought that it was the worst place in the world to be. (Laughs.) Anyway, we survived that too. Then, I remember when we were walking, these P-47s started buzzing us. We were coming down a mountainside, and we were waving and doing all these things - trying to let them know we were G.I.'s. I was with a bunch of guys from the 101st Airborne Division. About fifteen hundred of them were on the trail I was on. We couldn't figure out what in the world they were strafing. All of a sudden they hit something over in the forest. We saw these Red Cross trucks. They were white with red crosses on them. What they actually were, were ammo trucks. They had them dressed up to try and keep them from getting shot up. By gosh, they hit one, and you never saw such an explosion in your life. That's what those planes were after. They weren't after us. (Laughs.)

"We finally ended up in what was called a permanent camp at Nuremberg, and there were from twenty thousand to fifty thousand of us there at Nuremberg, I guess. There were P.O.W.s from every country in the world - mostly Air Force - because this

B-17s returning from a German mission.

(Photo courtesy Tom Brown)

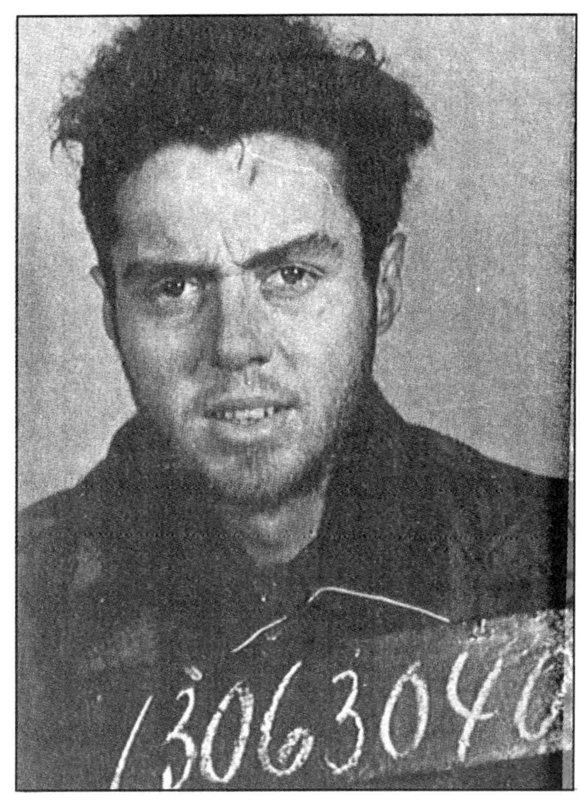

German P.O.W. mug shots of "Red" Graves which he obtained by going through his P.O.W. camp office on the day he was liberated.

(Photos courtesy "Red" Graves)

was Stalag Luft 13-C. The Americans were closing in all the time. As they came towards us, the Germans started evacuating us from this camp. We went from there to a place called Moosburg, which was not a Luftwaffe camp, it was Stalag 7-A, about twenty miles from Munich. That's where we were liberated by Patton's army.

"We didn't get a lot to eat, that's why I didn't weigh but ninety-one pounds. The P.O.W. thing was pure misery: freezing cold, hungry all the time, sick, dysentery. It's no life you'd want to lead."

After he was liberated, Mr. Graves was flown from Germany to a repatriation camp called "Camp Lucky Strike" in France. From there, he and 5,500 others sailed on the S.S Admiral Benson , a troop carrier, to New York Harbor. They were welcomed home warmly and the song, "Don't Fence Me In" was played for them over and over again. Another thing he remembered about that day was that the harbor had very thick fog. The fog was so thick that he couldn't even see the Statue of Liberty. They were then sent to Fort Meade for several days. He received a uniform and was sent home to Virginia for sixty days of leave. After his leave was up, he was sent to San Antonio, Texas, where he received a discharge from the Air Force.

Robert Harnden

392nd Bomb Group
578th Squadron
Bombardier

by
Chistopher Wolfe

Robert Harnden is a retired railroad worker in Pittsburgh, Pennsylvania. He is a typical American in many ways. He and his wife have two children and several grandchildren. As grandparents should be, they are both eager to tell the story of their grandchildren's latest accomplishments. There is one thing, however, that sets Mr. Harnden apart from the rest of the population. All of us enjoy the freedoms of this great nation, but few of us truly understand their cost. Robert Harnden does. He has seen first-hand that our freedom is not as free as we are sometimes fooled to believe.

Robert Harnden entered the service in February of 1943. He attended Cadet School in San Antonio, Texas and signed up for pre-flight school. After passing the rigorous tests, Mr. Harnden was unable to fly due to an eye condition. From there he moved on to bombardier school. In March of 1944 Robert Harnden graduated as a bombardier and soon made his way to England where he flew on a B-24 Bomber. After flying thirty-five missions with the same crew, Mr. Harnden traveled back to America where he was awaiting reassignment when the war ended. The most exceptional part of Mr. Harnden's story, however, is not the technical garble about things such as the Norden Bomb Sight or the guns on B-24s; it is about the people, friends, his crew, and himself.

Bomb craters at Coxiyde.
(Photo courtesy Gene Hinchberger)

A very interesting part of Robert Harnden's story is the close camaraderie that existed between the members of his crew. In his own words, Robert Harnden recalls the close bond between those men:

"We were very close, extremely close. If we'd go anyplace, we'd go as a crew. We went every place together. We'd go out to a club or someplace, and they'd say, 'This is officers only.' We'd just turn around and walk away. They'd say, 'Oh, this is enlisted men only.' We'd go until we found a place where we could all stay together, which made for a lot of friendships. I still correspond; we still get together."

Such good friends were often prone to

mischief, but they stuck together in the end. Mr. Harnden tells the story of an incident that occurred over England during the war:

"They might call on the pilot and the copilot and the engineer to take a ship up, off the base while we were in a combat area, but not on a combat mission. If they'd replace an engine on a aircraft, you'd have to put time on it. In other words, they'd want it to run before you actually take it to combat. So they'd call the pilot, the copilot, and the engineer to slow-time, they call it, slow-timing an engine. Every time they went, we went. The whole crew went! We didn't have to. That just shows you how close we were. The rest of us could have done anything we wanted to: gone to the movies, or stayed home, or slept, or read, or anything, but when they went, we went. That was just how close we were. One day, we were out slow-timing an engine, and you flew at relatively low altitudes; you didn't fly very high. We were about ready to go back when we passed over the vicinity of an English air drill where they were playing soccer, and somebody made the smart suggestion, 'Let's go down and get a closer look.' Everybody knew what he meant. So we came in going the length of the soccer field and I mean we came in low! Those guys were running like the dickens and falling on the ground. And the tail gunner said, 'You ought to see that soccer ball. We just drove that son of a gun three miles from here.' The backwash from the props threw the ball. So I said, 'Gee, I didn't get a good look at that goalie's number; could we do that again?' And we did. We went around and came down over again."

Of course this was not what they were supposed to be doing. When their superiors found out, the pilot and copilot were severely reprimanded. Mr. Harnden said, "I know they fined the pilot fifty bucks." We all collected the money and gave Phil [the pilot] his money back."

The most touching story of this close-knit crew occurred fairly recently. A member of the crew, Tex, the top-turret gunner and assistant crew chief, was very ill and near death.

"We went to see him; he'd been paralyzed with a stroke and all that bit. But he just brightened up when he saw us. He lit up and he smiled. 'Do you know who we are?' 'Sure, I know who you are.' And his son and wife said that they're sure that he just lived for that moment. They feel that he hung on, knowing we were coming. He died three days later."

World War II was not exclusively an American effort. Our men fought alongside men from countries such as Britain, Australia, and others. Mr. Harnden comments on his foreign acquaintances:

"The British airmen, you kind of took to but as far as the other soldiers in Britain, they didn't have any time for us, and we didn't have much time for them as far as that goes. They used to say of us that there were three things wrong with the Americans. We were over there. We were over-paid. We were over-sexed. That was their tribute to us. But they didn't hesitate to take a cigarette or a pack of cigarettes if you'd give it to them. They'd even ask you for them - so there was no love lost. We did have some crew that stayed at our base over the Christmas holidays in '44. They couldn't get back to their base because of weather, and I got to meet some of the Australians that were on those crews, and they were an excellent bunch of guys. They were fine men."

War was not all about friendship and camaraderie, though. There was fighting. Mr. Harnden tells a story about a particular target in Germany and his feelings about combat:

"One of the places that we didn't like was Hanover. There were oil refineries there, and it was heavily protected by antiaircraft fire. You didn't care to see that_. As you approached it [the area] all you'd see was a big huge box of shells going up and you knew that you had to fly through it; there was no choice. That was sticky. I can tell you this: anybody who says they weren't scared didn't see anything. You had to be frightened! There was just no way you could avoid it. 'Cause you knew that there was the possibility that you'd get killed. It was that easy! There were no 'ands', 'ifs', or 'buts', you know. You were either going to go through it, or you were going to get killed; one or the other. So anybody who says, 'Ahh, I wasn't afraid,' you can tell that person never saw any combat, of any kind, 'cause that's the only reason you wouldn't be afraid. I don't care whether you were a foot soldier, or a tanker, or a Navy man, or what.

"We got a lot of holes in the aircraft over a number of courses from ack-ack. We only had one man injured; that was the copilot. He got hit with a piece of flak on the shin. It wasn't real severe, but he was the only one on the crew that was actually struck and injured. We did take one hit that knocked out a couple of engines. Of the four engines on the ship, two of them went out, and there was hole, oh, I would say, eight to ten inches big right behind where I was. The navigator worked behind me. We had our backs to each other, and the shell went off literally between us; and neither one of us got hurt.

"Another amusing thing you found when you were on a bomb run, [was that] you had your eye on the bomb sight, and you would get a burst of shrapnel that would be quite removed from the aircraft, but in the bomb sight with the effect of the telescopic features of it, it would look like it was right in your face. More than once you'd find yourself pulling back from the bomb sight like it was going to come right through you. It was amusing. You had to chuckle at yourself after you did it because you knew it was stupid.

"We had one flight to Berlin, which was our longest mission, if I'm not mistaken. That was late in the war. We got quite a bit of antiaircraft fire there. But the main thrill of that was getting to the seat of the German government and getting the chance to lay some bombs on it."

Although some missions could be frightening, Mr. Harnden still remembers some fondly:

"The most fun mission we had was the last one we flew. It was right after the Americans had pushed over the Rhine. The troops were moving quickly and they needed supplies. So for our last mission, we were loaded with food, guns, and all that stuff to drop by parachute. They were in the racks, but when you dropped them, they parachuted down, to help all these soldiers that had crossed and were trying to go deeper into Germany. We flew that at about two hundred feet. Now that was a thrill - all the way over Europe and all the way back, down at two hundred feet or less. On the way back, we flew under high-tension wires, and I don't think anyone on the ship saw them. It was too late to go over them; the best shot was to go under them. We were under them and gone before we realized what we'd done and how close we'd come to hanging ourselves up in the power lines."

These stories involve just a few of the experiences that Robert Harnden and many others like him had during World War II. The kind of friendship that existed during the war is something to be emulated. They learned firsthand what this country's freedom is all about. These lessons have lasted. Robert Harnden said, "If I knew the outcome, I wouldn't mind doing it again."

A. Clair Hetrick

457th Bomb Group
751st Squadron
Waist Gunner

by
January Sta. Romana

It was a Thursday afternoon when my friend and I found ourselves sitting on a couch across from Mr. Hetrick's desk. Mr. Hetrick was the waist gunner in the 457th Bomb Group. I had asked him a couple of days before whether he would be interested in talking about the war. His reply was sure it was okay, but he did not really remember much. He was either kidding or being modest at the time. When my friend and I left Mr. Hetrick's office, it was similar to stepping out of a time machine. Mr. Hetrick was able to share events with us he did not think he would be able to recall.

I was at home at the time Pearl Harbor was bombed. I was about fifteen or sixteen. Everybody was so patriotic, and they couldn't wait to get to the so-called enemy. My uncle was in the Army. I guess that was one reason I enlisted. He was in North Africa. I enlisted while I was in high school before I was eighteen. I enlisted because it was the patriotic thing to do. Everybody was patriotic. There was no burning flags and such. When the Japanese bombed Pearl Harbor it made us all pretty mad. After I was in the service my uncle got killed in Italy. That made me mad again. I just couldn't wait to get at the Germans. I wanted to fight them. I wanted to shoot them down... that's the way a lot of people felt. I'd say ninety-nine out of one-hundred wanted to go. Everybody was sick of it by the end of high school. I wanted to join earlier and lie about my age, but my parents had to sign papers. I enlisted in the Navy when I was sixteen, but my parents wouldn't sign the papers. When I was seventeen and in my senior year in high school, I enlisted in the Air Corps.

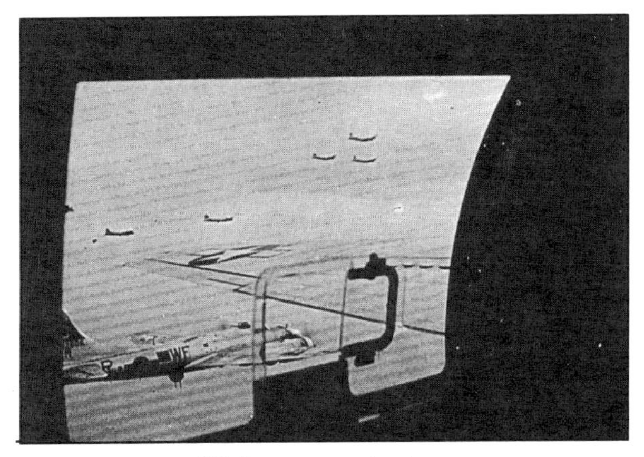

Waist-gunner's view.
(Photo courtesy William Bowers)

The training was very good. The armed forces really knows how to train people. They're good at it. I never throw anything on the ground to this day. They would make us pick up anything that wasn't growing. That was the first thing they did, and we weren't even in our uniforms yet. They said, "Police the area." We didn't even know that meant, "Pick up everything that's not growing."

Then we got into the barracks. The C.O. says, "We want that floor so clean you can eat off of." It was a hardwood floor; and if there was dirt in the cracks, then we had to clean it with our biscuit knives. That's the kind of stuff they made you do. (Laughs.) They're good trainers. There's no doubt about it.

Then I went to gunnery school. I never saw a machine-gun before. You learned to take them apart. You learned that gun so well you could do it in your sleep. You learned how to work with it blindfolded and with gloves on. Then after that, they shipped us to Tampa, Florida. For six days and seven nights, we were in a train. Once

(Photo courtesy Jim Doerr)

a day we'd stop the train, and everybody would get off. We would get off on a big field, and we would do our PT [physical training]. They would exercise us, and they would let us run off a little energy. Sometimes, at those places where we stopped, people might be there with apples or sandwiches or something like that. At that time they wouldn't run a troop train in a direct line. They were afraid it would get sabotaged or something, so they would zigzag around. It was done very smartly and intelligently.

So then we got our crew. They sent us to Mississippi. We were trained together—us ten people. We learned to work with each other. They called it OTU, Overseas Training Unit. Then they said, "O.K., you're going overseas." They took us to Savannah, Georgia. They gave us an airplane. We flew it to Massachusetts, the first day and then from there Goose Bay, Labrador. Then we jumped from there right over Greenland to Iceland. We stayed one night in Iceland and then flew down to Wales. We left our airplane there. They had to rework us to get ready for combat missions. We weren't totally ready. They made us all sergeants because when you got shot down, the enemy treats the sergeants better than they do the privates.

Sometimes we got seventy-two hour passes, and we jumped a train, and ran over to London, and had a big time. It was quite an experience for very, very, young people. I was the youngest one in my crew. I was eighteen.

My pilot was from eastern Pennsylvania. My copilot was from Mount Pleasant, Pennsylvania. My navigator was from upstate New York. The bombardier was from New York City. The flight engineer was from the Boston area. The radio operator was from Columbus, Ohio, and the armorer was from Tulsa, Oklahoma.

We'd take off in the dark. The pilots had predetermined the areas we would fly, and we flew in formation. I still don't understand how we got into formation without having problems.

I never met an enemy, but I did get close enough to one to see his eyes. I didn't know why they did that. We just shot them down. When the jets came out, we didn't know what they were. They flew so fast, and we flew so slow, that they couldn't hit us. They didn't stay up in the air too long anyways because they used up so much fuel.

The first mission everybody called a milk run. Hardly anything happened. We went to a target that was apparently not well-defended. The second mission I was on, which was three days later, nine of our airplanes got shot down. Eight of them were out of my squadron. That was my worst experience. This was the time I saw the eyes of that German. He was about fifty feet away. We shot off his wing. That was pretty nerve-wracking, but it didn't deter us. We were ready to go for the next one. We kept our morale up by saying that this was our duty; we have to do this. Everybody else was doing it, and we were going to do it too.

(Photo courtesy William Bowers)

We didn't know we were flying until that day. They would come, wake us up, and tell us that we were flying. This might be three in the morning. They would tell us to go to the assembly point after we had eaten breakfast. There was a platform on the stage up there. When they found out that everyone was there they pulled a string, and this presented you with the map to tell you where you were going. We didn't really have time to worry about the mission we were about to do. That was the routine. You didn't know where you were going until they opened those curtains.

There was a number of scary moments. One time we were flying out of Germany, and one of our bombs got stuck. This was very dangerous because it could blow up our plane. We tried to pry it loose. Then, we finally got it loose, and by that time we were over Belgium. We couldn't have landed with that thing. We should have dropped it over water, but we had to get that thing out of there. Another scary time was when we were going to Berlin on a mission, but we never got there. During formation we were pretty high up, and we lost an engine. With one engine out, we couldn't manage to stay in formation. Then, all of a sudden, another engine went out. We dropped like a stone. We turned around and headed for home. We threw almost all of our ammunition out, and we dropped our ball turret. We managed to maintain about six-thousand feet or so. We landed on a steel mat that they had just put down in Luxembourg. Our army had just taken that ground. Then, another crew from England picked us up.

I never thought that I wouldn't make it out of the war alive. The war did make a difference for me and my family. If it wasn't for the war, I wouldn't have gone to college. I went on the GI Bill.

One of the funniest moments I recall was during one of those dances they held for us. My buddy had arranged it so that he could see his girlfriend at this one particular dance. She was there, and so was her fifteen-year-old sister. I was eighteen at the time, and I ended up babysitting. The girls ended up missing their bus, so we had to drive them back ourselves. Of course, we didn't have a vehicle to do this. My buddy was an assistant of the colonel's at one time, so the guards at the gate knew him. We went to the colonel's place and started rolling his jeep down the driveway. The girls and I weren't allowed to ride with my buddy until he passed the gates, so we had to crawl through the barbed-wire fence. After that we met him and drove the girls home. My buddy and I stayed at the girls' houses for a little bit; then we drove back. Again, I couldn't ride with him in the jeep, so I had to crawl again through the barbed-wire fence. As I looked up, there was a guard with his gun pointed right at me. Of course, he wanted to know what I was doing. He ended up letting me off. I think he thought it was funny.

I arrived at Natrona Heights on V-E Day. I'm probably one of the few guys that can ever say that throughout the whole time I was overseas I never cheated on my girlfriend. Not many guys can say that.

Gene Hinchberger

492nd Bomb Group
858th Squadron
Flight Engineer

by
Steve Wasko

Gene Hinchberger is a quiet but extremely fascinating man with a wealth of stories to tell. We conducted this interview in his downstairs office, which was decorated with a rifle collection amongst other hunting memorabilia. Several books about WWII and other historical subjects were contained in an enclosed bookshelf by the wall.

Upon the conclusion of this interview, he showed me several pieces of WWII memorabilia, which included a survival kit and flash cards with the names and vital information about all the types of airplanes that were pressed into service during the war. The most interesting piece of memorabilia came from his survival kit. That being a roll of money from all the nations of Europe.

He also provided me with a wealth of photographs. To me, the most interesting were the aerial shots of the war's aftermath.

At the conclusion of our two-hour interview, I knew much more about the personal side of a war in such a way that history books can never cover.

I got into the service because Uncle Sam said so. (Laughs.) I was drafted. I received training in the Medical Corp. I said, "This ain't for me." So I signed up for Aviation Cadets. But when I signed up, I could not get into that, plus, I didn't have enough education either. They wanted college boys for pilots and navigators. I went to school for two years to learn to be a flight engineer aboard the B-24s. With that training I was also instructed on all areas of the plane, the engines, structural frame, hydraulics, maintenance, survival, gunnery school, parachute training and flight training with the crew I was assigned to. My training as a gunner whose position would be located above the main fuselage, would be necessary should any enemy planes attack from above our plane.

Were there any close calls that stick out in your mind while you were overseas?

One night we hit the coast, I think it was Norway. We flew real low at night so that radar would not pick us up. As we hit the coast the enemy let loose with rockets. You ever see those rockets? Salvos of them! One of them went up above the plane and blew up. We didn't get any damage then. You know, in our missions we would fly real close to the ground; and a lot of the time any damage we would get, we would not know about it until the next day when we could see the damage in the daylight.

One time we inspected the plane the next day after our return to base and saw that we were shot through the back turret right over the gunners head - (laughs) - and makes

Gene Hinchberger in a flight suit. (Photo courtesy Gene Hinchberger)

(Photo courtesy Gene Hinchberger)

a hand gesture of about six inches to show me how close that gunfire came to hitting the gunner's head. No one ever got hit, but we picked up a lot of small arms fire at night and a lot of tracers, that was on low altitude missions, and on the high missions we would be flying at about twenty thousand feet. We would fly Pathfinders for the RAF. That's the English Royal Air Force. Our planes were well equipped with radar, which very few had.

We flew B-24s. called Liberators. Our mission was to find our target and then light up that area, and the Royal Air Force would come in behind our planes and bomb it. Our planes would not fly in formation at night. Instead they flew about a half a mile apart . Their planes had these little pipes on the wings, and there was an orange light, a green one and a red light, in case a pilot got out of line. Since the lights were located back inside the pipes nobody could see them except the guy behind you.

When we would be going out on a mission , we would be driven out to our plane on a big truck. During the ride nobody had anything to say, but coming back from the mission - boy - everybody was talking.

Since our flights were to help the underground, we would usually fly over Norway or Denmark. We couldn't go on to land; so we stayed over the water across the North Sea.

We carried twelve containers of supplies. These containers were about twelve feet long with a parachute on the tail end of them. This was done by cutting back our speed to about one hundred forty-five miles an hour - just about as slow as it would fly. Then we would lower flaps, drop the landing gear and pull the nose up. This was so we wouldn't rip the parachutes.

The way the pilots would find our targets - the underground would have a red light flashed with the code of the day. This code would be in Morse code and would change daily. Then they would set out three white lights to show you which direction was downwind so the planes could slow down and drop their supplies.

We carried very few bombs. There was another bomb group known as the "Paperboys" who would drop bombs that exploded and this released propaganda leaflets. They

Bridge between Bonn and Weisboden. (Photo courtesy Gene Hinchberger)

also would drop pigeons in little wooden cages which were attached to a parachute. These pigeons were useful ways to send messages attached to the pigeons' legs. They had a heck of a setup. Now when we'd go on the low mission in Norway, a lot of the time we were flying lower than the mountains. One night we almost got it. We were coming in through the coast and someone gave us the wrong setup. It was too high. The pilot had to bank the plane sideways and we headed back out over the North Sea. Two or three times we got the job of flying the cooks and maintenance men all over Europe so they could see the damage done to those areas. There was a big camera located where the waist guns went on the plane, and we took some pictures. A lot of those pictures we weren't allowed to bring back home because they didn't want folks back home to see all this stuff.

We'd see all kinds of damage. We went over a city, about the size of Butler, and there wasn't one building standing, and the trees on the outskirts just looked like toothpicks. I don't have any pictures of that city. We only were supposed to bomb factories. Didn't you know that?

I have a pilot's license. I flew for years around here. My wife says, "Who's going to keep these kids when you get killed?" (Laughs.) Our missions were about eight to twelve hours long; and when the pilot or copilot got tired, one of them would go back and take a rest and I'd crawl into his seat and the navigator would call corrections. Since it was on autopilot, anyone could fly the plane. (Laughs.)

During one mission the automatic pilot malfunctioned, and by time the pilot was able to pull the nose up we were very close to the water. The rest of the mission we had to fly without the autopilot. The reason you fly on autopilot is that it corrects any problems before something happens compared to being unable to correct the problem by hand when something happens.

Did you witness any devastating accidents?

One time this Polish pilot took off from our field after loading up with ammunition. I guess he was showing off. Because he was carrying too much weight he couldn't get the plane turned over, and he hit some trees, came down, and hit the back end of a building; and him and that engine flew the farthest out into the field. He only lived a couple of minutes.

Another time one guy's engine was on fire, and he did what you should never do. He turned and came back in the downwind. He hit, and that thing just cart-wheeled. I'll bet the fire flew three or four hundred feet into the air when it went off. Some of them got killed. One guy got the top of his head peeled off. That was a mess.

I went on twenty-nine missions. After one year of flying I went back Stateside. Luckily, nobody in our crew was ever injured. We were a little bit more fortunate than the other guys flying.

Joseph Hines

398th Bomb Group
602th Bomb Squadron
Radio Operator

by
Kevin Tritch

Joseph Hines is a man who loves life and when someone tells him, "Have a nice day." he responds, "I've never had a bad one." He begins this tale of his experiences in the war as an eighteen-year-old who just graduated from high school.

I graduated from high school in June of 1941, and the war started in December of 1941. It was very evident that I was going into the service whether I enlisted or was drafted. I was eighteen, and in February of 1942 I enlisted. Everyone who enlisted took a two-year college equivalency test. I graduated from Central Catholic High School which was like going to a two-year college. Anyway, I passed the test and was sent to Miami Beach. I rather enjoyed this, since we got to do all our morning exercises on the beach and lived in the hotels. About this time I was sent to school to learn math, such as calculus, decision-making skills, and Morse code. Next, I was assigned to a crew and went to gunnery school in Arlington, Texas. There they sat a bunch of us in the back of a large truck which was being driven around a race track. They gave us each a shotgun, and we shot at various targets to teach us how to lead our target. When you're in a plane and moving at six hundred m.p.h., and the enemy is moving in the opposite direction even faster, you have to know how to compensate. I guess this is how trigonometry and calculus come into play. (Laughs.) Then, I stayed at an airbase in Santa Anna, California. This is where they decided I was too short to be an officer. I'm 5'5" right now, but at the time they told me I was 5'3 3/4". They didn't realize that I wasn't planning to be an officer anyway. While I was at Santa Anna I met Joe DiMaggio. He was my PT [physical training] instructor. All the athletes got the good jobs, but he really did his sincerely. From Santa Anna, I went to Wittenberg College, where I learned to fly on an L-5. At this time, I also got to train with my crew on the B-17. Our journey to England consisted of a stop in Nebraska; South Louisiana; Aberdeen; and finally Belfast, Northern Ireland. I completed my twenty-five missions as a radio operator. You really had to have the proper frame of mind because you never knew if and how you were going to come home. You couldn't get attached to other crews because you didn't know who would make it back after a mission. I'd see a plane getting hit by flak or enemy fire, and I knew who was on the plane; you had to learn to live with it.

We radio men thought we had an advantage; along with operating the radio, we also got to fire a gun when you weren't the active radio man of the group. So, most of the time I got to shoot the gun, since you only needed one active radio man at any time, and we had thirty-six in our group. Another misconception about radio on the planes was that you carried on conversations like on CB's today, but in reality, under combat, you just listened for emergencies.

One day when I was scheduled to fly a mission, my brother, who was a flight chief, came down to visit me from Norwich, England. He was only about forty-five miles away, but you couldn't just take a direct route, so it ended up taking him about half a day to get down there. It just happened that I was in combat that day. Now my brother was nervous; I mean he was jelly

Joseph Hines and his young interviewer Kevin Tritch.
(Photo courtesy Kevin Tritch)

in a ball rolling around—nervous as hell. He'd go up to the tower to find out our location, how long we'd been out there, and if anyone was turning around. These were things he went through almost every day, given the fact that he was in charge of thirty-six planes and crew chiefs. Every time a plane would come into sight he became really anxious and kept asking the sergeant if that was my plane. I came home safe and sound, and he was very relieved. When I got a chance to talk to my ground crew. They told me, "Don't let your brother come down while you're flying again." So I talked to my brother and asked him next time to check with my instructor to see if I was flying or not. (Laughs.) My brother and I were always good buddies. Another neat experience I had while I was stationed in England was I met Clark Gable at a base near ours.

Well, I did my missions. They were just a job you were trained to do. Go out and do it, and pray to God you come back. Religion played a major role with me. We'd get up at three-thirty or four o'clock in the morning, walk down to chaplain's house, which was actually a Quonset hut, and he would give us total absolution and the Eucharist and say, "See you when you get home."

Next, we'd take off, which was an ordeal in itself. I don't know how many planes collided during takeoff. After circling around and forming into our group, we would take an indirect route to our target. At about the time we were crossing the English Channel, Axis Sally would come on the radio and tell us exactly where we were going and that they'd be waiting for us. Also, on the other side of the Channel there were these two little guys who as soon as they saw a plane would start firing like hell. It was kind of funny because I don't think they ever hit anyone.

The war was a memorable experience. I had a lot of friends who never returned. I miss them; but you can't live with those thoughts all the time. But, I enjoyed the experience [the war]. Why? Because I was single and had no attachments. My mother and sister were safe back home, and both of my brothers were in the service with me. A neat sidelight was I met a girl who happened to be the daughter of the King of England's barber. So, one day I got to go inside and visit the royal palace. Sometimes I kid my wife that if the war had lasted three more months, she would have been English. (Laughs.) I guess my best experience was that I met a lot of nice people during the war. The only two people I looked up to were my navigator and pilot. In addition to getting us where we needed to go, they were both taller than me.

I was fortunate enough to get through the war in one piece. Only once, when we had taken some flak, did we almost go down. You had to be ready to jump at all times, and I was; but our pilot pulled us out, and that's even better.

After I completed all twenty-five of my missions, my C.O. [commanding officer] asked me to stay with the squadron. He told me, "Why fly home? You've got all this experience. Stay here. I'd like you to be my driver for off-base activities." So, I was having fun; and I decided to stay, since officers weren't allowed to drive a vehicle off of the base. I also became permanent C.Q.

[charge of quarters] from midnight to eight o'clock in the morning. I would get every other day off, so I only had to work three or four days a week. What I did was get the orders from headquarters and alert the crews I was in charge of. I would just tell them to get up, and they were going to fly a mission. I had no idea where they were going.

Finally, one day about three o'clock in the morning I got the order to evacuate my quarters, because they were sending us home. It was kind of funny; because officers weren't supposed to touch the men, and this posed a problem to me when I tried to wake them up. So we packed up and shipped out; and taking another indirect route, we landed back in the States in Connecticut. This was top secret since the war was still going on in Japan. I phoned my mother when I landed and told her, "Hey mom, I'll probably be home in the next couple of days, but don't mention it to anyone because it's top secret." So, she said, "We just heard on the radio that the 602nd Bomb Squadron had landed in Connecticut." I mean this was top secret! (Laughs.)

Its kind of ironic that I didn't get the slightest injury during the war. Then one night after I was out of the service, I was driving down the Fort Pitt Tunnel and was hit head-on by a drunk driver. I was in the hospital for five months, but I survived, so I still hadn't had a bad day.

Joseph Hines graduated from Duquesne University with the help of the G.I. Bill and became a food broker for the next forty-three years. He is now retired and living happily, at the age of seventy-three, with his wife Nellie in Cabot, PA. To this day, Mr. Joseph Hines still responds to the comment, "Have a nice day," with, "I've never had a bad one."

Destroyed bridge at Cologne.
(Photo courtesy Gene Hinchberger)

David Inman

353rd Fighter Group
Pilot

by
Jolene McConnell

David Inman is a very interesting man with a subtle humor and a silent intensity. He speaks with a smile, ready for a question. He comes off as an intelligent, sweet man. He seems to have a very comfortable demeanor.

Before the war, he worked at a division of Dupont. He was transferred to the Manhattan Project, where he was placed in charge of unloading trucks. In December of 1942 he enlisted in the Air Force, and from there, his story begins...

I had no intention of being drafted. I wanted to choose what I was gonna be. That's when I signed up; and they said, "Oh well, it'll be six months or so until we call you, because there are so many people in the pipeline now to take flying training. And...well...we'll call you." I was sworn in, raised my right hand and all that stuff. The next thing you know, in February, they said, "Come on, we're ready for you."

Training Begins

So they called me in, and we went down to Florida for our basic training. We were always marching or sleeping, marching or sleeping. We were on Miami Beach, living in a hotel. But all of our activities took place out on the drill field.

After Miami beach, when we were supposed to be at least good foot soldiers, not airmen by that time, they sent us up to Kent State. We had what they called "college training detachment." But to this day, I don't think we simply needed the training. They were stalling because they didn't have enough flying fields open... because of the large influx of men coming into the Air Corps. We were there about five months. Then we went to San Antonio.

Base at Raydon, England
(Photo courtesy Joe Haynos)

[In San Antonio we were] weeded out. They either kicked us out or we couldn't meet the qualifications. There you were segregated to be either a bombardier, a pilot or a navigator, based on the results of the test they gave you. I got what I wanted - to be a pilot. From there we went to flying-training school.

I went out to the panhandle of Texas in December of '44 and started my flying training there, flying a PT-19, a little low-winged plane. I got about a hundred hours in the air in my class, 44-F. It was cold. We wore big...enormous, teddy-bear, sheep-skin jackets, and sheep-skin gloves and sheep-skin boots and sheep-skin helmets. In winter in open cockpits at a hundred or so miles an hour, it was pretty chilly. That was the beginning of flying training. I soloed there in December. That was a thrill. About one-third of the guys got washed out there. We moved onto what they called basic training - bigger airplanes, more powerful. That was about a four hundred twenty-five horsepower plane. We got our hundred hours there and soloed that one. I flew the AT-6s for the advanced trainer. I got my wings on the 27th of June 1944.

After a brief, one-week leave, the first he had gotten since he joined, Mr. Inman went to overseas' combat training in P-40s in New Mexico...

I remember, we got off that plane and all we saw were burrows on the horizon and nothing but tumbleweeds - no town, no nothing. It was only noted for two things. One, it was where Billy the Kid was killed; and two, it had an air base. Of course everyone went to see Billy the Kid's grave. Then we put in another 150 hours into the P-40, and that completed our training.

Shipping Out

By that time, the war was drawing to a close. By the time we got processed and got our equipment in Kansas, we headed to our point of debarkation. We went to New Jersey for our final checkpoint and went out on the U.S.S. Monticello an Italian liner that we had captured, refurbished, and made into a troop ship. There were about sixty of us pilots and the rest were foot soldiers. We spent about two weeks crossing the North Atlantic. That was an experience. We didn't get a whole lot of sleep because depth charges kept going off. It's a funny sound, as if a hammer hit the side of a metal drum. While we were on the sea, we got the message that President Roosevelt had passed away in April of '45. By the time we got there, and got our P-51s, the air war was just about over. I didn't get to go on any missions. I was either lucky, or very unlucky that I didn't get called. I'm not sure which one.

The Dove of Peace

Our commander was Col. Duncan. He was a red-hot pilot. Everybody liked him. He was shot down in France, and he joined the French Underground. He stayed there for three months. Then he came back and assumed command of our base again.

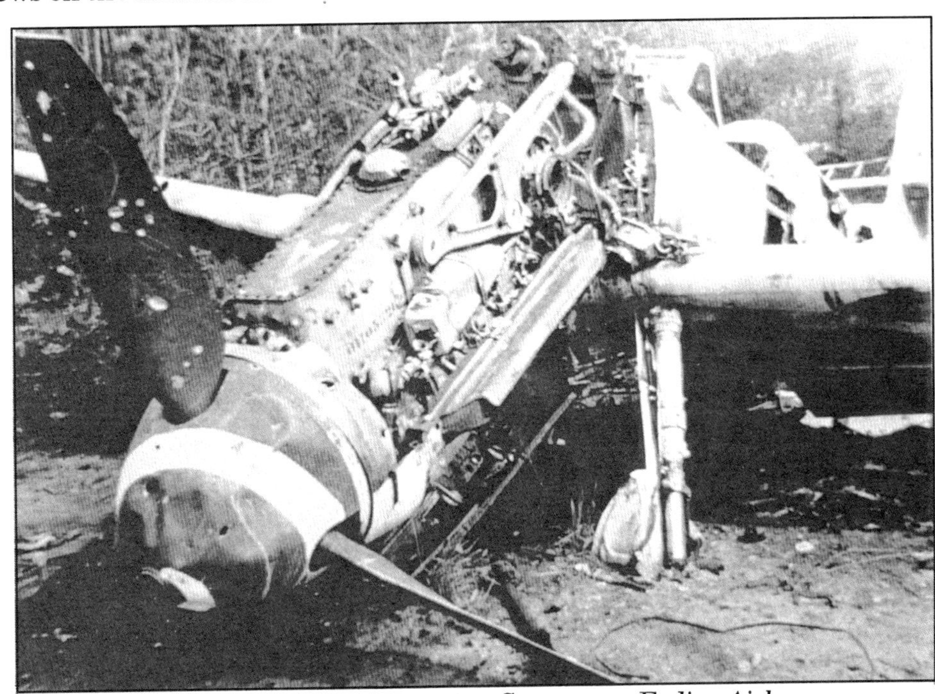

Me 109 destroyed by retreating Germans at Erding Airbase.
(photo courtesy David Inman)

Me 262 German jet airplane sitting on assembly line of bombed-out factory in Augsburg, Germany.

(Photo courtesy David Inman)

The new plane was called "The Dove of Peace." His first plane was originally named "Murder Incorporated." Since the German intelligence knew everything about us, (they had great spies along the way to feed this information to them), they picked up on this and used it as propaganda against us. "See how the Americans call these things 'Murder Incorporated' to murder all of the poor German civilians." Orders came down to Col. Duncan and said he had to change the name. He changed it to "Dove of Peace."

At this point, Mr. Inman told me about what he did after V-J Day.

V-J day was in August of '45. Before you could come home, you had to have eighty points. Since I got there so late I didn't have the points, so what they were gonna do with us was send us over to Germany for occupation. About ten of us from my squadron went with me. First of all, we landed in France. They flew us over in a DC-3 which is a twin-engine transport. We lived in tents there.

An Unearthly Encounter

One of my jobs, I had to take forty-five two-and-one-half-ton army trucks from France on the Autobahn to Munich to deliver them. We started out in France on back roads. One of my guy's trucks broke down, so we had to tow it. It got going down the hill, and the guys weren't paying attention, and it flipped over on its side. Nobody got hurt. I didn't know anything about it until we got to the next town because there was a big string of trucks behind me. I turned around and went back in the jeep. I was standing there talking to the sergeant and trying to decide what to do with this crazy truck. My hands were at my side. All at once, I felt something in my hand. I looked down and there was this little, yellow-haired, German boy who had come up and put his hand in my hand. That was a moving experience because I didn't see **anyone** around. Where that boy came from, I'll never know. I went on talking, then I looked around, and he had disappeared. That was the last I saw of him. He was a cute little kid - hair like corn silk.

The Secret Weapon that Could Have Changed the War

On this truck trip, I passed through an experimental aircraft station. This was an assembly line for the brand new German jet fighter. It was pretty bombed out, but one of the planes was still on the assembly line.

Putting on the Ritz

I was transferred then to another place. I want to tell you, life in the service wasn't always tough. It was pretty good sometimes. This place was in France in a place called Crepy. We were forced to live in this place.

He said this as he showed me a picture of a colossal, four-story, white, Elizabethan-style mansion.

My buddy and I had a bedroom all to ourselves. The walls were not papered, they were with cloth-covered padding. [There was] Louis XIV furniture all the way through. It was owned by a count that was French, but was living in Belgium at the time. We had French maids; we had a French chef, and we had parties. We had a good time, but somebody had to do this. (Laughs.)

We had a party, a big dance, one Saturday night. We had a French combo come in, and they were playing music. We invited all the local girls. I was dancing with this one mademoiselle for most of the evening. I asked her if I could take her home and she said, "Oui." I had my jeep ready. I still, to this day, don't know how I had a jeep. I shouldn't have been authorized one. I didn't steal it! (Laughs.) The jeep was enclosed. What I didn't know was that she had her entire family there with her. I had the whole family in the jeep. But we squeezed in. I think there were five of us all together. That was the life there.

In Germany

From there, I was transferred to Hanau which was our base for the air depot. We just took over an old, German air base. We had parties there too. I was there about five months. I was commander of the truck squadron. I had about sixty-five trucks. We supplied the entire base with transportation of all kinds including jeeps, and command cars, and ambulances. At the base we had Germans to do all of our work for us. The cooking staff, the cleaning staff, the carpenters, the electricians were all Germans. I had about 130 men in that squadron.

We had our own little college on base. I was the dean of the college. I had classes teaching German, teaching physics, and in some cases, teaching English. That lasted until June 1946 when I was discharged.

The End of the War

I went back to DuPont, and I had no intention of going to college, but my friends at DuPont said, "You're just wasting your time here. Go to college." So I went back to Kent State. One of my classmates said to me, " I'm an operations officer at an Air Force Reserve unit flying out of Cleveland. They're flying these light, twin-engine bombers which are very nice aircraft. See if you can enlist, and we can fly together." I said, "Okay." I went up and got interviewed; and the recruiting officer said, "Sorry, you're too old." I was twenty-six years old then. How lucky I was that they turned me down, because that unit was one of the first that went to Korea.

Back to Europe

We [Mr. and Mrs. Inman] went back to Europe in 1979, to the air base. There were lots of signs everywhere that said "Property of Her Majesty. Keep Out." We went in anyway. The door to a Quonset hut flew open and a man walked out. "Here during the war, were you? Would you like a tour?" We looked around awhile, and he said he wanted to play golf, so we left.

We went back again two years ago to a reunion at our old air base. The group that sponsored us was the Raydon Air Field Preservation Society. It was as if we had never been away. We weren't just Americans coming back, we were brothers and sisters and cousins of these people. That was the impression we got. They put on a feast for us, a dinner, a lunch, entertainment during the day, trips to their homes like long-lost relatives. Their generosity was amazing.

Mr. Inman has traveled all over the country. He is currently living in Upper St. Clair, Pennsylvania enjoying his retirement. He lives in a comfortable home with his wife, Della. He looks on his war experience as a great adventure. He and his wife traveled to Europe a number of times and once discovered that he was a distant relative of Winston Churchill's wife. He enjoys golf, photography, and genealogy.

Frank Kacinko

447th Bomb Group
708th Squadron
Waist Gunner

by
Emily Johnson

Frank Kacinko is a quiet man with a low, raspy voice. He is seventy-two, but he doesn't look older than sixty-five. This is exceptional, considering he recently has had some serious health problems from which he is recovering quite well.

Frank Kacinko flew 30 missions on the "Radar Queen."
(Photo courtesy Frank Kacinko)

"I was seventeen when I graduated in '41. I was eighteen when I enlisted. [I enlisted] because I didn't want to be in the infantry. [Laughs.] I was twenty years old when I was over there fighting. I was in England ten months - that's how long it took me - thirty missions. I went over there in March and came home January first of '45 - that was about six months before the war ended.

I was in aerial gunner school in Tyndall Field, Florida where they taught us how to shoot before we went overseas. When we got over there, they told us that after eight missions we were living on borrowed time. I have 233 combat hours all together out of thirty missions, so the other twenty-two I flew with God's help, I guess. I was glad when I had my thirty. When I went over there, you only had to fly twenty-five, but they had so many getting shot down, they made it so everybody had to fly thirty. On my last mission I got out of that plane and kissed the ground.

Well, when I was fighting, we didn't have any funny incidents. [Laughs.] They were all scary. I guess the most scary one I ever had was going down through the Ruhr Valley - Cologne, I think it was. We had the engine shot out right next to the copilot. It was burning like mad. The pilot pulled out of formation. I put my parachute on, and he says, "Hold on!" and he puts it in a steep dive and turned on the fire extinguisher. We went from about thirty-two thousand feet down to ten thousand feet, and the fire blew out, and then we just flew back home. [Going to] Berlin, a plane on each side of us got shot down by fighter planes. We had seventy-two holes in our plane, and we just flew back home. We had ten airplanes shot down, and lost one hundred men.

Some of these missions were easy, some were hard. We had a lot of close calls. Over half the fellas I went over with are buried over there. Every mission, someone went down. Our first mission, the plane next to us got shot down. It got hit with flak, and the engine caught on fire. The pilot pulled over to the side and everybody bailed out. A few seconds later it just blew up in a big ball of fire. Then we went to Frederickshaven right down near the Swiss border. We were over the target and just dropped the bombs. The top-turret gunner - right up behind the pilot - he gets down, and looks in the bomb bay, making sure all the bombs dropped. He no sooner than got down when flak exploded above him, and a great big piece went right through where his head would have been. And where our bombardier was, flak burst up in the glass part and just shattered the whole thing. He never flew after that.

Frank Kacinko's plane "The Radar Queen"
(Photo courtesy Frank Kacinko)

Everyone was scared. Every time you went over they shot at you. You go to Berlin and they have six hundred guns shooting at you from the ground. You went down through the Ruhr Valley - that's where all their steel mills were - and you had about a thousand guns shooting at you. You just had to keep flying - straight as ever - don't move. You never turned back. Once you start over, you keep going, no matter what happened. We'd come back, and they'd fix up the planes, and you'd fly again the next day. It's not like the movie shows, you know, "I'm ready to go!" A lot of times we went to a briefing room, and they had a great big target up there covered with a big curtain. The colonel comes in and tells you where to go. He pulls the curtain. It could be a fairly short mission, but if it's a long mission everybody groans and moans like mad! One mission we dropped supplies - guns, food, ammunition - to the French Underground.

But we still kept on flying. Nothing stopped us. The only thing that stopped us was the weather - when you couldn't see. You only flew when the weather was good. Most of the time the weather was bad. We almost ditched in the English Channel one time. We had two engines shot out, and we kept coming lower and lower - foggy as hell. Everybody got into the radio room and prepared to ditch. We all got our parachutes on. We came down out of the fog and a few hundred feet... there was the coast of England. There was an English airfield. We landed, and about halfway down the runway the other two engines quit.

When you came back off a mission, you went to this fella that was sitting there with a bunch of bottles of liquor, and he gives everybody two shots of whatever they wanted. I used to drink one and give the other to the copilot. By the time he went back to bed, he was half drunk.

When I came back from Europe, I landed in the U.S. on January first of '45. They sent me to a hospital in Florida for six months for battle fatigue - right on Miami Beach. Then I went to Dodge City, Kansas, and I was flying B-26s. We were training Frenchmen how to fly. Then, from there, I went to Fort Lewis, Washington to learn how to fight forest fires. Summer of '45 I went down to California into Sacramento,

B-17 Flying Fortress bombing a German airfield.
(Photo courtesy Tom Brown)

and for the rest of the summer we were fighting forest fires. There were so many of them - the Army was fighting forest fires. When the war with Japan ended in August I was on top of a mountain fighting a forest fire. In September they let us out. We weren't there very long. I never told my mother and father I was coming home. The only time they knew was when I knocked on the front door at almost four o'clock in the morning.

To Frank Kacinko, serving in the 8th Air Force was not a time to get away from home or see the world. He had a job to do, and he meant to do it thoroughly. Mr. Kacinko was awarded many medals, including the Air Medal for "courage, coolness and skills," and the Third Oak Cluster to the Air Medal for "exceptional meritous achievement." He was also honored with the Distinguished Flying Cross for "excellent marksmanship, courage, presence of mind and devotion to duty." These awards truly represent the kind of soldier Frank Kacinko sought to be - and achieved.

Joseph Kasacjak

448th Bomb Group
713th Bomb Squadron
Radio Operator and Gunner

by
Erin Brady

It is December 23,1942. A young man named Joseph Kasacjak parts from his family and friends in his hometown of Leechburg, Pennsylvania. He is destined for Baltimore, Maryland where he will begin basic training. At this time the United States is well entrenched in World War II, and our armed services desperately need all the qualified help they can get. After completing his training, Joseph decides that he would like to be a gunner in the Air Force. He passes all the necessary tests for this position, including the physical exam; however, he is refused admission because his height just barely exceeds the six foot limit.

Undauntedly, Joseph changes courses and attends radio operating school. However, he cannot be dissuaded from his desire to become a gunner, and he goes to take the tests once again. He passes the tests as before, but this time he bows his legs during the physical examination with the hope of disguising his true stature. Joseph insists that he is naturally bow-legged, and the doctor can't help but admire his dedication, so he marks him down as being only six feet tall.

Because gunners are in such short supply, a nine-week training course is breezed through in just two short weeks. After completing all of the necessary preparations, Joseph is assigned to a B-24 squadron. Soon the group is whisked away to an unknown destination. First, they are flown to South America, then to Africa, and finally they arrive in England.

It is almost overwhelming to imagine leaving one's hometown and accompanying total strangers to an unfamiliar country, without adding the knowledge that one is heading off to war where only fate will determine who lives and who dies. All this and more were undergone by Joseph and the nine other crew members of the plane on which he worked. Working as a radio operator on a B-24, Joseph also was responsible for taking the place of any gunner who was incapacitated. The rest of the crew consisted of a top gunner, belly gunner, nose gunner, two side gunners, pilot, copilot, and navigator.

Joseph's crew flew thirty combat missions over German territory. American squadrons were escorted by British fighters across the English Channel but only as far as France. After that the fighters had to turn back, and the rest of the mission was flown unescorted. During such a mission there was always the fear of enemy aircraft lurking where one least expected them. One common tactic used by the German planes was to climb above bombers keeping the sun behind them. From this position they could fly down upon American planes whose crew members could not see them due to the sun. Being unescorted, this gave the enemy ample opportunity to destroy American planes. During World War II there was no such thing as a safe mission.

The primary targets of the American bombers were factories. It was important to try to destroy all factories which produced ball bearings and other parts used in planes in order to prevent the production of more German planes. This was so vital to the safety of American forces that when the bomb bays on Joseph's plane failed to open, and it was necessary to manually release the bombs before landing, Joe pulled the pin out of every bomb before dropping it, only to realize later that the bombs would

P-51 formation.
(Photo courtesy Tom Brown)

detonate on their own.

Joseph's height turned out to be a real problem throughout his service. Because he was so tall, Joseph had difficulty sitting in the lower turret and at the tail of the plane when he was operating the guns. On top of that his insulated suit did not fit him properly. On one mission, while flying at a high altitude, his ill-fitting suit got a huge rip in it, rendering it virtually useless against the cold. At a temperature of minus forty degrees Fahrenheit, he spent a miserable mission fighting the frigid conditions. Nothing more could be done to protect himself than jumping up and down and rubbing his hands together to keep warm. Fortunately, after a flight that seemed to last for an eternity, Joseph was able to receive the attention he needed and escaped with nothing more serious than mild frostbite on his fingers.

Several flights later, the squadron got off to a late start. Due to inclement weather, the mission was delayed until late afternoon. Typically, the planes would leave England at three o'clock in the morning, fly across the channel, attack their target, and fly back in the early afternoon. On this particular day, however, the late departure would mean that the planes would have to fly back in the dark.

Everything began smoothly. The bombs were dropped with surprisingly little enemy resistance, and they began the late trip back to England. With their lights on in the dark, the planes were sitting ducks. The Germans took this opportunity to try to wipe out the entire squadron. A surprise enemy attack necessitated that the planes turn off their lights and fly out of formation with no visibility - a very dangerous thing to do. The enemy persisted, even following the planes as they went to make their precarious landings, easily spotting their targets on the lit runway. The squadron decided to radio in and request that the runway lights be extinguished, forcing all of the pilots to attempt landing with no lights on any of the planes or on the runway to guide their descent. Many planes were destroyed in this undertaking, including the one that carried Joseph Kasacjak and his fellow crew members. As their plane descended onto the dark runway, it was steered off course and into several parked planes. Assuming the crash position (head between knees) was the only thing that saved the copilot's life when a wing from another plane went through his windshield.

All the crew members survived, but as Joe was climbing out of the plane and up onto the fuselage, he fell and hurt his knee, an injury which still troubles him today. A lieutenant pulled him away from the wreckage, and he was taken to the infirmary. Joseph will never forget when the doctor who bandaged his knee placed a bottle of whiskey next to him, sensing how badly his nerves were shaken.

Unlike the British, the American Air Force bombers stationed in England flew in formation as a means of protection, leaving only the tail-end Charlie, or lowest and last position, extremely vulnerable. This was effective under most circumstances, but it was rendered useless by the flak shot up randomly in large quantities by German antiaircraft guns. Many people were killed as a result of flak.

For Joseph, another near-fatal mission occurred when their plane was hit with flak over Germany. Many mechanical problems followed, and a decision had to be made as to whether the plane could make it back to England, or whether the crew should bail out over Sweden, a friendly nation. As they continued on their flight, Joe was covered with gasoline while attempting to repair a fuel line. It was also very cold that day. Because of the dangers associated with bailing out of a plane, the pilot chose to try to reach a base in England. As they started to cross the Channel, they began to lose altitude rapidly. Everyone feared that the plane would not make it to England, and suddenly they realized that they were below the minimum altitude for bailing out. The navigator plotted a course for the closest airfield on their line of flight to England. Because of the pilot's skill, along with good luck, they were able to safely land the plane at the closest airfield. Unfortunately, the people at this base were somewhat less than hospitable to Joe and refused to give him a change of clothes. Joseph was forced to endure a long ride back to his base in the back of a truck wearing a gasoline-soaked uniform in the middle of Winter.

When asked to recount his experiences in World War II, Joseph does not immediately tell of the aforementioned narrow escapes. Rather than dwelling on the horrors of war, he likes to talk about the interesting people that he met and the humorous or pleasant experiences that he had.

Being an adventurous young man, Joseph took every opportunity he got to leave his base and visit London with his friends. More than the dangerous flights over Germany, Joseph remembers the British soldiers who showed him the best hang-outs in London. Stronger in his mind than the bombs and the guns are the pranks he played on the officers to sneak off the base and go to the theater or get out of KP duty.

Joseph retained his sense of humor under even the most harrowing circumstances. On many missions one terrified gunner found it impossible to endure the stress and anxiety of his job. After leaving his position in the plane, this man would throw up in Joseph's helmet, while Joseph operated his comrade's gun. With a smile Joseph remembers how, after the mission, this man would clean out the helmet and return it as if nothing had happened.

These are the memories that matter the most to Joe, and it is clearly this positive attitude that helped him to maintain his morale and courage during the war. This fortitude still emanates from Joseph as he relates his stories. It took the combined bravery of ten crew members to successfully complete all of their required missions and not suffer a single casualty, but one will never hear Joseph bragging about this. He is very modest about his part in World War II and doesn't believe that he is a hero. Instead, he says that the members of the infantry underwent far greater trials than he.

Joseph returned to the States just prior to D-Day, and to this day he wishes that he had been able to take part in it. In fact, on both V-E Day and V-J Day, he and his comrades were restricted to the base to perform their duties while the rest of America celebrated.

Joe was honorably discharged from the service on October 18, 1945 from Madison, Wisconsin. During his service, he earned the rank of Tech Sergeant and was awarded the Distinguished Flying Cross for meritorial duty while serving in Europe.

After his discharge, Joseph returned to his home in Pennsylvania, where he resumed his job at Allegheny Steel Corp. He has since married and raised a family. Sadly, he lost a cousin on a bombing mission over Europe; however, all of his brothers, who also served in the war, returned home safely. Remarkably the same was true for the entire crew that he served with. They have kept in touch over the years and have had many reunions since World War II. Five of them are still alive today.

Few people's lives were not affected in some way by World War II. Besides losing a loved one, Joseph's opinions on war were greatly influenced by his service. Like many veterans who have experienced combat, Joe now does not believe in war as a means of solving political problems.

L. Robert Kimball

100th Bomb Group
351st Squadron
Navigator

by
Stacy L. Geibel

Although he accomplished much throughout the course of World War II, Mr. L. Robert Kimball is also a very successful businessman with great pride in family. He is an alumnus of Penn State University, as well as a big fan of their football team. He is a straightforward, honest man with a past, as well as present, to be very proud of.

I was...oh...nineteen when I joined the Air Force. I just wanted to win the war. Things were different in those days. Young guys wanted to join the services. Now they run away from it. Everyone wanted to be in the war, probably not the smartest thing in the world, but we felt we needed to be there.

I started out in the pilot program. They were going to try and make a pilot out of me, and they had so many aviation cadets that they didn't know what to do with them. So in the course of that, they decided they needed navigators. I'd had two-and-a-half years of engineering, so I fit that bill pretty well. They stuck me in navigation school. From February of '43 until probably February of '44, somewhere in that area, I was in training. We had very intensive training. We learned to navigate by the stars, how to shoot guns, jump out of a parachute, and everything you needed to know about how to fight the war.

When I first went overseas to the 100th Bomb Group it didn't even mean anything to me. It was fine until I had about six missions in and I got a pass to go to London. I was in the cab with some other fliers and they asked, "Where are you from? What do you do in your group?" and "How many missions do you have?" I told them I had six missions and I was in the 100th Bomb Group. They said, "Well, you don't know the story of the 100th," and I told them, "No." Well, it turned out that they weren't allowed to tell us when we came there because we were just kids, about twenty years old. On one of the missions, one of our guys - I don't know whether he thought he had problems - dropped out of formation. At that period of the war if you dropped your wheels you were escorted by German fighters. The pilot put down the wheels, and two fighters pulled up beside him. Anyway, he shot down the fighters, pulled up his wheels, and went home. So, from then on we had to land with others from the 100th Bomb Group. A couple of times [the Germans] wiped out a whole group. They didn't want us to know that. [After that] everyone called us "The Bloody 100th."

[My first battle experience] was very frightening, and so was the last one, and every one in between. It was like going out in front of the firing squad every day, twenty or thirty times, and having them miss you, but say, "Oh well, we'll get you tomorrow." We'd feel that way even when we weren't in combat. We'd be taking off the runway in the fog where you couldn't even see the end of the runway. We'd be going one right after the other, and every once in a while you'd hear a big boom. One would crash before it ever got off the ground. Either that, or we'd be circling around from one airfield to another and they'd run right into one another. Then you'd get up there and have a young pilot who only had a couple of hundred hours in the air, he'd have a load of bombs, a full crew, 2700 gallons gasoline, and he wouldn't be used to any of these things. He'd start to lose control of his airplane, spin out, and crash. There are just so many things that would happen over there. It's hard to believe.

As for bombing cities, that didn't bother me. They were shooting at us, trying to kill us. Heck, I didn't care if it were a lady down there running those guns or not, because that's what they were. I didn't feel any different about the first mission as I did the last one, but it never became just a routine duty to me. [The day before a mission] we had no way to prepare because we had no idea where we would be going the next day. We'd go to bed, and the next thing you'd know you'd hear the jeep pull up. You'd hear the door open up, and this guy would say, "Captain Kimball, you'll be flying today." That's how I always found out.

When we left, we had some things that we always had to carry with us in our flight suits. We carried these [silk] maps (holding one up), a little compass about as big as the end of your thumb, a .45 automatic, and a picture that you could use on a French passport. They'd take pictures of us looking like civilians, and we carried them. When we got to the underground we'd have to show them our picture, and they'd help us along. It was all fixed so we could make it home, and a lot of them did. They found their way back through the underground. We had a flak map too. They had red circles on them to show us where the flak was. We had to fly between the circles.

I remember one Sunday morning we were bombing Nuremberg. I suppose it was about ten in the morning. There was a lot of flak and they could trace you right on your altitude. They [the flak] came at us in batteries of four. They would aim for us, the lead plane, and you could see these four things out in front of you. What we would have to do then is move slowly to the right and to the left so that by the time they fig-

Robert Kimball (far left) and fellow navigators.
(Photo courtesy Robert Kimball)

ured out where we were, we weren't there anymore. Of course that didn't help the wing men any. I remember it [the Nuremberg mission] specifically because I saw like five or six airplanes going down right in front of me all at the same time. I remember saying to myself, "You dummy, you volunteered for this." I figured we were next. Anyhow, we did get through it.

There are some funny stories. This one happened before I got over there. The 100th Bomb Group flew in, the whole group from the United States, when they first moved to England. They were not the best organized bunch in the world. They had trouble even finding England, I heard. Anyhow, they flew some missions, and they were having a lot of problems. The people up at where they call wing headquarters decided they better replace some of the top people there, so they put a new colonel in and kept moving down from there until they got to the group navigator, a man named Major Crosby. He's in a picture I have here (looking at the picture), and that's me. Anyhow they brought this new guy in and he'd never flown a mission. They [The 100th Bomb Group] didn't like him, and of course they were going to ship Crosby out, and everyone liked Crosby. So, they decided they would just do something to get rid of the new guy. They told him maybe he ought to go on a mission to get a little experience. So he said, "Oh yeah." He wanted to do that. They took him over Germany, of course they had this all arranged ahead of time. The pilot pretended he was having trouble and hit the bail-out button. The guy jumped out, and they just closed the door and went home. The guy spent the rest of the war in a POW camp. (Laughs.)

I remember Christmas Eve of '44. We went out on a mission, and our primary target was covered with clouds. We couldn't see it [the target], so we went to a secondary target, which was great because secondary targets usually didn't have any flak. Well, it turned out to be an airfield with lots of flak. We got hit and didn't know how badly. That wasn't odd, we often got hit. It was nothing. We were leading, so we were the first plane to land. Here our tires had been shot out, and when we hit the runway we lost control and skidded around. So all the other guys were flying around, and they couldn't land until they got us off there. No one got hurt though, luckily.

Oh, I remember lots of missions, but the worst ones were the oil targets. Germany really protected the industrial areas. The flak in these areas was so heavy that everything was just black. It would just make clouds. Those were the scariest.

I never really had my own crew. I was a lead navigator, and they had what you called lead crews, so I just kept switching around. They would pick a certain lead pilot, and his crew would sign a lead navigator. I flew my missions with a variety of planes. I flew twenty-four missions, then they stopped me from flying so I could train other navigators. I stayed until after the war. I think I had bombed just about every city in Germany.

We had all kinds of people over there: tough ones, meek ones, brave ones, cowards. We had guys that just couldn't do it. We couldn't get them in an airplane. They'd just sit there and cry. My first bombardier, Smith, was scared. I wasn't a lead navigator the first couple of missions; so we would be sitting up there, and all he would have to do was watch the lead plane. He couldn't even do that. We had a little door where we bailed out, and he would just sit back there with his parachute on. All he did was ride, so the next thing you know they shipped him home. Every once in a while you'd get someone that just couldn't handle it, and you could understand that.

Another character, Lt. Graham, a navigator, got hit on one of the missions. The pilot and copilot got scared, and they didn't know whether they should go back to England or crash land in Germany. They were frightened bad, and the copilot wanted to fly back to England; so Lt. Graham got the fire extinguisher and hit the pilot on the head and knocked him out. The copilot then

(Photo courtesy Robert Kimball)

took the plane back. Split-second decisions like that had to be made, or they'd be made for you.

Sometime in November of '44 I was the lead navigator for the whole Air Force, two thousand planes. You can't believe what that would look like. That's when we were trying to end the war, right after the Battle of the Bulge. The ground troops were in there pushing, and what we were trying to do was cut off their supply lines. We got all of their airfields, then their railroad tracks and rail yards. We cut off everything so they just couldn't fight. They had no ammunition, no fuel. We're the ones that really broke their backs.

When the war was over we were going back to the States to retrain. They gave us an old plane that had been shot down in Switzerland, and we took it down through Africa and across the Atlantic back to Florida. When I got out of that plane, the first thing I said is that I'd never get in one again. Now I own five planes. Anyway, I came back and finished school. I went into business here in Ebensburg, and I've been here ever since.

L. Robert Kimball was an extraordinary veteran of World War II, with three Air Medals and the Distinguished Flying Cross. His accomplishments have not gone unrecognized, and his efforts have been greatly appreciated.

Harold Kornman

392nd Bomb Group
579th Squadron
Navigator

by
Dennis Whalen

During most of the Second World War, Mr. Kornman was stationed in Wendling, England, on an old RAF air base. He was a lead navigator for the 392nd Bomb Group, and had flown twenty-three successful missions before April 22, 1944. His twenty-fourth mission was a bomb raid on Hamm, Germany. The objective was to destroy the railroad martialing yards. Considering that the crew had run two bomb raids to Berlin during their earlier twenty-three missions, the crew felt lucky. Sadly, there wouldn't be a twenty-fifth.

While flying over Hamm, they took some damage. The waist gunners bailed out immediately and were taken prisoner by the Germans. The rest of the crew held out until they were over Belgium. The men had been instructed, if forced to bail, to wait until nearing the ground before opening their parachutes. Only Mr. Kornman remembered those instructions. The other men were immediately captured.

"I delayed the opening of the chute until I was at only about two thousand feet. What happens when you open a chute is that any of the enemies in the territory can see you floating down. I had noticed that there were some German troops coming out of this small town, oh, maybe just a couple miles away. As I hit the ground, I rolled over and released the chute. I noticed a small piece of woods there. They were trying to search the woods, which were right across the road there. I had to cross the road, and the troops were coming down the road, and they saw me go in. I tip-toed through a pretty good-sized woods. I got to the other side, where I was in a wheat field. The wheat was about this high [indicating to his knee] but I laid down there and hid. For three or four hours, they searched the woods."

From his vantage point in the wheat field, Mr. Kornman was able to watch the search. After dark, he wanted to get away, because he knew that the Germans would be back looking for him the next day. "After they left, I took off."

A report was written about him for the Beaver Times. It read:

"As daylight approached, he recalled the Air Force briefing that he had on the procedure to follow in order to contact underground personnel in occupied territory. This advice was to locate a house outside of town in a remote location, watch the house, and at the right time approach the house, knock on the door. There was a strong probability that they would be in a position to contact the Underground Resistance Movement to help you get through the country. With this in mind, at daylight, he located a house on a small farm, laid out in the orchard, and watched the lights go on in the house. In about half an hour, the man in the house walked out of the house with his lunch bucket, got on his bicycle, and rode away to his work. At this point, Harold then approached the house, knocked on the door, and was greeted by the lady of the house in wooden shoes. She appeared to recognize him as an airman with the flying suit he wore, and he indicated to her that he was hungry, and she walked to the kitchen stove, he thought to prepare a breakfast. Instead, she grabbed a pan of boiling water from the stove and came after him, she threw it as he was bounding off the porch. Obviously and understandably, she was concerned for the safety of her family if the Nazis found a U.S. Airman in their home."

Mr. Kornman did, however, find members of the underground who were willing to help him.

"After watching several farmers go past, he saw a black horse pulling a covered type wagon with two young men in the driver's seat. He thought that they could possibly be helpful, so he jumped out in the middle of the road as they approached. They immediately stopped and appeared to recognize that he was a downed flier in need of assistance. They motioned for him to get into the back of the wagon, which turned out to be a beer delivery wagon, and they immediately opened a bottle of good Belgian beer, which tasted extremely good at the time..."

Mr. Kornman feared their intentions. He didn't know whether or not they were legitimate members of the underground or if they were bounty hunters trying to earn their pay by turning an American Airman over to the Nazis. But they were trustworthy, and the following day, they took him to meet Marcel Windels.

"Mr. [Marcel] Windels was a leader in the Underground Resistance Movement. Harold stayed at the home of Mr. Windels for two days while he [Windels] prepared a fake passport for him after taking his picture in the civilian clothes that he [Windels] gave him to wear. After a couple of days, he followed another member of the underground on bicycle to the home of a local priest where he stayed in his attic for about ten days and learned a little bit of Flemish from the priest. From there on, it was a matter of moving from one place to another, always in the direction of France."

From France, Mr. Kornman was able to escape to England, where he arrived on September 9, 1944. After nearly five months, he got back.

Mr. Kornman stayed in Europe until 1946, when he returned home. He and his wife moved around the country before settling in Beaver, Pa. Then in January of 1989, something unexpected happened.

"In early January, Mr. and Mrs. Kornman were aroused from their sleep with a phone call at 6 a.m. Mrs. Kornman answered the phone; the call was from Belgium...This call came from Bob Coangelo, a U.S. citizen...[who] was a friend of Paul Windels, the son of Marcel Windels... Paul had been trying to track Harold down without any success...Marcel had been machine gunned down by a crew of retreating Nazis at the end of the war along with the father of Paul's good friend, Piet Duthoy and two U. S. Airmen that they were escorting.

Bob Coangelo gave Harold the address where he could reach Paul Windels and he immediately wrote a letter to Paul which started a series of communications between the two of them, plus a number of communiques with Andre Noielle, who is currently the head of the American Legion of Belgium and who was also a leader of the Resistance Movement during WWII."

Because of the letters and communiques, Mr. Kornman was invited to return to Belgium for the first time in forty-five years to attend the 1989 Flanders Field Celebration, a ceremony to honor American soldiers who gave their lives on Belgian soil.

He arrived in Belgium on May 24. He retraced his steps from the Nazis shortly after landing. He spoke to the Belgian people, thanking them for their courage and their help. He returned to the U. S. a week later.

Howard Langston

306th Bomb Group
423rd Squadron
Toggelier

by
Randy Krampert

Howard R. Langston is a mild-mannered, optimistic man. Being drafted for WW II in 1943, he volunteered for the 8th Air Force Division. He was placed with the 4th Squadron in the 306th Bomb Group at the age of nineteen. Even though it was difficult to leave his pregnant wife, family, and friends, he always felt that the war's outcome would be a "good one." He never feared the possibility that he might not make it back home. For this I feel that the 8th Air Force and the U.S. were more than lucky to have someone like Mr. Langston on our side.

I was a toggelier. I went over later in the beginning, and they were developing the Mickey scope. It was really radar. The advantage of that was that we could now drop bombs through cloud coverage. So they had to get somebody to run this Mickey scope. They took the navigator of each crew and sent him to a school to learn how to use it. They replaced the navigator with the bombardier, and the bombardier was replaced with someone, such as myself. I was a sergeant at the time. It was up to me to drop the bombs at the right time...so I flipped the toggle switch. On the left side of the nose of the aircraft, there was a toggle switch. When I flipped that switch, the bombs would drop out, thus the name toggelier.

I really didn't volunteer, I was drafted in 1943. I was nineteen. Do you think you could go drop bombs on cities and people?

It is a different atmosphere...different conditions.

I was stationed in a little village about two miles from Bedford, England, which is pretty much due north of London, about forty or fifty miles.

My barracks was right near a farm house. As a matter-of-fact, two or three of the fellas of my crew got really acquainted with the family. We used to go over and have tea at tea time. Sometimes we'd go over for what they call "late supper." Supper over there was at about ten in the evening. You'd have a cup of Ovaltine and cookies or tarts or something. There were a couple young boys, and we knew the mother and father. It was like a home to us. Barracks' life was pretty drab, so it was nice to go into a home-like atmosphere. They had tea at four in the afternoon. I had to learn how to eat soft-boiled eggs out of an egg cup. Matter-of-fact, I bought my own egg cup. An egg cup is like a small glass with a stem, kind of like, maybe, a small wine glass. You'd put the egg in it with the pointy end up and crack the shell with a spoon, then you'd scoop out the egg.

I've never gone back, but I'd have liked to. My wife developed heart problems and wasn't able to travel. I stayed in touch with the family for a while. We used to send Christmas cards back and forth. Then, the father died. The mother and the two boys must have moved somewhere else 'cause I lost track of them.

I gave those boys my bicycle when I left. That was one of the first things I bought over there. I bought a bicycle -(laughs.)- then I bought an egg cup, 'cause you had to have your own egg cup, then I got a set of darts 'cause that was the game they played over there. (Laughing.) So, I had my own personal darts, egg cup, and my bicycle. So I fit in pretty good there.

I remember one time, it must have been my birthday...My mother and my wife baked an angel-food cake, and they didn't have Styrofoam packing then so they used puffed wheat. They got this box and packed the cake in puffed wheat, so it wouldn't get crushed. It arrived in good shape. I thought, well, I'm always eating over at the farm house with the family, why don't I just take my cake over there? So, I took it over and cut it so everyone could have a piece. (Laughing.) The boys noticed that puffed wheat...They didn't want the cake; they started eating the puffed wheat like pop-corn. They thought, Wow! This is great! I got a kick out of that. I had to write back and tell my wife and my mother that the boys liked the puffed wheat better than their angel-food cake. (Laughs.)

I had quite a few scary moments over there. One of the most outstanding was on one of our first missions near Berlin. It must have been about my twelfth mission. I recall that the flak was very thick. It was so thick that I...I was afraid to look. But, I had to; my position being the guy who dropped the bombs. I had to watch the lead squadron, because the lead squadron used the bomb site. I didn't use the bomb site. When he [the squadron leader] opened his bomb bay doors, I had to open the bomb bay doors on my aircraft. I would watch his bomb bay, and when I'd see the first bomb come out, I'd flip my toggle switch, and out came our bombs. Anyway, I really didn't want to look because there was so much flak. I really felt... very uncomfortable. I don't know if I was scared, but I remember being very, very uncomfortable. So I held my hand over my eyes and just looked

B-17 bomb drop.

(Photo courtesy Tom Brown)

through a crack like this, (Putting his hands over his eyes), so all I could see was his bomb bay doors. That was probably one of the scariest times.

Another time, we were on a mission, the lead navigator kind of got a little lazy. It was up to the squadron lead navigator to fly us around the red zone. The clouds were so thick, apparently, he just wanted to get home. He took us straight through the middle of the red zone [Flak]. Unfortunately, when we got to the twin city of Mannheim there was a big hole in the sky. A big hole. We could see the city, and they could look up and see us. And, ah, we had a new tail gunner on this mission. He said, "Oh! Look at all those flashes down there! What is that?" Somebody said, "Well, you can count to about twenty and you'll know what they are." That's when flak just completely surrounded us. It knocked out the oxygen system. We were very low on oxygen. We were flying at twenty-four thousand feet. We needed the oxygen. Flak hit one of the hydraulic control lines for one of the inboard engines, and the prop just ran away. I don't understand why, but for some reason, the propeller was spinning so hard that the whole craft was shaking. We were told to snap our parachutes on. We were all ready to bail out. Then suddenly, the plane got quiet again. I looked out the window, and here the prop had flown off - flew out into space somewhere. (Laughs.) The propeller could have flown right through the nose where the bombardier, myself and the navigator were sitting. It would have gotten all of us. Fortunately it flew in some other direction. We had come down low because of the oxygen situation, but we got home all right on three engines. When we got those mission assignments, much like the ones I've explained, it didn't really bother me. We knew about it the night before. When I woke up the next morning, when they called us at four o'clock in the morning, then it would bother me. But even then, it really didn't set in fully. The full intensity didn't set in until we went to the briefing. When we went to the briefing, they showed us what cities we were bombing. Then you would feel it. Up on the maps there would be a lot of red paint. Wherever you saw red up on the maps that meant there was heavy flak activity. The more red there was around your target, the more nervous you would get. The more nervous I would get. I...I couldn't eat breakfast. I would be so tense...We could eat breakfast before we would go on a mission, if you wanted to, but I never could.

After we flew over, dropped the bombs, and started back home, all of the sudden, I would be so hungry. Ah, man, I could eat a horse! (Laughs.) So what they used to do - they used to give us a little box of hard candy. It was called hard tack. Anyhow, they used to pass these out. I'd always save mine and make sure I had my hard tack for the way home. It was just funny how you could get rid of your tension so quickly. I can still remember how hungry I would be. That's one time we'd really get a good meal was after a mission. I really enjoyed those meals.

When I got back, I worked at Armco. Veterans were entitled to go to college free. We were given $90 a month to live on, if we went to school. I went to Carnegie for two years. It was called Carnegie Tech. Now it's Carnegie Mellon. That helped me get the job at Armco.

I feel that people may have forgotten or don't appreciate what happened, but it doesn't bother me. We just did what we had to do. Like I said, we weren't heroes; we just did what we had to do. I don't think some people appreciate it, but it really isn't their fault.

Now retired, Mr. Langston golfs three to four times a week, and is the treasurer for his church. He is a very honorable man. Even though he concludes that he is not a "hero" and his stories aren't interesting, I feel that my short visit with him has heralded him a hero to me permanently, and also to many others.

William C. Leasure

91st Bomb Group
324th Squadron
Navigator

by
Elizabeth Marquez

It was a rainy October afternoon when I first met Mr. William C. Leasure. As I was driven to his home, I tried to imagine what this veteran of the 8th Air Force would be like. I surmised that he would be quite similar to my grandfather who was enjoying his retirement by just relaxing. I soon found myself to be quite wrong...

We, my friend Matt and I, rang the doorbell and were greeted by Mrs. Dorothy Leasure. A man not much taller than myself rose from a chair and greeted me. This man was quite different from what I had pictured. He wore a denim shirt and jeans which seemed pleasantly odd to me. He took our coats and then led us to his kitchen table. It was obvious that Mr. Leasure was no stranger to interviews. The table was covered with pictures, papers, and books, all awaiting us. The first thing that Mr. Leasure did was hand me a two-paged itemized description of what lay before us, and then he began to explain them. The first item on this list we examined was his biography which he had written for the 20th Air Force Directors' Committee in 1995. This biography detailed Mr. Leasure's life, from his birth to the present.

William C. Leasure was born in Clymer, Pennsylvania on September 9, 1918 to a coal miner. When he was old enough, he commuted to Indiana State Teachers College, which later came to be known as Indiana University of Pennsylvania. After two-and-a-half years, his money ran out, and he went to work for Railway Express, until the Air Corps Cadet Program came into being.

Mr. Leasure enlisted on April 19, 1941, and in September he was called to service. He entered the Spartan School of Aeronautics, and completed his primary flying training. He was then sent to Randolph to gain more experience. *At this point, Mr. Leasure stopped for a minute and commented, "I thought I could fly. Evidently, they didn't." He was then sent to Navigation School at Mather Field, Sacramento, California in February. On July 4, 1942, he graduated first, in a class of one hundred.*

Mr. Leasure then handed me a small cream-colored folder. Inside of it were two pictures. The first was of he and his wife on his wedding day. The second was taken fifty years later, on their anniversary. Next, he proceeded to tell me the story of his marriage. It was just eleven days between his graduation from Navigation School and the day he was to leave for Scotland. Many of the "higher-ups" were against the idea of the boys marrying before they left. So, Mr. Leasure and Miss Dorothy Holmes, along with another couple traveled to Reno, Nevada. On July, 5, 1942, Mr. Leasure married Miss Holmes of Clymer, Pennsylvania. Sadly, the gentleman in the other couple died in the war only months later.

On July 15, 1942 Mr. Leasure traveled to Walla Walla, Washington where he awaited further orders. He was assigned to join pilot Bill Crumm's crew, of which Rufus Youngblood, who would become famous for throwing his body over Lyndon B. Johnson when President Kennedy was assassinated, was also a member . From there the crew traveled on to Boise where they picked up their plane which they named "Jack the Ripper." *I proceeded to ask Mr. Leasure why he and the other crew members called their plane "Jack the Ripper." He answered by saying, "We were going to England."* Before reaching England, they made further stops at Bangor, Maine, and Gander, Newfoundland.

The next item that was placed into my hands had the word confidential typed at the top of it in underlined, capital letters. These papers, dated September 27, 1942, were the orders that sent Mr. Leasure and the other nine members of the crew to Prestwick, Scotland. The orders also applied to the thirty-two other crews, including the crew of the "Memphis Belle." These men were the "pioneers," the first to arrive in Britain. The crew of "Jack the Ripper" arrived at Prestwick, Scotland on September 30, 1942. They were then sent to Kimbolton, before being finally stationed at Bassingbourn on October 14 as a member of the 91st Bomb Group in the 324th Squadron. Between November of 1942 and February of 1943, Mr. Leasure flew in thirteen missions, eleven of which were with his own crew. These thirteen raids, which gave Mr. Leasure more combat time than any other man in the 8th Air Force, were among the first sixteen flown in the war, and the eleven that the crew flew was two more than the famed "Memphis Belle" had flown.

At that point, I asked Mr. Leasure if he was ever scared of flying. He said that he never remembered being afraid. Part of that, his wife chimed in, was due to the plane's pilot, Bill Crumm. They both described Crumm as a very enthusiastic man, who was very confident and a good leader. He then gave to me a portion of Crumm's diary. All throughout the war, Crumm had kept this diary, unknown to his crew mates. In the diary I found detailed accounts of the crews raids. In France they had bombed Brest; Abbeville; St. Nazaire; twice; Lille; Rouen; Romilly Sur Seine; Lorient, twice; as well as Vegasak and Rhur/Emden in Germany. It was in the diary where I found a description of Mr. Leasure's first of two kills. Crumm wrote, "Meet F.W. 190s before hitting French coast - Little trouble, but they came within one hundred yards dead ahead. Light flack at F. coast. Then more pursuit to the target. Bill Leasure got his first Me 109 with a fifteen-shell burst. It stalled belching black smoke then spun down thru the clouds."

After "Jack the Ripper" finished his Emden journey, on which Mr. Leasure was injured by flak, the crew was deemed the "most deserving crew" to return to the United States and report on the success of daytime bombing raids. On March 1, 1943, the crew arrived in Washington, D.C. Mr. Leasure, Mr. Crumm, and copilot, Mr. Mark Gilman spoke with General Arnold and his staff for two days in the War Room of the Pentagon, answering questions, and voicing their opinion that two hundred planes per raid, with fighter support, were necessary for the crews to survive during daylight bombing raids.

Instead of returning to Britain, the crew was given three assignments in the U.S. First, they traveled to the Air Force School of Applied Tactics in Orlando, Florida. While there, the crew wrote Bombing the Nazis. Each of the crew members wrote about their duties. This manual was then distributed to bomber training commands. *Now, I was handed a blue book with ring binding, a copy of Bombing the Nazis. Mr. Leasure seemed very happy to show me his part of the work, and I was excited to read it. It told exactly what a crew member could expect, starting the day before a mission and concluding when the crew arrived back at the base.* Next, the crew went on a promotional tour. In all, they were featured at thirty-six mass rallies at industrial plants. Before about 235,000 workers at each rally, they spoke on the importance of industrial production, war bonds, and blood donations. However, the tour wasn't all work. In both Los Angeles and San Francisco the crew was wined and dined at the best establishments the cities had to offer. *Mr. Leasure picked up an old green folder, and opened it, inside was a picture of the crew at a stop on their tour. They were all smiling and looked happy to be away from the combat which took so many of their friends.* Their last mission together was at the headquarters of the Second Air Force. While

Pilot Fred Rutan shows a souvenir helmet after an emergency landing at Cherborg. (Photo courtesy Tom Brown)

there, the crew was interviewed about possible improvements that could be made on both the planes and equipment.

Mr. Leasure rejoined the war, but this time he was sent to the Pacific. He became Staff Navigator and Tactical Plans Officer of the 315th Bomb Wing on Guam. Also he served as General Frank Armstrong's navigator on seven missions against Japan. *Mrs. Leasure rose from the couch and came into the kitchen. She then asked if we had ever seen the movie "Twelve O'clock High" Neither Matt, nor I had. She went on to say that the movies character, Frank Savage, was based on General Armstrong. Then I asked him how he had found out that the war was over. He answered, "I must tell you that story." While on a mission to Japan, Armstrong's crew was listening to the radio. They heard President Truman announce that the war was over. They turned off the radio, and awaited further notice. However, they never heard the code word, "Utah" which was the signal to abort the mission, and continued on.*

Then, he continued on, telling me about how he came home. General Armstrong and his crew was offered the opportunity to fly to Washington D.C., via Chicago, with all the hoopla a returning war hero deserved. However, a higher ranking general decided that he would take on this mission. Mr. Leasure then became a troop commander on the USS George Clymer in order to get home. As he sailed into San Francisco Bay, he heard on the radio that General Armstrong had just landed in Washington D.C. The higher ranking officer had changed his mind and General Armstrong had gone as originally planned.

Upon returning home, Mr. Leasure moved to Houston, Texas and worked as a sales manager for the Syntron Company of Homer Center, Pennsylvania. After eight years in that position, he quit, and invented automatic packaging machines for flexible packaging of snack foods. He started Mira-Pak Inc. which became a leader in its field. In the late 1970s, Mr. Leasure sold the rights to his twenty-five United States patents, and one hundred foreign ones. Since then, he has been involved in ranching and cattle operations in both Texas and Pennsylvania, coal mining operations in Pennsylvania, gas operations in Texas and Pennsylvania, and real estate in both Texas and Pennsylvania. *Mr. Leasure's final comment was that he keeps trying to retire, but has so far been unsuccessful. Matt and I left Mr. Leasure's home absolutely amazed. For the rest of the day, we talked about nothing else. He had lived the history that we had only read about, and, for us, he had made that history come to life.*

Duane Le Breton

493rd Bomb Group
861st Squadron
Gunner and Bombardier

by
Beth Rutkowski

Duane Le Breton, the youngest of ten children. His father died when he was just a young boy. You could say he was the handyman around the house. Even though he was youngest of the children, he ended up being the one to fix anything that broke down. Just before the war, Duane was working on cars and driving truck for "Lightning Express" in Pittsburgh. He retells his experiences of World War II.

I had just come from my Sunday football game. Once we reached the area where I lived, everyone kept asking, "Did you hear the news? Pearl Harbor was bombed this morning!"

I said, "What? Are you pulling my leg?" I was sixteen then, and I never thought I would live to see the war. I thought the war would be over by then. If you think about it, things were leading up to it. Germany was sinking a lot of our ships. We had to get into it. If we didn't, things would have turned out totally different.

I was drafted, but I felt that I was ready to go. Everybody else was. Why shouldn't I? My family didn't have much to say about the war. It was only my mother and youngest sister who told me I should try and stay out and make an appeal to the draft board. I signed up on October twenty-sixth. In December they called me up for the blood tests. My best friend and I enlisted together. We thought if they asked us if we had a preference between Army or Navy, we were going to say "Army." We did. They stamped mine "Army" and they stamped his "Navy." We wondered why, and if there was something behind it, unless they thought he would make a better sailor. It wasn't like he could swim any better than I could. (Laughs.)

My overall training was good. I took basic training in Miami Beach if you could believe that one. I couldn't believe it myself. (Laughs.) I thought this was out of this world. I mean, what more could you wish for? Down there living in hotels, and marching on the beach. Of all places, Miami Beach!

I remember one instance that my temper got a little out of hand. I was combing my hair under a spigot. This guy comes beside me and he, too, begins to comb his hair. He puts his comb under the water, the same water I'm using. He finishes up before me; and when he is done, he shuts the water off. You see, that was just like waving the red flag in front of me. Boy, did I ever nail him! I hit him the whole way to the bathtub. One punch and he bounced around like a ping-pong ball. He told me he was going to tell the major. Well, I didn't care; he could do whatever he wanted to. But, do you know what? He was to become my best friend. (Laughs.) After that little scene of letting him know who was boss, we became real good buddies. Everywhere I went, he tagged along right behind me.

After our basic training, we went to Fort Meade, Maryland. It was there that we took our aptitude tests. One day I got called up to the orderly room. The captain was waiting for me. He welcomed me and told me to sit down. The next thing I remember is him asking me how I would feel being in the Air Force. Strange as heck, I told him my real feelings: "Honest to God, no, I wouldn't want to be in the Air Force."

With a surprised look on his face he said, "May I ask you why?"

"Well," I replied, "I don't even like roller coaster and you want me to fly?"

He responded with a simple, "Yes."

Boy, oh, boy! I thought roller coasters were bad. I hated to see what planes were like. The captain tried to boost my confidence by saying, "You can't compare airplanes to roller coasters. They are very different."

I left his office, but he still hadn't convinced me. The captain wouldn't take "no" for an answer. He told me, "I'll tell you what, go back to the base and talk to the guys. See what they have to say. Then come back and see me. Think about it." That was the extent of our conversation.

Well, when I got back to the barracks, my buddies wanted to know what he wanted. I told them he wanted me in the Air Force. They told me, "You lucky son-of-a-b. You must have brains!" But when they heard I turned it down, they told me that anyone who turns the Air Force down can't have brains. You know what? They changed my mind immediately. At that moment I could have walked straight back to the captain and told him I would be more than happy to be in the Air Force. But I decided to wait 'til morning. However, I wasn't able to dodge them constantly making fun of me and calling me "bonehead."

The Air Force wanted young guys because it is easy to "wash out." (You can't handle the pressure, and get sick. It is possible to get the bends.) To prepare for the war, we had to take many tests. The tests we took ran on for days. While we were training, an order came out from the government that we were all washed out. They said they already had enough pilots and copilots. Why in the world did they get us? No sooner do you get down there and take the tests, than they tell you that you are washed out. Couldn't they foresee this happening? They told us that they would use most of us as gunners, and the rest of us would be radio men and engineers.

I wound up in Texas in the gunners' school. Now that was tough. They first started you out shooting clay pigeons. Then they put us in a truck, and the pigeons would come flying out at you from any direction. We needed to react fast in order to shoot the pigeons. They had a set number of pigeons to get, or we would not qualify. We needed to go to school every day. They drilled thing after thing into our brains. I remember we had airplane identification. The teacher would flash an airplane on the screen and we would have to identify it. The only problem is they flashed picture after picture consecutively. There was no time to think. Surprisingly, after awhile we would barely miss one. I was in gunners' school for about two months. I entered in the middle of April, and we got out the sixteenth of July. Another drill they had us do was dismantling machine guns and putting them back together again. Once they felt we had it down pat, they blindfolded us, and again you had to take apart the gun and put it back together again.

U.S.O. performers entertaining the troops. From left to right - Mitzi Mayfair, Kay Francis, Martha Raye. *(Photo courtesy Tom Brown)*

After I was done with the training, we

had a sixteen-day delay. We were then sent to Camp Kilmer, New Jersey, where we prepared to head overseas. We went to New York City and boarded the Queen Elizabeth. It was the biggest ship, and it held lots of people. The ship would change direction every fifteen minutes. This was so a submarine wouldn't be able to follow. However, every time the ship changed its direction, everything would sway to one side. I remember when we were eating dinner, they didn't let us in on any secrets. As soon as the ship began to change direction, all of our food and everything on the table slid right off the table. (Laughs.) They could have been kind enough to tell us this would happen, then we could have started grabbing for something. It took us six days to get there since we were zig-zagging across sea.

When we got on, it was about eleven o'clock at night, and they told us to go to our cabins and go to bed. They didn't want us to fool around. I told one of the guys that once we woke up in the morning, we would be able to see the New York sky line. The first thing in the morning one of the guys goes up and takes a look. He comes back down and tells us, "You ain't going to see a New York sky line. New York ain't even in sight." No sooner did we get on, they started moving us out. (Laughs.)

The first plane I flew was a B-24. I only flew it in the States. When we got overseas, they put us in B-17s. I was glad about that. I never feared of dying. I can remember the nights before our missions. Our tail gunner would lift up a toast and say, "Drink and be merry, men, for tomorrow we will fly."

We lost our bombardier. He flew with another crew, then it was shot down. They made me the bombardier which I liked. I liked being up in the nose. When I first got in I thought you would never get me in the airplane because I would be too scared. Just to look down, I would get scared. But not at that height. It is so high that you can't even relate.

I always wondered if with every target we hit, people were killed; or whether the guys shot down were your friends?

I was fortunate in so many ways. It first started with my basic training in Miami Beach. Then I was able to go overseas in the Queen Elizabeth, and coming home I flew a brand new B-17 back to the States. However, the most incredible incident was when we had a forty-eight-hour pass to go into London. I had a terrific time, especially picking up women. (Laughs) We were issued these passes once a month. We got the pass for the 7th and 8th of May. When we first got in London, we stopped at a bar. The bartender asked, "Hey, Yanks, have you heard that the war is over?" He told us that the news was on the wireless [radio]. Ain't this something? The next day was declared V-E Day. You wouldn't believe the crowds. They were up on poles celebrating. Ain't that funny?

After the war we headed for home. I was in Lincoln, Nebraska, in charge of fifteen planes. One day the headquarters called me in, so I reported to them. When I reached their offices they instructed me to pack my bags and go home. I was twenty then, and a free man. I was just discharged.

Mr. Le Breton did what he needed, and was able to come home to his family. He comes from McKeesport, but for the last eleven years he has resided in Wilkensburg. A disabling sore on his ankle, complicated by diabetes, caused him to retire early. Never having been married, he lives in a small apartment by himself.

At the end of our conversation, he pulled out a letter and some pictures that he received from a female friend he met while in Miami Beach. From his facial expression, it is obvious that he still has fond memories from the war. Finally, he shows me a picture of himself in his flying jacket. He was young then. He was also proud.

Alexander Lee

100th Bomb Group
418th Squadron
Radio Operator

by
John Hanratty

[On] our mission to Bremen in 1943 we lost seven planes. The following day we lost twelve planes. That's how this 100th Bomb Group got its title "The Bloody Hundredth." The reason it got that title was not because it lost more than any other, it was how they lost them - twelve at a time - seven at a time.

These are the words of Alexander Lee of the 100th Bomb Group. Mr. Lee was born in England but became a naturalized citizen of the United States prior to the Second World War. During the war Mr. Lee served as a radio operator while serving a tour in Europe.

I was born in England, and I had a sister there along with several cousins. I was sort of, in a way, looking forward to seeing them. One day I went to the squadron commander and told him I wanted to go and see my sister, and he was like, "Hey! Come on, I'd like to see my sister too." Then I explained to him my situation, and he said, "That's odd. I never heard that story before. Go ahead." So I was given three days. They [my family] lived on the west coast of England, outside of Manchester. I got off the train very early in the morning, and I was walking up the street when this girl comes toward me, and walked past me. I didn't think much of it, but something told me to turn around. As I turned around, she turned around. It was my sister. I hadn't seen her for about ten or twelve years. (Laughs.)

There was another humorous situation. Well, it was humorous, but it could have been tragic. While we were in training in Walla Walla, Washington we used to do a lot of cross-country flights, and the pilot of our airplane was a very excellent pilot. He insisted everyone on the plane switching positions so we could get used to each others jobs. I was a radio operator and my turn came to be in the ball turret. My good friend was at that time the ball-turret gunner. I got down in it and rolled it back, and closed the lid. It had two handles to close, and when he closed the top he would slap on there and say, "Roll it back." I rolled it back. The door opened. It's about ten thousand feet up. The only thing that saved me that day was the strap that I had coming around my back. It kept me from falling out. I finally got out, but left the door open. So we radioed back and told them what had happened. They said, "Bring your plane in." Well, when we landed, the door caught, snapped up, hit the tail gear, blew that out, and then it went down the runway by itself. We got out okay, except the squadron commander busted everybody on the plane. That was humorous but almost tragic.

I was married when I went overseas. My wife would ask me all kinds of questions, and I couldn't answer. The letters were censored. They would say they read this in the paper and ask me if I did it. I had a code with my wife. I smoked terribly. A lot of guys did. I would tell her I smoked so many cigarettes, and she would understand how things were going just by that.

It was scary as hell. The first [mission] we flew was July '43 to Trondheim, Norway. At that time, we did not know it, but up there the Germans were experimenting with atomic energy. We were told it was a submarine plant, which it was. The Luftwaffe at that time used that area as a rest place. They thought Trondheim was

(Photo courtesy Stephen Kinzler)

as safe as you can get. But they got surprised that day. A few of them came up, and we got a flat tire that day. But we had to sweat out that flat tire on the way back, and we landed with the flat.

The night before a mission oddly enough I did some praying by myself. They had a Catholic service, a Jewish service, and a Protestant service, but I'd go to town. We were alerted before we went. I didn't know where [our mission would be] or what, but we were alerted and told to be back.

I thought the officers on our plane were God - especially the pilot. He was exceptionally good. We were in his hands, and that's it. I really looked up to them.

When we were returning after our tour was over, we were shipped home aboard the New Amsterdam. The ship was carrying POWs. Many Luftwaffe people were there. Yeah, we met them. We used to wear jackets with bombs on the back. They didn't like that. They'd start arguing with you in German. You would just turn your back and say, "Take a good look." (Laughs.)

Probably the best time I ever had was the night of our last mission. They threw a party for us because we were the first crew to finish a tour without loss. We had pheasant under glass that night. Where they got it I don't know, but I suspected they shot the King's pheasant. (Laughs.)

The engineer of our plane was from Texas. After we finished our mission, he and I went to this Royal Air Force base. We stayed there for a few months. We were sitting there reading our letters, and I looked at him, and he had the funniest look on his face. I asked, "What's the matter?" He said "Look at this." He was married, but his wife was also writing to this other guy and got the letters mixed up. (Laughs.) He was fit to be tied of course.

I went back to England for a reunion once. There was a little church and the town was called Diss, and we went in there. It was a very small church, but when we got there they [the British war veterans] all lined up. When we came in, boy! They came to attention. It was very heartrending.

Mr. Lee currently resides in Monroeville with his wife. He has three children, nine grandchildren and one great-grandson. He continues to attend some of the local reunions that are held. He is interested in the British culture and his British heritage.

Billie E. Miller

92nd Bomb Group
327th Squadron
Waist Gunner

by
Nathan Tagg

The year was 1943. Billie Miller was a junior at Butler High School. When he turned eighteen in January, he enlisted in the United States Army. He was assigned to Armor in a training unit, the 699th Ordnance, in Fort Knox, Kentucky. In November he was given the opportunity to join the Army Air Corps. "There wasn't much basic training as such, we already had done a lot of training in the Armor . Then we went into the aerial gunnery. They had an advanced gunnery course for us because, in the armored force, you fired everything from pistol through 75mm. We had a lot of .50 caliber machine gun training, and all they had to do was get us used to turrets and what they called the RAD sight."

After completing the aerial gunnery course, Billie was sent to meet his crew in Ardmore, Oklahoma. Miller was assigned as a waist gunner. After several months of additional combat training, the crew was ready. They flew their B-17 to England but soon found out that they had to surrender it. Miller and the others were stationed in an airfield at Podington, England, about fifty miles northwest of London. Their B-17 was one of about forty in the 92nd Bomb Group of the Eighth Air Force. The crew underwent a week or so of orientation and then were sent into combat.

On August 3, 1944 Miller went out on his first mission. The destination was Merkwiler, France. The target was an engine factory for German aircraft. It seemed as if his luck would run out on this, his first time out. The plane had lost an engine before even reaching the target. After releasing its bombs, the crippled B-17 limped toward home. By this time, the other engine which had been "sick" was giving out. The B-17 carrying Miller dropped back from group to group until they were alone. Then a couple of P-51s picked them up. All this time, the crew had been trying desperately to lighten their weight and gain altitude. Anything that could be removed was tossed from the plane. This included all the guns, the floorboards, and even the spare clothes.

The plane finally landed with one engine out and one on fire internally. As soon as it taxied to a stop, one of the tires blew out. "Our ground crews counted anything an orange would fall through as a hole, because they were always chewing oranges. Anything smaller than that they didn't count. So the vertical stabilizer about blown off was one hole. The prop and part of the engine blown off was another hole. We had 285 holes." No one was injured despite how badly the plane was shot up. The pilot received the Distinguished Flying Cross. It was only his second mission.

Miller also remembered an interesting occasion concerning a Lockheed P-38 Lightning. "A lot of the people didn't like the P-38 Lightning...they should have been really good aircraft, but they had a lot of engine problems. It wasn't until well after the war that they found out that they were really using the wrong engine in it. It wasn't the one they had designed for it anyway. You got so you felt a little uneasy with certain outfits, and if they were flying 38s, you felt a little more uneasy than usual...Our commanding officer seemed to dislike the P-38s, immensely. I remember one coming down through our squadron with a Me 109 on his tail. He was trying to come through us to get us to shoot the Me

109 down, because evidently he was having trouble. The old CO came through with the Lockheed slogan 'Look to Lockheed for Leadership.' I thought he was really leading!"

There weren't that many attacks until the mission on which Miller was shot down. The bomb group was returning from an attack on the synthetic oil facilities at Mersburg, Germany when they were hit. "...The outfit was called the 'Butcher birds.' They were a Focke-Wulfe 190 outfit. They hit us so hard, so fast, and with so many. By this time in the war we didn't fly ten-men crews. Our missing man was a waist gunner, so I had both waist guns then. The newer planes made it more difficult. The plane we usually flew was an older G-model, and they [the guns] were back to back. In other words, all I had to do was turn around to get to the other waist gun. However, on the newer G's, they were giving the waist gunner more room so they staggered the waist positions. By the time you got turned around, sometimes, it was all over.

"The weak spot in the B-17 was right at the wing root on the right wing, the starboard wing. The German aces knew right where it was. And, what they did was, they worked over your fuel tanks on that wing...Then they would work into that wing root because that's where all of your oxygen tanks were stored. Most of the time, you saw them going down. A lot of the time, at the wing root, was where the fire was."

When Miller was shot down "...the plane was flaming and we had to go out through fire. That was always scary because a few days before we had seen nine guys go out with their 'chutes on fire. If any sparks would get into the parachute pack, the nylon could ignite when the chute opened, incinerating the parachute." As they jumped from the plane, the radio operator raised his head up, and the tail decapitated him.

Billie Miller and crew pose for a photo in Podington, England on August 30, 1944. Twelve days later on September 11 this crew was shot down. Top row, left to right - Lt. Max Cook (Pilot, K.I.A.), Lt. R. Willett (Copilot, P.O.W.), Lt. F. McDonough (Navigator, P.O.W.), Lt. S. Crivelli (Bombardier, P.O.W.). Bottom row, left to right - Sgt. W. Young (Ball-Turret Gunner, P.O.W.), Sgt. Billie Miller (A. E. Gunner, P.O.W.), Sgt. L. Mohr (R. Gunner, K.I.A.), Sgt. C. Smith (E. Gunner, P.O.W.).

(Photo courtesy Billie Miller)

327th Bomb Squadron Patch
(Photo courtesy Billie Miller)

It ripped his dog tags from his body. The pilot had remained in the plane. His body landed in a bomb crater and was covered up until four years after the war. The tail gunner was a substitute, the regular being in the hospital from serious wounds, and this had been his first mission.

The seven crew members, excluding the pilot and radio operator, landed safely in Germany near the birthplace of Martin Luther. Miller lost a section of his parachute from some type of a projectile and landed in a stone quarry, fracturing his leg in nine places. All the crew members were immediately captured. At the prisoner camp of Dulag Luft, Miller was kept in solitary confinement for two weeks. "What they would do was take a person who was wounded, but not likely to die from his wounds, and then they would try to get information out of him by not giving him medical attention. I did not know what had happened to the pilot so there was no sense in telling them about that. I did know what had happened to the radio operator, but I wouldn't tell them anyway. Evidently, they could not locate the pilot immediately either, and they could not identify the radio operator. So they were trying to find out from me. They used all types of methods. I'll tell you. I don't like solitary. I don't think I could take much of it anymore."

Miller was eventually taken to the hospital where his leg was x-rayed and wrapped in crepe paper. He was then sent to another hospital at Obermassfeld where his fractures, which had started to heal, were rebroken without anesthetic. His doctors were mostly Scottish and British who had been taken at Dunkirk. They put him in a cast and he was sent to yet another hospital at Meiningen. He ended up in the prison camp of Stalag Luft IV in northeastern Germany.

On April 26, 1945 Miller was liberated near the town of Bitterfield. He and the other prisoners had been moved from Stalag Luft IV as the Russians approached. In fact, the Russians had been trying to capture the prisoners to use as hostages. Miller then spent several weeks in a hospital in France. He finally returned to Butler, Pennsylvania in mid-June. Coming home was "pretty wonderful." Billie E. Miller soon settled down into civilian life : marrying, raising a family, and eventually becoming a teacher.

Joseph Miller

392nd Bomb Group
557th Squadron
Tail Gunner

by
Tina Snyder

Mr. Miller is a bright, lively man who barely looks old enough to have served in World War II. He is a devoted father who clearly adores his family, and his wonderful sense of humor is immediately apparent. He served as a tail gunner and was awarded the Purple Heart for his ordeal as a prisoner of war, a tale that begins before he even left America...

We were in Boise, Idaho, on a training mission, and [a crew mate] said to me, "Joe, we're not gonna make it back." I laughed, but he said, "I'm not kidding, look at this plane." We were practicing in planes that were sent back from overseas, and this one looked like it had seen about three tours of duty.

We were to fly from Boise to Denver, down to Dallas, then back to Boise. Well, we were just about over Denver when one of the engines quit. We were able to land in Denver, but Josh and I never forgot that.

The day we got shot down, he said to me again, "Joe, we're not gonna make it back." I said that he'd told me that once in Boise, and we did make it back, but he insisted that he had the same feeling. There was nothing wrong with the plane. It was a beautiful new plane, so there was no reason...

We were to have our 25th Mission party, and we weren't supposed to fly, but they said that it was supposed to be a snap of a flight. We were just going to go over to Germany and come back...

On the first pass that the Germans made against us, they hit my power unit for the turret, and the turret stopped. Had it stopped any further to the right or to the left, I wouldn't have gotten out. The gun in my turret wouldn't move around, just up and down, and while I was trying to fix my gun, a 20mm shell hit. The impact knocked my helmet off and sent my gun down then up, when it discharged and hit a German plane. How I know I got him was that he ended up in the same hospital in Frankfurt as my waist gunner, and he said it was me who shot him down. (Laughs.)

We never closed the doors on the turrets, although we were ordered to, so I kicked myself out of the turret on my back. I grabbed for my parachute, but instead of grabbing the handle, I pulled the rip cord and opened the parachute in the airplane. The waist gunner threw me the extra parachute, and I got out with the rest of my crew; only the navigator and the upper-turret gunner were killed. I was the only tail gunner of the seventeen men who survived that day.

When we got captured and interrogated, the Germans said that they were sorry we'd missed our 25th Mission party, and that they had singled us out of everybody. Then, they took me to a farmhouse to see the local doctor, and he set my leg. (It was broken in the fall.) I stayed until they could prove my identity to get medical treatment, but my leg had already been bandaged, so I just sat there for four weeks and did nothing.

Then they had me in for interrogation, and when I got there the interrogator said to the sergeant, "Go get it." I thought, "Well, here comes the whip." I had no idea what I was getting into. (Laughs.) "It" was a book - and they told me that I was with Davis's crew, how many missions I had flown before I was shot down... The only thing they didn't know was why we had two tail gunners. I said it was in case I got scared; but he told me, "That's not a good remark. That sounds like an Englishman. You're an American...."

They put me in a big room and said that if I ran into anybody, don't tell them where I had been. There were twenty-five men in the room, and we each had a sack of straw to lay on and a blanket. When we got cold, we had to cuddle up. We were supposed to get a Red Cross parcel every week. Then it was every month. At the end, it was two for the whole room...

We had a stove in the corner, and we used to take the coffee grounds from our parcels with some margarine and put it in a tin behind the stove with our chocolate ration on top. After a while we'd take it out, and it made a delicious chocolate cake.

When we could get a hold of some white German margarine, we would take about eight boxes of prunes, two boxes of raisins, and seven quarter-pound packets of sugar and put them into a fifteen-gallon jam cake jar that had never been cleaned out. We'd put it behind the stove and sit there while it would pop and hiss and jump around. We watched for the Germans while it fermented. Well, the Germans knew we had it and let it be known that they were going to raid the barracks. So we barred to door with a board. We got this fellow from the next room who could play a fiddle standing on his head, and he did. (Laughs.) We danced, and we drank, and you never saw twenty-five sicker men. The next morning for roll call, not one man from our room made it. We all got five days in solitary, but it was worth it. So there's your recipe for prune brew.

In the Red Cross parcels, you got a pack of cigarettes, and even though I didn't smoke, I learned, because it took your mind off the hunger. Next to the cold, the hunger was the worst thing. We really didn't have it any worse than the Germans, though, because they didn't have any food either. The hardest part was sleep; the floor was made of tree trunks, and all we had was a straw mat. It just got so cold....

We were ninety miles straight north of Berlin. When the war was over the Russians came from the east, and the English and Americans came from the west. The Russian prisoners were all majors and up. Anyone below that was shot. So the Russian Army was out for blood. They had every telephone pole in the area marked with a German. When the Germans saw them coming, they fled west because the English would be kinder....

I went home with ten thousand people on a boat that was supposed to hold five thousand. We slept on the floor, the deck, or anywhere

Generals Woodbury, John Henry, and James Doolittle.
(Photo courtesy Tom Brown)

else we could find. On the first night, we were served spinach. I dearly loved spinach, so I ended up eating probably twenty people's spinach. Since I only weighed ninety-seven pounds, I got so sick that I got to go to the hospital that had beds and sheets and everything. I was riding in the lap of luxury the whole way home.

The real story of the war, though, wasn't the fighting, because the German was just like me, doing his job. The Russians were a little weird, and the English, let's just say they're tough as nails, but we were all the same. The heroes, really, were the civilians because they put up with that nonsense day in and day out for years.

After the war, Joseph Miller returned to his home in the Pittsburgh area and still resides there with his wife, Agnes, in Greensburg, Pennsylvania. They have three daughters and several grandchildren, to whom he is a devoted and active grandfather.

Nose art.

(Photo courtesy Edward Jones)

Vernon Mock

96th Bomb Group
337th Bomb Squadron
Tail Gunner

by
Sara Giallombardo

Mr. Vernon Mock is a charming and pleasant man whom I enjoyed talking to a great deal. The many stories he had were told with pride and a touch of humor. He had many unique war experiences, whether in the air or just on the base.

I came out of high school in 1942 on a Friday and went to work for Penn Electric on Monday. Then in March of '43, I was drafted into the service. I was nineteen years old when I went in. Uncle Sam said, "I Want You!" so in I went. After training in the United States we went over [to England] on the H.M.S. Andes. I didn't know I was going to be a tail gunner. When we got there, we went out to the skeet range and practiced shooting. Those who were the best went to the Air Corps. I don't know what happened to the other guys.

I flew with the same crew during the whole war, except for our pilot and copilot. We all had to learn how to fly, though. Our pilot wanted us all to be able to fly in case of a real emergency, so we all got to fly for about twenty minutes or so. Our waist gunner was the oldest man on the crew, and at the time he was the only one that had a child, and of course we named our airplane after his daughter, Candie Anne. I still keep in touch with her. She lives in Oregon. So every time we go out there we'll call her up, and meet somewhere, and just yak.

As far as missions go, we flew thirty-four total. I kept a record of my own, starting with my first mission. I took a little piece of paper and just jotted the mission down, and then the next day I'd look in the Stars and Stripes [military paper], and get the clipping from the paper. This one mission [the fifth mission] we came back with 150 holes in the plane. I was wounded on the twenty-fifth mission - wounded in the back while I was advancing. How 'bout that? Now, we wore flak suits, and these suits had these metal plates in them. They overlapped, and the shrapnel hit me right in between the plates. The flak suits looked like a catcher's suit in the front, but in the back it only came down as far as your waist, and you had to wear a helmet. There was also a piece of flak that hit my helmet, went out through the window beside me, and left a dent in my helmet. Well, after I got wounded, old Sid Huster, our radio man, was gonna give me a shot of morphine, and he was gonna put it in my face! But the waist gunner stopped him and said, "Put it in his arm or something," because you had to put it in where there was exposed skin, and our flak suit, and our jackets, and everything covered us all up.

The thirty-four missions were all done in a few months. There are two though, that stick out in my mind; the one that I was wounded on, and the next one when we went back to the exact same place. It's kinda scary doing that. You think, "Holy Cats, here we go again." But the one that I remember the most was the one where we dropped supplies to the French Underground [the tenth mission]. It was the longest mission, it was ten hours, but the thing is, it was a milk run, so to speak. We took off from England, then climbed up to altitude, then dropped down to almost treetop level, oh about five hundred feet from the ground. Well, in our bomb bay we didn't have bombs. We had canisters that had parachutes attached to them; and the canisters had food, and ammunition, and supplies for the French Underground. We dropped that stuff, and when we dropped it you could see those men running out from the trees then running back under the trees again. Well, we climbed back up to altitude and come back to England. But we didn't see one fighter. We didn't have any flak, no antiaircraft of any kind at all. The only thing is I almost started shooting at one of our own fighters. Whenever we were up in altitude, everything got cold. It gets thirty to forty below zero. On the window I looked through...that thing frosted over, solid frost. I could not see out through it at all. I had to look along the sides. Well, we were down there on low altitude, and I saw this fighter coming down underneath us. At first I thought it was German Me 109, but then I looked a little closer, and here it was one of our own P-51s! But I almost started shootin' at it. There was a couple times when we came back by ourselves [out of formation] because we had engine trouble. Matter of fact, the one time we came back we were losing altitude, and two engines weren't working, and we started throwing stuff out. Anything we could find, we'd throw out, anything at all.

Whenever we would fly they gave us what they called an escape kit. There would be a map, a little compass, and our picture so that we could make fake passports in case we were shot down over enemy territory. We could get in touch with the underground, and then they would make us fake passes. But the Germans got wise and said, "Hey, these guys are all dressed the same." because in the pictures, we all wore the same tie. Well, like I said, they gave us a little compass about as big as my thumbnail, and if you got captured you were supposed to swallow this thing then in a day or two, take a look in your BM, and dig it out, and find your way home. (Laughs.)

We were all real good friends, and we goofed around a lot on base. We even had a mascot. That's Lady Moe [small burro]. They had what they called a shuttle flight. They flew from England, bombed Germany, landed in Russia, bombed Poland, and landed in Africa. They filled up and bombed up in Africa, then flew up again, and bombed Germany, and then went back to England. Well, when they were in Africa, they got two of these African donkeys and put them in the bomb bay to bring back.... The one burro died, but this one survived. That was Lady Moe, and she had the run of the base.

On the base, we slept in these Quonset huts, and there were three crews in each one. Well, at nighttime, when the evening came along, 'course the guys would get bored and start a game of cards. Well, Mattie Quinn and his crew was supposed to go on a mission the next day, and he wanted some sleep. 'Course there was one light hangin' in the Quonset hut, and he said, "How 'bout putting the light out so we can get some sleep? We got to go on a mission tomorrow." But nobody paid attention to him. Everybody was issued a loaded .45 semiautomatic. Well, boom! he shot the light out and everybody went to bed and got some sleep. (Laughs.)

The entire time there [at the base] there were no German airplanes up over England, but there were what they called the buzz bombs and the V-2 Rockets. Matter of fact, one evening there was a buzz bomb come over real close, went on past our base, and then after a bit we heard the engine quit on the thing. We heard the explosion, but we didn't know where it was at. The buzz actually had wings, and a tail with a little jet motor up on the tail. In the early part of the war, when they were sending those over, the English fighters would go up and they'd shoot em' down - explode 'em in the air. But then the Germans went to the V-2 Rocket. Boy, you could really hear those coming. Most of 'em they aimed at London. I was in London when a few of those hit, and boy, the whole ground would shake!

I came back on the Queen Mary. I had to sleep on the deck on the way 'cause the ship was really overloaded, but I didn't mind.

After the war Mr. Mock went back to

B-17 Flying Fortress over Schweinfurt.

(Photo courtesy Tom Brown)

work for Penn Electric. His courage and efforts during the war earned him the Distinguished Flying Cross, the Air Medal, The Good Conduct Medal and the Purple Heart. In the spring of 1947 he met his wife of forty-nine years. They have six children and thirteen grandchildren. He still flies today and is also part of the Experimental Aircraft Association. From his bomb group there were 938 losses. The experiences Mr. Mock had are remembered fondly. For all of his courage and selflessness, he truly is a hero, and I feel very privileged to have been able to share his memories.

The Crew

Rupert Cornelius - pilot
Louis Campbell Jr. - copilot
Charles Wagner - navigator
Earle Flesher - bombardier
Raymond Wolfert - top-turret gunner
Vernon Mock - tail gunner
Samuel Schreckendgust - waist gunner
Markham McEnroe - ball-turret gunner
Sidney Huster - radio/gunner
Warren Newton - waist gunner

Fielder N. Newton

389th Bomb Group
564th Squadron
Navigator

by
Tara Lynn Washko

It was only appropriate that I talked with Fielder Newton in the "Penn State Room" of his home. Penn State memorabilia covered the entire room. Mr. Newton was even wearing his Penn State class ring. It was in the fall of 1942 that he passed the Army Air Corps exam and the physical test that allowed him to join the reserves. By doing so, it allowed him to stay in school at Pennsylvania State College where he was majoring in mechanical engineering. At the end of the spring term, on May 14, 1943, the Air Force called on him. He graduated from Selman Field as a second lieutenant on August 7, 1944. He became a member of the Eighth Air Force, Second Air Division, and served as a navigator in the 389th Bomb Group at Hethel, England.

We went to the Brooklyn Naval Yards, and I was chosen as the loading officer for our group of ten crews, which was one hundred men. So I went the day before, and going there I met a man by the name of O.J. Nash, who was a Canadian. He was on his second tour over to England as a volunteer. However, the troops that he brought with him were the first Canadians that were conscripted to go overseas. He had a group that was terrified, these guys were jumping the train all the way down from Montreal, and a couple of the men got away. I helped him get his group in their quarters, because mine was done so quickly and simply.

Going over, we were really a conglomeration of people. We went on the Ile' de France, which was one of the three largest ships afloat at the time. They were the Queen Mary, the Queen Elizabeth, and the Ile' de France. We had, in addition to these Air Force crews, a bunch of infantry men, and OSS girls, who were secretaries for the officers of strategic service. They were in the Secret Service really, but they were girls that were going there to be secretaries. Probably in London is were they would have been stationed. We had MP's and nurses. There were five thousand troops on one ship. The Ile' de France, because it was so fast, didn't go in convoy. We went by ourselves, and we were only about five days in getting across the ocean, or seven, I don't really recall.

It was sort of like you were going on a cruise. You know, the thing that was different about it was the fact that when you are twenty years old, nothing in the world is ever going to hurt you. You don't really worry about those things. That is why the Eighth Air Force, and all the air forces during the war were such great fighting groups, because everybody was young. Even the higher ranking officers were young. Older than twenty, but younger than thirty were a lot of these guys that were colonels and lieutenant colonels.

Strangely enough this was November. We knew that when we left the Brooklyn Naval Yards we went south and then swung east, north of Bermuda. We then hit the Gulf Stream, and the weather was just delightful. We were out on deck. It was very warm, but it wasn't delightful enough that some of us didn't have the discomfort that you get from seasickness. One of the funniest things I remember was that some of the guys had smuggled a dog on board. We would have these periodic, unannounced boat drills for abandoning ship if we were hit. We were coming in from one of these, and I was going through a passageway. I looked down, and here's this dog, his head hanging down, and his eyes glassy. I am sure he was seasick, and it was really a funny thing to see.

Over in England

We were in England at the end of November [1944]. We then had a lot of exposure to the intelligence officers and various things you needed to know, and we flew some local missions around England. The reason I know that it was after Christmas was that we were asked on the afternoon of Christmas Eve to go with another crew to another air base that was closer to London. We were to pick up a B-24 that was down there for repair and bring it back. We got on board. It was just the pilot, the copilot, the flight engineer, and the radio operator. We flew down and landed in a snow storm. They dumped us out, hit the throttles, and took off. By the time we got the plane, it was too bad to leave, so we had to go into this little English town and to spend Christmas Eve at the USO. We went out on the town and hit the pubs that night. The next day it cleared up, so we flew back to our air base. I neglected to tell you something else about our crew. One of our guys, in fact our flight engineer, was from Brooklyn. He got a forty-eight-hour pass to go see his family before we received our orders to sail to England. The only trouble was he never came back. He went AWOL. To this day we don't know what ever happened to him. We had another flight engineer assigned to us when we got to our air base. It was sometime after that that we flew our first mission.

On a mission..., you wouldn't go on a straight course naturally, you would zigzag around, so you wouldn't tip your hand as to where you were going. Ultimately,

Fielder Newton and crew - Top row, left to right - J.C. Dodman (Pilot), Paul Rochett (Copilot), Fielder Newton (Navigator), L. E. Dewell (Bombardier), Cliff Brace (Flight Engineer). Bottom row, left to right - Ron Ring (Tail Gunner), Gene Richardson (Radio Operator), Dick Bidlack (Waist Gunner), Bill Denton (Waist Gunner), Jim Ward (Nose Gunner).

(Photo courtesy Fielder Newton)

you would reach a point, which was called the "initial point," and at that point you were committed. You knew your heading to go to the final target and it would be maybe fifteen or twenty miles. Your whole group at that point would turn and start in. That's when things got really tough because the targets that you were heading for all had antiaircraft. They were all shooting at you, and the good thing was that they didn't always have the right altitude. Those things went up and burst at a certain altitude, and they would have to guess at that. We also had another little trick, we called it the "daily mail". They were little packets, and there was a chute in the back of the plane where you would push out the packets. They would break up, and go down. That would foul up the radar.

We flew just seventeen missions. Probably the reason for that was that we became a lead crew. We took extra training, and lead crews didn't fly as frequently as they said. The pressure was harder than it was for the others.

We had one occasion where we were hit with flak over the target at Berlin and lost an engine, forcing us to return on three engines. That was a little bit scary. We had to drop out of the bomber stream and come back alone, because at that point you can't keep up, speed wise. This is the most dangerous position you can get in, because when you are alone the German fighters just love to attack. Fortunately, we weren't attacked, and after we got closer to the American lines (we called them "little friends") the American fighters came, and they flew formation with us until their fuel got low. We were by that point probably into Holland, and the pilot had asked me to keep plotting different courses. We were first going to go to France. . . our concern was running out of fuel, so he had me plot a coarse to an emergency field in France. Everybody cheered "Hooray, we're going to France!" Unfortunately he changed his mind, and said there was another emergency field right on the coast of England, right at the Channel, which was prepared to take us. We started to go there and got halfway across the Channel when he said, "Give me a course to home." So off we went to home. We did land and fired the red flares as we came in so we had a clear track to land. We had fifty gallons of gas left in our tanks.

We had one very sad circumstance over which we had no control. We were coming back from a mission and were still over Germany when one of the bombs had hung up in our bomb bay. We certainly did not want to land with an armed bomb hanging in our bomb bay. So the flight engineer and another one of the crew went back to shake it loose. They messed around and finally got it loose, and then we all watched it go down. Would you believe, we were flying over the country and it sadly hit a house. Well, if they tried to do this, they couldn't. It was just one of those flukes. Some poor farmer lost his house and we hoped no one was in it at the time. War is a strange thing.

Fielder Newton was married before the war, and his wife Marjorie faithfully wrote him all the time, although at times it may have been hard to read. Mrs. Newton has the unique talent of being able to write backwards. Mr. Newton remembers having to go to the latrine to read some of her letters by using the mirror. Marjorie Newton rented an apartment at Penn State at the war's end realizing that her husband would want to return to earn his degree. When Mr. Newton was discharged on December 8, 1945, he returned to the University and received a mechanical engineering degree in 1948. He worked in steel industry sales until his retirement in 1988. He and Marjorie have four sons and are the happy grandparents of seven grandchildren.

Ralph A. "Hap" Nicholas, Jr.

448th Bomb Group
714th Squadron
Navigator

by
Stephen M. Heasley

A "hero" can be seen as many different things to many different people. Some would say that a hero must possess and exhibit the quality of pride in all that they achieve and accomplish. Others would say that a hero must display a certain degree of modesty when discussing and explaining their courageous endeavors. Others would state that a hero must possess an extreme degree of self-motivation and determination combined with a solid, loyal, and sensible work ethic. Regardless of which definition of "hero" is most widely accepted, aspects of each definition are amply evident in the life and times of Ralph A. "Hap" Nicholas, Jr.

In December of 1942 Hap Nicholas embarked upon the journey of a lifetime when he enlisted into the United States Army-Air Force, which would later become the United States Air Force. A student at Washington and Jefferson College, Hap planned to receive a college education and, in due course, get into business. Motivated by patriotism, Hap decided to enlist to fulfill his obligation to fight for his country in the armed forces. "My parents, being parents, understood why, but, being older, they recognized the danger. So they were concerned."

On May 12, 1943, Hap was called upon for service, and he gladly accepted his call to duty. Pearl Harbor had been bombed on December 7, 1941 and, by this time, the war was already over one year old. "I remember exactly where I was. I was at the home of a girl I was dating, and I can remember the bombing as if it were yesterday."

The training to be part of the war itself was a long and tedious process. "They shipped us out of Pittsburgh on a train for basic training down to Miami Beach for six weeks, then from there, back on the train up to eastern Pennsylvania, where we had a few months of what was known as CTD, College Training Detachment, prior to going to Nashville, Tennessee where we would take our classification test. We were known as Aviation Students at that point. We took our classification tests to learn if either we had been "washed out" or were being sent to pilot, bombardier, or navigation school. I found when they posted my name on the bulletin board that I was qualified for pilot training and navigation training, but, for whatever reason, not bombardier school."

"I can remember going into a second lieutenant's office. He was not a very personable fellow, and he was a ground officer. We being aspiring 'fly-boys,' derisively called any ground officer a 'paddlefoot,' or ground pounder as they were never destined to fly.

I said to him, 'Sir, I see that I am qualified for pilot training and navigation training, and since my father was a pilot in World War I, if it is possible I would prefer going to pilot training.' He said, ' You do have a choice, mister. You can either go to navigation school or to gunnery school.' I snapped to, saluted and said, 'YES SIR' and hustled out of there, and in due course, was shipped down to Selman Field outside of Monroe, Louisiana, where I began my navigation training."

After graduation from navigation school in September of 1944, Hap was shipped to Walla Walla, Washington to form a crew with nine other recent graduates and learn to "run" a four-engine B-24 Liberator Bomber along with many dozens of other ten-man crews.

"Some distance away from our base was a Marine Air Force Base at Pendleton, Oregon and 'boys being boys,' every once in a while a few HELLCAT or WILDCAT fighter planes would scream in over our base at fifty or a hundred feet and demonstrate to us below their recently acquired "HOTSHOT" piloting skills. It was done so that we might 'eat our hearts out,' for all bomber pilots are would-be fighter pilots.

"Although these show-off tactics were not permitted, they did happen and happened often enough that they planted conspiratorial seeds in our minds, and we sought revenge.

"I still don't know how-the-dickens we got away with it, but this one day a twelve-plane squadron or two of our B-24 Liberator Bombers were loaded with many cartons of revenge-related cargo.

"The planes were 'revved up'; we took off one by one circling into the sky. We completed our formation and soared off at modest altitude toward the Marine base.

"We were indeed a mirthful bunch looking forward with great glee toward retribution against 'the enemy.'

"We approached the base. The runway stood out like a sore thumb, and the formation roared over at almost no altitude.

"The cartons had been opened, and upon a given radio signal, the enlisted men unloosed from the waist hundreds if not thousands of rolls of toilet paper which dropped ridiculously over the concrete with ever lengthening tails.

"We circled, turned 180 degrees, and to add insult to injury, we flew back over the field to enjoy our premeditated desecration. It was one hell of a mess.

"Our C.O. understandably took a dim view of these shenanigans and meted out the worst possible punishment that his imagination could conjure up.

"We had to endure and suffer through two days of being restricted to the base.

"Once our skills were honed, and the many squadrons able to fly in tight formation, we shipped out to Hamilton Field, California, and were given many fever-inducing shots for whatever jungle malady...certain we were going to the South Pacific. Naturally, the Army shipped us east."

Hap left in December on a ship called the New Amsterdam from New York City. Taking the North Atlantic route, he arrived in England, which would remain his base of operations for the duration of the war. "The English liked the Americans because they realized that we were putting ourselves on the line against a formidable, despicable foe, and they opened their doors to us and we were always made to feel a warm welcome in their homes."

During his war experience, Hap navigated a total of twenty-one missions over Germany, the first being in December of 1944. On the mornings of missions, each person was briefed individually upon their specific duty, and prepared for the task they were to perform. Not the least of Hap's preparation was the quiet recitation of the Lord's Prayer and the twenty-third Psalm, evidence of his strong belief in his Heavenly Father.

Like any other group activity in life, Hap met many new and interesting people during his war experience. "It was like anything else in life. ninety-nine percent of us got along, and the other one percent didn't count." Although he has lost track of most of the guys, he can still remember many of their names and faces. Supporting the theory that there is no such thing as work without play, Hap recalled a night when, out of boredom, a craps game broke out in the barracks. "A bunch of us were down on our hands and knees, using British currency (a florin was worth forty cents, a half-crown was worth fifty cents, and a pound note was worth four dollars). We began shooting craps. In due course, I got hot, was winning, and we got down to the point where there were only two of us...a fellow by the name of Lt. Joe Steffan, who was the pilot of one of our associate crews. I cleaned him out, and I said to him, 'Joe, I'll throw down half a crown, and you throw

"Hap" Nicholas and crew - Top row, left to right - Stanley Jurkanis (Bombardier), Ed Schreiber (Copilot), Ruf Nichols (Flight Engineer), Tom Horton (Pilot), "Hap" Nicholas (Navigator). Bottom row, left to right - Tom Brehm (Tail Gunner), Jerry Staley (Waist Gunner), Troy Jones (Nose Gunner), Kearney (Waist Gunner), Kelly Smith (Radio Operator). (Photo courtesy "Hap" Nicholas)

your dice in.' He said, 'Oh Hap, I can't. They're my lucky dice.' 'Oh, go ahead.' I badgered him. So he relented, and he put the dice down and I threw down a half crown, and rolled a natural. I gathered his dice and my half crown. We went to bed and were roused out of the sack the next morning for a mission. Joe and his crew did not return."

Death and devastation was something that Hap had to deal with. One of the major advantages to being in the Air Force was that he didn't have to deal with the enemy one on one. "We never met the enemy one on one. We were always four or five miles high in the sky. This was a matter of world survival. We had absolutely no problem in countering, and hopefully whipping, the enemy. It was impersonal from the point of view that when we were 25,000 feet in the air dropping bombs on whatever cities. We knew there would be desecration. We knew there would be people killed, but I never, thank the good Lord, had to have a rifle with a bayonet in my hand having to kill or be killed face to face with the enemy."

Another form of death Hap had to confront was the death of fellow crew mates. "It was always sad because we became friends from all portions of the nation, whatever the state, and none of us expected to get killed. I had a number of friends who were shot down over whatever target, and one doesn't get over it. You don't get over it... it lasts. It lasts a lifetime. I can picture the loss of my friends as though it were yesterday, and that was fifty-plus years ago. It's an experience I, sure as blazes, wouldn't want anyone to go through."

One particular mission stood out as probably the scariest of them all. "My cubicle was in the nose of the ship, forward of the wings and four engines, and I can remember applying my trade, as it were, and then all of a sudden I found myself suspended in mid-air with my head glued to a plastic bubble above and outside of the plane that we use for celestial navigation at night, and I had no idea why in the world I was suspended. I could see the pilot and the copilot as I'm hanging there, in what seemed to be an eternity and then all of a sudden I was thrust to the deck and simply could not get up. That seemed to go on forever, and then suddenly the plane righted itself. I gathered up my instruments and got organized again...and continued the mission over the target and dropped our bombs.

"Our 448th Bomb Group comprised of four squadrons of twelve planes plus other bomb groups continued to a predetermined rallying point, still 'at altitude' and began our descent only when we reached the French coast. It was at this point I climbed out of my cubicle, went up to the flight deck, squatted between the pilot and copilot and asked them what in the world had happened."

"For our own protection it was imperative that our formation be 'tight', almost wingtip-to-wingtip. Our position was known as flying 'bucket-on-the-bucket' which meant that we were slightly behind and lower than the two planes in front of us."

Jerry Staley and "Hap" Nicholas.
(Photo courtesy "Hap" Nicholas)

"This was our first experience being attacked by the newfangled German jet, a Messerschmitt 262 which came head-on at our formation firing canon. The plane above us to our right was hit, fell off to the left locking wings with the second bomber and they both, as one, hurtled bellies-up, down and back at us. This was when our pilot Tom Horton, thrust the stick forward, and we dropped like a rock out of formation to avoid impact and certain death with the two entangled bombers."

"It was at this point I was suspended. A few thousand feet lower our pilots realized we were 'a sitting duck' because of bandits-in-the-area [German fighter planes], pulled back on the stick hopefully to ascend to the protection of our formation which was when gravity pinned me to the deck."

Morale remained high throughout the war, but the happiest day was the day the Germans surrendered. "You knew you were going home! We flew the North Atlantic route stopping once in Ireland to refuel. We landed in Connecticut, went to Camp Kilmer, N.J., and then it was a matter of being transferred to Texas to form new crews to fly to the South Pacific to end the war with Japan. Luckily, however, the war ended before they had to leave."

Hap returned home in November of 1945. He continued his studies and entered Pitt in January of 1946. As repayment for his time in the service, Hap was given a free education and $90.00 per month by the federal government. Hap had a relatively easy time adjusting to society and moving on with his life, but he sympathizes with those who did not. "I can appreciate the foot soldier or the marine who, be in Europe or the islands of the South Pacific, became ill with malaria, dysentery, you name it, or to have been wounded - I can certainly understand their coming back and having severe emotional problems. I did not, thank the good Lord."

Hap now spends much of his time with his family, business, and the Western Pennsylvania Wing, which he co-founded, of the Pennsylvania Chapter of the National Eighth Air Force Historical Society. Their wing, comprised of 121 veterans who served in England, gathers quarterly to reminisce at lunch. At one such gathering, Hap was relaying a story about his plane wrecking in a random part of the countryside during the war. Much to his surprise, the man sitting two seats away from him had been standing there that day when the accident had occurred.

"After a particularly long bomb-run, while circling our base to land, we ran out of fuel. Our engineer was frantically pumping the last of the vapor into the four engines with one engine, then another 'conking out.' Our pilot had no choice but to 'peel out' of the formation and we were forced to land in a field nowhere near a runway at a nearby base. As we screamed through the grass toward a forest and certain death, the right wing hit a wooden shack, the right tire blew and we spun like a top.

"Two luncheon seats to my right sat Tony Chardella who had been stationed at that fighter plane base. I can still see his widened eyes, his mouth agape as he blurted...'WAS THAT YOU!'

"As my gooseflesh subsided, he told me that he was standing perilously close to where we had come to rest. Since the plane was beyond repair, they 'liberated' (i.e. stole) our ten fifty-caliber machine guns to be retrofitted to their P-51 Mustang fighter planes as well as our survival rations.

"He grinned and said, 'We particularly enjoyed your candy!'

"Chilled to the marrow, our ten-man crew was abjectly trucked after dark...back to our 448th Bomb Group at Seething Air Force Base to be assigned a new bomber and to continue out part in the war."

Hap was born and raised in Butler and knew all of his life that he wanted to live there. After graduating from the University of Pittsburgh, he bought, with his father's help, through the Ford Gum and Machine Company of Lockport, New York, penny gum-ball machines. Hap's territory was Allegheny County, and about thirty-two Kiwanis Clubs sponsored the placing of the one-thousand machines. He opened a real estate office in 1950 for a dozen years and followed his family business—the O.H. Nicholas Transfer and Storage Company on S. McKean St. Now he has three sons-in-law, a daughter-in-law, and a son that will succeed him in Nicholas Enterprises, which is composed of barge, rail, and truck terminals on both the Ohio and Allegheny Rivers.

As one can see, Hap Nicholas has earned his title of "hero" in many ways. His lack of desire for fame and attention and willingness to simply "get on with life" show his modesty. Hap's solid, loyal, and sensible work ethic enabled him to continue his education upon his return to the United States and enabled him to build a future for his children and grandchildren to expand upon.

Ralph Patton

94th Bomb Group
331st Squadron
Copilot

by
Michele Van Deusen

Ralph Patton is a very intelligent, colorful, and giving man. His den embraces memorabilia from World War II, including pictures, books, awards and plaques. He is rightly proud of his many accomplishments.

In April of 1942, I voluntarily enlisted in the Air Force because I was single, healthy, and knew I'd have to go sooner or later. I was twenty-two years old at the time and had to leave my family and girlfriend behind. It was tough because I didn't know when I was going to see them again, or even if. Four months later I was called up to active duty, and I had never even been off the ground. By May of the following year I graduated as a second lieutenant from flying school.

I remember my first mission very vividly. It was in November of 1943, and I flew to Paris. The irony is that there were some clouds below, and we couldn't see the targets, so we were unable to drop our bombs. We carried them back and dropped them into the English Channel. But a German fighter plane did fly head-on into the aircraft in the formation behind us and exploded. The whole mission was just absolutely wasted. We went to all that trouble-to lose airplanes and to have so many men killed - just to have dropped the bombs into the English Channel. The scary part of it though was that I had the wrong parachute with me that time, and if something had gone wrong with our plane I would not have been able to bail out. So that was all part of only my first mission.

But up until my ninth mission, they were fairly easy and routine. We were on alert before each mission. They would come around and wake us up maybe at two or three in the morning. We would go to the mess hall for breakfast and then go to briefing where they would inform us of our target. Then we would check in with our airplane. That all took a few hours, for each station was miles from the other. Only on one mission were we ever hit with anti-aircraft fire, and that put a hole in the tail. Other than that, things were uneventful. Basically, you were told to go, and you went. If you came back, you were happy and would put a mark on the wall.

One night I remember we all went to a dance somewhere in England. It was, I think, after our eighth mission and the first time we were allowed off the base. When we Americans walked into the dance, those poor British guys didn't stand a chance because all the gals wanted to dance with an American. We were really well paid compared with the British soldiers, and even though we weren't all handsome, we all looked good in nice uniforms. So I walked this little girl home and asked her if I could see her Monday night (this was Friday), and she said, "Sure." Unfortunately, I was shot down on that Sunday. That broke up any budding romances. (Laughs.)

We were shot down on our ninth mission in the middle of Brittany, the westernmost part of France that sticks out into the English Channel. Three of the crew were killed, seven of us got out alive. We lived in the French Underground for two and a half months. One was there for nearly eight months. I was in a school house for five weeks, a bistro for two weeks, and a hotel for two weeks. While we were in the underground the British Intelligence Service set up an escape network and parachuted two French Canadians into France to organize this effort. They had a radio with them, and with it they were able to contact London and arrange for a motor gunboat to come from England into the coast of western France. All told, this operation rescued ninety-four of us in January, February, and March of 1944.

The night we came out, there were twenty-six of us. We were brought to the northern coast of Brittany and marched through the mine fields and down a cliff to wait for the gunboat to come in. It waited two miles off shore and then sent in rowboats to pick all of us up. This whole operation was arranged with the British Military Intelligence Service, Canadian secret agents, members of the French Resistance, farmers, priests, and teachers, all of French civilian population. They were all in great risk because the men would be shot immediately if they were found harboring an American airman. The women would be sent to concentration camps. Fortunately though, the operation was so closed-mouth, so secretive, that most of them were not caught.

This was a coordinated operation and everyone involved was a volunteer. They were courageous people who knew that they had a job to do and did it freely; and some ended up losing their lives. Totally, the one hundred people involved in helping me personally get out of France got 134 people out of there; ninety-four of whom were American. Ten years later I went back to visit them, and still keep in touch with some today. The relationship is very wonderful.

I went back to England in March of 1944. The invasion of France was not until June. I was back home long before the ground troops invaded France. At that time it was very secretive - we weren't allowed to talk to anybody. We were locked up for three days while we were interrogated by

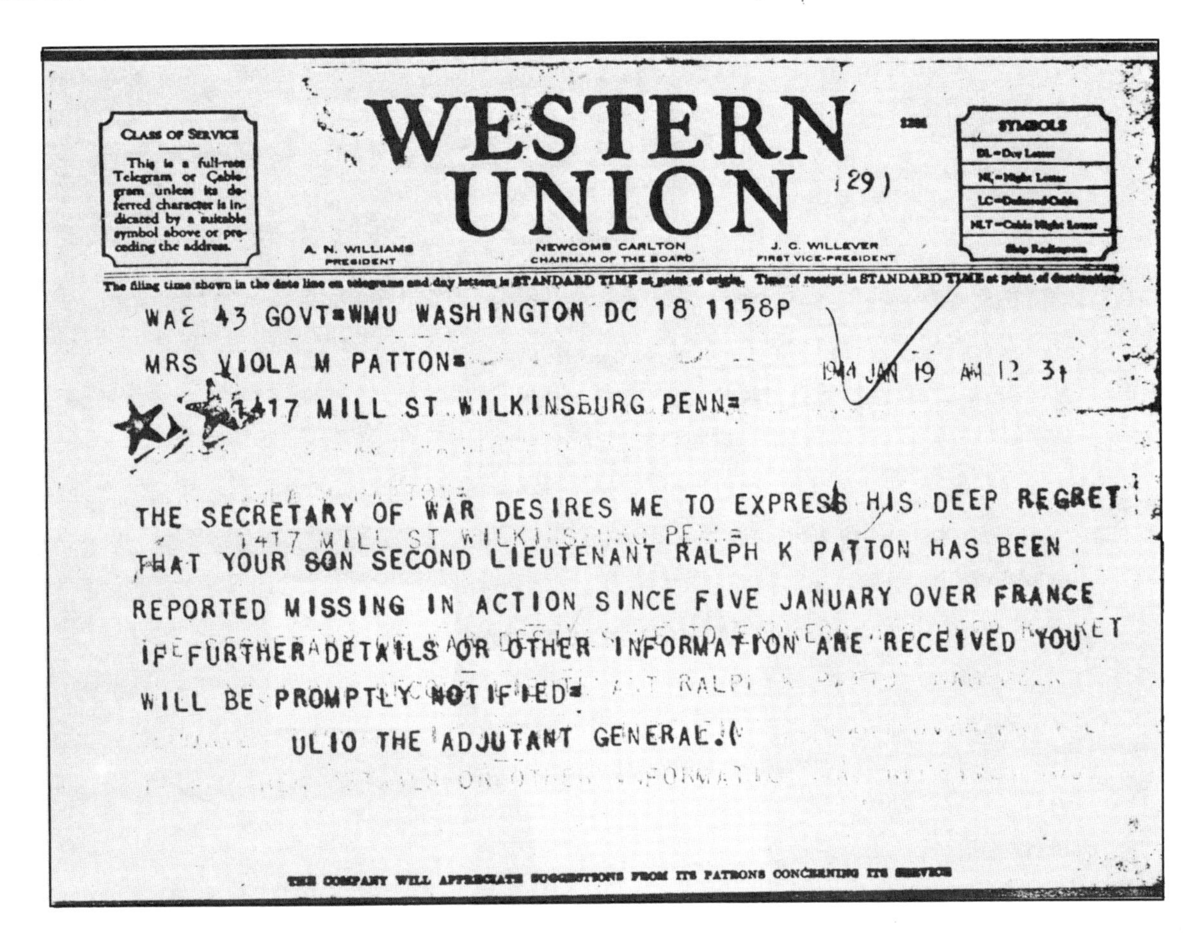
WESTERN UNION

CLASS OF SERVICE
This is a full-rate Telegram or Cablegram unless its deferred character is indicated by a suitable symbol above or preceding the address.

A. N. WILLIAMS PRESIDENT — NEWCOMB CARLTON CHAIRMAN OF THE BOARD — J. C. WILLEVER FIRST VICE-PRESIDENT

SYMBOLS
DL=Day Letter
NL=Night Letter
LC=Deferred Cable
NLT=Cable Night Letter
Ship Radiogram

The filing time shown in the date line on telegrams and day letters is STANDARD TIME at point of origin. Time of receipt is STANDARD TIME at point of destination

WA2 43 GOVT=WMU WASHINGTON DC 18 1158P

MRS VIOLA M PATTON=

1417 MILL ST WILKINSBURG PENN=

1944 JAN 19 AM 12 31

THE SECRETARY OF WAR DESIRES ME TO EXPRESS HIS DEEP REGRET THAT YOUR SON SECOND LIEUTENANT RALPH K PATTON HAS BEEN REPORTED MISSING IN ACTION SINCE FIVE JANUARY OVER FRANCE IF FURTHER DETAILS OR OTHER INFORMATION ARE RECEIVED YOU WILL BE PROMPTLY NOTIFIED=

ULIO THE ADJUTANT GENERAL.

THE COMPANY WILL APPRECIATE SUGGESTIONS FROM ITS PATRONS CONCERNING ITS SERVICE

(Courtesy Ralph Patton)

the Intelligence Service (Army, Navy, Air Force, British), all asking us questions about areas of France we had been in. We were told we were never allowed to fly combat again. The rationale was that if we were shot down a second time, the Germans would have known that we were shot down a first time, and would pursue the idea of who helped us the first time. They didn't want those people to be killed. Nor did they want the underground networks to be broken up. So I was sent home as a Navy instructor pilot out of Columbus, Ohio.

One thing I learned from being over there is that I'm lucky to be alive. Therefore, no one should make a big deal out of little things. You have to zero in on those things that help the cause or that help your future. People have to understand that promotions and salary increases will take care of themselves if you do a great job. I think my war experience served me very well.

Ralph Patton married his high-school girlfriend, Betty, in May after he returned from Europe. He had homes in Buffalo, Rochester, and Detroit but eventually moved back to Pittsburgh, close to his home town. He retired in 1982 as the vice-president of the same coal company he worked at before he left for the war.

He's been back to England about ten times with his family and friends to visit the men and women who helped to save his life. He is the Chairman of the Board of the Air Force Escape and Evasion Society, a group he began in 1966. He is a very dedicated man who puts a lot of time and energy into what he does.

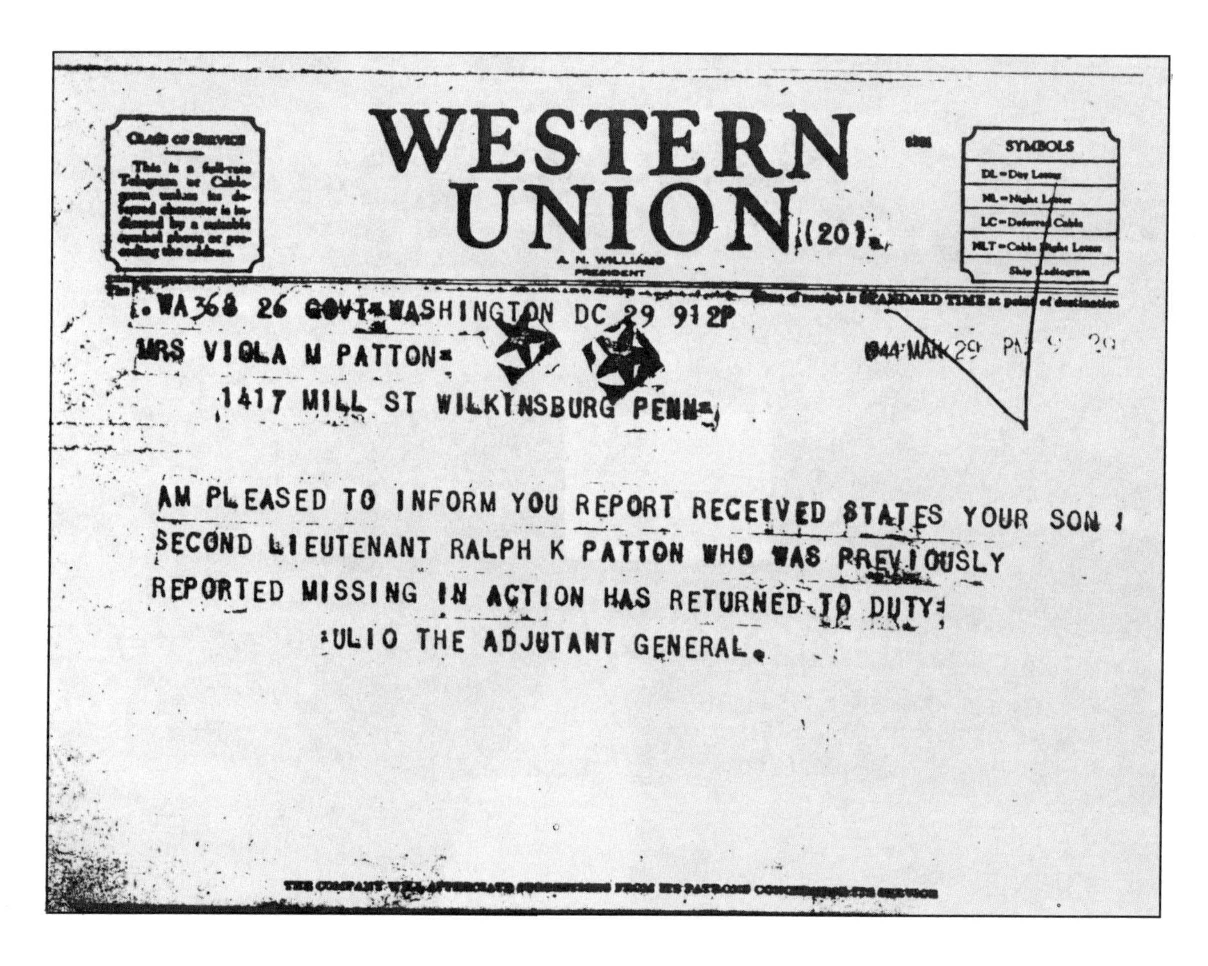

WESTERN UNION

WA368 26 GOVT=WASHINGTON DC 29 912P

1944 MAR 29 PM

MRS VIOLA M PATTON=

1417 MILL ST WILKINSBURG PENN=

AM PLEASED TO INFORM YOU REPORT RECEIVED STATES YOUR SON SECOND LIEUTENANT RALPH K PATTON WHO WAS PREVIOUSLY REPORTED MISSING IN ACTION HAS RETURNED TO DUTY=

ULIO THE ADJUTANT GENERAL.

(Courtesy Ralph Patton)

The boat which secretly took Mr. Patton and other rescued Allied personnel back to England.
(Photo courtesy Ralph Patton)

Walter Pawlesh

388th Bomb Group
563rd Squadron
Tail Gunner

by
Nicole Webster

He is a kind, outgoing man, with an excellent memory and recollection of details and events. He was a tail gunner, and also a POW. His plane, in the 388th, was called "Heaven Can Wait," after a popular song at that time. He showed a model B-17 and a couple of his books. He was open and relaxed throughout the interview.

I went into the service in 1944. I was captured March 23rd. We were fortunate that all our crew got back. Nobody was killed [in combat]. Four or five of us were wounded.

I was a tail gunner... [in a] ten-man crew. Everybody else was captured and I wasn't. When I bailed out at three hundred feet, I bailed out very low. My parachute opened, and I hit the ground at the same time. Because I bailed out so low, they couldn't see me - I got my 'chute down, hid it, and started my escape. I slept in the woods. I came to the edge of the woods... underneath the roots of the trees, the dirt had pulled out. I separated the roots, crawled in there, and went to sleep. I figured if they looked for me they wouldn't think to look in under the tree. I slept there 'til it got dark, [then] I took off trying to find my way back to Belgium and France.

My buddy Ralph... bailed out ahead of me, then the radio operator, then me. When I got down, I tried to figure out where they would land, and I started back lookin' for them. Ralph and I had a pact, "If anything happens, we'll try to keep together." I couldn't find him. He [had been] captured right away. The rest of the crew crash landed the airplane, and they all got out. The pilot and the copilot did a marvelous job of bringin' the airplane in. My buddy Ralph was wounded pretty badly. He was shot up with 20 mm cannon shrapnel. He was the only one who was wounded badly.

When you're in Germany, your life is in their hands. The civilians would do you more harm than the military, because we were constantly bombing them, and we were putting up thousand airplane raids. We were dropping bombs galore, devastating the cities and the civilians took after us a couple of times. We were fortunate to get away when we were with the Germans. The civilians did capture some of the airmen, and they hung them. I never gave it a thought until... I saw The Great Escape. Most [of the guys killed] were British, and when I saw that, I thought to myself, "Boy, I was pretty lucky." 'cause I was by myself. They could have shot me anywhere along the way, and nobody would have even known about it.

When they captured me, they took me into a little town, and they put me in a home of these People's Army... and I waited. The door opened, and in came this high-ranking Luftwaffe officer, and he spoke perfect King's English. We respected their rank, and they respected our rank. When the door opened , [and] I saw that he was an officer, I snapped to and jumped right at attention. He wanted to know if I had a pistol. The first thing he said was, "Sergeant, do you have a pistol?" I said, "No, sir!" He said , "Did these people harm you?" I said, "No, sir!" [Then] he said, "I'll be back." I sat down, then he came back, and he said, "I'm gonna ask you once more - Do you have a pistol?" I said, "No, sir!" He said, "OK, follow me."

There was a touring car out there just like... you would see in the [German war] movies. A private was driving it, a lieutenant was sitting with him, and I was in the back with this major lieutenant colonel. They took me to a jail in an airfield. Then they moved me with one German guard from city to city. I went to the railroad station, got on the trains with this guy... mingling with the German population. Most of the people on the trains were military too. They'd just look at you. You didn't know what they were thinking. We would get to a different airfield [every day], and they would put me in jail 'til they got me all the way to Frankfurt.

The Germans had an interrogation center there for American airmen. All American airmen went through this interrogation center. They put you in solitary confinement, and they would interrogate you every day. We didn't have any information for them. I told them, "Hey, I'm a tail gunner." [I] gave them my name, rank and serial number. That's all we were allowed to give them. [We didn't] know anything about the outfit. They would tell me who my commander was, and who my supply sergeant was. I said, "You know more about the outfit than I do!" They did [know more than we did]. They had all this espionage. They knew more about us. They told [some other guys] when they went home on furlough, where they were located here in the States. They knew all this. They knew every thing about our government, and every move we made. Their espionage was just as good as ours, if not better!

There was a picture of Hitler on one wall, Goering on another- just like you would see in a movie back here. Everything was just like in the movies. They gave me a demitasse cup of coffee, and a couple slices of bread. In came the Gestapo, and he had a riding crop. I thought, "This guy's gonna beat the daylights outta me!" (Laughs.) He

Ruby Newell voted the prettiest WAC in the E.T.O. (European Theatre of Operations) is seen here with her P-51 namesake. *(Photo courtesy Tom Brown)*

had young kids with him. They couldn't have been no more than about fourteen years old, and they had big squirrel rifles. There was a blond woman with them, and she was the only one who could speak English. She said, "For you, the war is over." (Laughs.) She said, "Now you're gonna go to a prison camp, where you'll meet the rest of your comrades."

Never once was I ever afraid that anything was gonna happen to me. But they were [abusive to us] to some extent. If you were with the Air Force; the Luftwaffe, respected your rank and everything. If you happened to get caught by the civilians, or some of the infantry, they may do you in. Most of the time, I was with the Luftwaffe. They treated me pretty good, and there was no reason for me to be afraid. I was in the company prison at the airport, and there was a German sergeant getting ready to eat his dinner, and he came over and gave me a canteen cup full of hot vegetable soup. (Laughs.) That really hit the spot!

He described the concentration camps that he saw while on the forced march. The descriptions are detailed and graphic, but he had one very important point in this.

This actually happened. A lot of people don't believe that it did, but this actually did happen - to men, women, and children. When we were on the forced march, we were going through Linz, Austria. That was a big city, and there was only one bridge standing; we had bombed all the rest. While we were going through, the air raid sirens went off. All of the Germans were running to the air raid shelters; we were marching. The ones that could speak English were yelling, "Now you're going to get a dose of you own medicine!" (Laughs.) We were marching out as fast as we could - we got out just in time!

Our prison camp was thirty - seven kilometers from Vienna - outside of a little town called Krems. It was way up on top of the hill. When they [the Germans] brought us in there, they brought us in by train, and then we had to walk this big hill - all the way up. It was like a mountain! We were up on a plateau on top. It was actually the foothills of the Alps. So many people [have] gone back to the prison camp, but there's nothing there.

Whenever they took us into prison camp, they gave us a shower. They deloused our clothing and they cut all our hair off and shaved our heads. When we went in the big shower room, the first thing that came to mind was, "Is water gonna come out of the shower heads, or gas?" We didn't know what they were gonna do to us. When your hair grew back in, they'd give you another shower and cut your hair again. Our guys would take this oleomargarine, rub it in their hair, and put sand in their hair. That would ruin the German clippers. After they did that a few times, they quit giving us haircuts.

When we got in prison camp, you wouldn't believe the American ingenuity - it was superb. We had a cardboard playhouse. These guys got together and they put on "Hell's - a - Poppin" and "The Man Who Came to Dinner." These guys were good. They portrayed women. A lot of guys were from New York, and they had been on Broadway. Even the Germans came down to watch the shows.

A lot of [the Germans] understood English, more than what you thought, because they wouldn't let you know that they knew English. When they were around you, they were always listening. They had ferrets, these guys that would come around at night and crawl around under the barracks and listen to the conversations. [They understood because] a lot of the Germans were educated in England, and they spoke really good English.

The Red Cross parcels had Spam, oleo, powdered milk, five packs of cigarettes, three D bars, and a box of either raisins or prunes. There were times we got barley soup, but we didn't get very much from the Germans 'cause they didn't have anything more than what we had. We got potatoes from them, and some ugly canned stuff that

(Photo courtesy Robert Kimball)

we ate because we were hungry.

Cigarettes, candy bars, and soap were the biggest trading commodities - you could trade for almost anything. We had these "D - bars" They were pure chocolate. They were put in hot water to make hot chocolate. With that, you could trade for anything.

The bread that we got [as a ration] was sawdust bread. Sawdust was mixed with the dough, and it was good bread. (Laughs.) We would get a small piece, and it had to last a whole week, and you would cut it paper thin. (Laughs.)

He talked about sports in prison camp, and how the Red Cross sent them more sports equipment than food.

When Patton's Army liberated us, I had about six fresh eggs in one of my socks. They put us in an old aluminum factory; it was warm in there, and I scrambled those eggs in there. I got dysentery. I was as sick as a dog! They put me in the hospital over there, and they wouldn't let me have anything but baby food, for about a week, until I got back on my feet.

At the end of the war, they marched us out of our prison camp, and took us all the way across Austria; it was 180 some miles. All four thousand of us airmen were in eight groups of five hundred in a group. I was in the last group. We used to go to town, and usually just the women were home. We'd trade them candy bars or soap. Soap was a big thing for them because the soap that they had was terrible. One time some Hungarian people gave me Hungarian goulash and some bacon. The people knew the P.O.W.'s had things to trade, so they were willing to trade.

We came into Nancy, France, and they knew we were coming. They got out the beer, wine, and whiskey. The doctors took one look at us and said, "Lock everything up, 'cause if we give these guys any booze, we'll kill them all." (Laughs.)

There were over four thousand American airmen in our camp. I never saw the rest of my crew until the war ended and I was in Le Havre. They moved everybody to "Camp Lucky Strike" in Le Havre. We stayed there a whole month and fattened ourselves up. We drank egg nog, ate good, and took it easy. When I was in Le Havre one of the guys I knew from training came by. He said, "Hey, Walt! I just ran into your whole crew up in the chow line." So I ran up there, and there they were - the other five enlisted men. There were six enlisted men and four officers on a plane. That was the first time I'd seen them since the day we got shot down, and I never saw them again until we got home. We slept in tents, then they finally marched us down to the docks, and we got on a Navy transport. We were back in New York in about four or five days. This Navy transport made quick time all the way across. I was on the U.S.S. Admiral Benson. Most of the guys were on these Liberty ships that just rode the waves. (Laughs.) Those guys were sick! It was real good for us that we got home so quick.

I said we got shot down on our fifth mission, but the rest of the crew didn't get the Air Medal. You got the Air Medal for every five missions. I told the [nineteen-year-old guy that was typing up the discharge papers] that I got the Air Medal, and he typed it on my papers. (Laughs.) I had the Air Medal, the Purple Heart with a Cluster, the POW Medal, the Victory Medal, the Good Conduct Medal, and the European Theater Medal. I had about nine ribbons I could wear on my uniform.

When I got home, I was in bad shape. I couldn't adapt real quick to our life, because of the noise and everything. I was sitting in [my friend's] living room, reading the paper, and the streetcar comes down and goes around the corner there. When the streetcar came down, it made such a noise, it sounded like a load of bombs. I threw the paper up in the air and I dove under the coffee table. (Laughs.) Everybody sat there and looked at me, wondering what the heck was happening. (Laughs.) It took years [to adapt].

The nightmares still come back, even today. For years, I dreamt about being chased by the Germans. I'll never forget the first time my wife said, "You look terrible." (Laughs.) I said, "If you were being chased all night by the Germans, you'd look like me." (Laughs.) This went on and on for years. Then I had this dream... where we were all laying on the ground and this German officer was coming by. He had a pistol, and he shot every one of us in the head. When that happened to me, I never had any more nightmares! But those dreams still come back, little by little, I can't get rid of them - it's just something that's gonna be with me 'til the day I die.

My pilot was Lieutenant McFall. This is from the 388th book I have. [He refers to his book.]

"Lieutenant McFall in the aircraft 42-31745 'Heaven Can Wait' was hit by enemy fighters, shot down near Nuremburg. The last man to bail out was the tailgunner when the plane was a few hundred feet in the air. Enlisted men were in Stalag 17B and Barth."

They were all in Barth; I was the only one in Stalag 17B. They have marked (from the crews that were shot down) "P.O.W. " But then they have "K.I.A." "K.I.A." - killed in action. It's amazing how many were killed in action. It gives all our missions in here - where we went, how long the mission was. We never had any pictures taken. We weren't over there that long.

It was a different world over there. There's so much, in fourteen months, a lot of things happened. When we talk, we're just touching the surface of everything...

Mr. Pawlesh recalled many interesting facts, both amusing and shocking. All that he hopes is that it opens someone's eyes and mind and sparks an interest in this country's history.

Edgar Powell

467th Bombardment Group
788th Squadron
Pilot

by
Rachelle C. Olenic

Ed Powell is an enthusiastic man who held interesting positions in the war due to his numerous talents and skills. When he talks about the war, he makes the stories come alive.

Before the war, I worked for a railroad train track maintenance equipment company in Aspinwall. I enlisted in 1942 when I was twenty-one and qualified as an aviation cadet with two years of college. I was sent to San Antonio, Texas for my pilot training from December, 1942 until October 1, 1943.

After my first days of pilot school, I was sent to a different base. We went through the West Point Cadet hazing system and soon learned to "hit a brace," to eat while sitting at attention, to occasionally "eat a square meal," to run between classes, and march, march, march. I had played trumpet in the high school band. When I got into the Aviation Cadet Corps, I was placed in charge of the drum and bugle corps where we marched daily in front of ten thousand soldiers; I played two trumpet solos and lowered the flag.

Since I could type and take shorthand, I was assigned to the office where I took dictation and typed letters. I also played the bugle calls over the P.A. system to call the men to the mess or assembly. I was even a ham radio operator, and I was able to fix our P.A. systems. I didn't have to go out and march or peel potatoes, and I didn't have to get a G.I. haircut. After ninety days of intense ground school, we were sent for another ninety days to Oklahoma City to primary flying school for our first hands-on experience with the single-engine trainer. Then came three months of advanced single-engine training (which included night flying, acrobatics, and instrument flying) in Kansas on a heavier 450 h.p. engine, similar to a fighter plane except without retractable landing gear. Then I went to two-engine school in western Oklahoma. My hope was to fly a P-38, but it didn't turn out that way. The day I got my wings and my commission, my wife came down from Aspinwall with her mother, her sister, and my mother; I was married in the base chapel.

I was sent to a classified center in Salt Lake City around October 15, 1943. When they decided they needed pilots for the four-engine Liberator, I was sent to a couple of bases for intense training and practiced bombing, night navigation, and just about everything you can think of. By the fifteenth of February, 1944 I was on my way to combat.

About the middle of March, we started on combat missions. I was a member of a lead crew. We only flew when we led the group - which means that we didn't fly every day. On the days that we didn't fly lead, we had to fly some airplane and test it out at high altitude to ensure that everything would work when it was our turn to lead the formation. The reason for this was that the lead airplane finds the bomb site very accurately so that when the lead takes out his bombs, everybody else hits the toggle button and drops their bombs at the same time. That's how they get their pattern of bombing a target. The Germans make all head-on passes at the lead. We're leading a thousand airplanes in a big raid, and we're the first ones out. If they miss us, they are going to hit somebody anyway. One of the unfortunate parts was that the Germans

Edgar Powell and crew. Top row, left to right - Bill Moore (Pilot), Ed Powell (Copilot), Frank Coslett (Navigator), Ed Verbosky (Bombardier). Bottom row, left to right - Clinton L. Watts (Engineer), James R. Anslow (Radio Operator), Walter T. Kilgore (Assistant Engineer), Henry H. Allen (Ball-Turret Gunner), Werner G. Braun (Waist Gunner), and Robert G. Staley (Tail Turret).(Photo courtesy Edgar Powell)

had such strong intelligence working for them and always seemed to know in advance what we were going to do.

On the day that we were shot down, our crew was selected to lead the whole division. On board, there were three pilots as well as my squadron commander (a major) who sat in my pilot seat. I was in the tail turret flying as formation control officer and also defending the airplane as a gunner. It's the formation control officer's job to get the formation together as fast as possible without wasting a lot of fuel. There might be a thousand airplanes popping up through the clouds at seventeen thousand feet wondering where they were and where their leader was.

We were bombing Berlin, and the Germans made an extra effort against us. In fact, the Germans shot down sixty-five airplanes in one day on just one mission, and there were ten crewmen in every plane.

I was in the 467th Bomb Group. Our plane's wing had been shot off in a prior mission. The wing had been replaced, and the plane was repaired. We got hit directly over the target with heavy artillery which knocked out one of the engines. Suddenly my hydraulic controls went dead. I called one of the gunners who looked and told me that a shell had gone through a hydraulic line. If it had gone off, we would have been dead. This was my first realization that I could get killed out there.

For protection, we obtained a good position in the middle of wounded B-17s. We started losing engines mainly from lack of fuel due to using fuel to fly on three engines. Over Holland, the fourth engine quit running. We pushed the alarm button for bail out at seventeen thousand feet.

We had picked up the clouds coming back again, and they were supposedly at three thousand feet under us and about thirty thousand feet over us. We had no real horizon to work by. We had talked it over and felt that the safest thing to do was not open our chutes until we fell to about three thousand feet .

I often had wondered what it would be like to do a one-and-a-half or a two-and-a-half off of a high diving board, so I pulled my knees up, and immediately started to tumble. Then I straightened out. I realized that I didn't know what was up or what was down; there was no horizon reference at all. It turned out that it had been raining and the cloud deck had dropped. When

"The Comet" with Lt. Johnson and his crew. Refer to Tom Brown's entry later on in this book for the real story behind this plane and photo.

(Photo courtesy Tom Brown)

I opened my chute, I was five hundred feet above the ground. As soon as my chute opened, I landed on two trees in a forest of huge evergreens.

The first thing you find out is that you don't have shoes or socks on because when your chute pops open, your shoes and socks are gone (except for paratroopers who wear the big high boots which is why they are worn) so that those who flew always wired an extra pair of shoes and socks to their parachutes. The only mistake I made was that I had placed the shoes at the end of a wire two and a half feet long so they wouldn't be in my way. They were at just the right angle so that when the chute opened, they came up and hit me in the mouth! I climbed down from the tree and ran as far as I could before I realized that I wasn't wearing shoes and socks. I ran back to get my spare pair of shoes and socks, then ran as fast as I could until I was completely out of breath. Meanwhile, my head was ready to explode from falling seventeen thousand feet at that fast rate of speed. The pressure had been intense. I stopped to put on my shoes and socks. I saw a road sign at an intersection. I got my map and compass out of the emergency escape kit which I always carried in order to determine where I was and which way I was to start walking. By now my hearing was coming back, and I could hear dogs barking. Fifteen minutes later, I was discovered by a group of about thirty Germans.

Of course, I had no gun or ammunition since we weren't to carry them. If we were spotted wearing a gun holster as we parachuted down, we would be shot before we reached the ground. I was placed in the back seat of a jeep. I was taken to a local jail in a little Dutch town called Apeldorn. In the back of us, there were five jeeps each with one driver and five men carrying submachine guns. We made a wrong turn into a dead-end street. The lieutenant in the jeep with us told the driver to turn around. Those guys couldn't turn those jeeps around. They would get them almost turned around and they would turn the wheels the wrong way and then go back the other way due to their lack of experience with vehicles. The more the lieutenant yelled, the more confused the drivers got. If I had laughed, that would have been the end of me.

The next day they transported us, as well as others who had been picked up, to a jail in Amsterdam. There I found my squadron commander (who had been sitting in my copilot seat) and the ball-turret gunner and the bombardier; we pretended not to know each other. A hundred prisoners were rounded up in a period of about three nights, and we were placed on a train to be taken to a Frankfurt interrogation center where every airman was questioned individually.

The Germans had heard that we had developed radar bombing equipment to bomb through the clouds. That was true, but I didn't know about it. They tried everything they could to get me to admit to something I couldn't admit to knowing about. They knew a lot about me. They knew I was born in Aspinwall and went to Aspinwall High School. They knew my wife's name, when I went into the service, and when I graduated. In this country, everything is in the newspapers; their intelligence clipped the articles on soldiers, and files were kept. But one thing the interrogator did tell me that surprised me was the names of everybody on my airplane that was shot down including the names of my regular crew plus a few of the extras. One trick they pulled was that the sound of a gun would be heard outside the windows; when you jumped, they would say, "Well, there's another POW who did not talk." I spent eight days in a cell about five feet wide by six feet long with no windows except for a little window at the top of the room to allow a little light in. We were given bread and water for eight days, and every day the interrogations continued. When I was captured, the interrogation people had that notebook of mine with them and said that possessing the notebook made me a spy since I had copied down some names of towns listed on the sign post located near the site where I was captured.

We were placed on trains and moved slowly, traveling at night to a place south of Berlin called Sagan which was a big prisoner-of-war camp for airmen. There were ten thousand POWs there.

Well, we were POWs now, and we were fingerprinted and made to look pretty bad. They gave us a German POW number. While I was in the POW camp, that's when life really became tough. Actually, the Red Cross tried valiantly to get food to us and kept most of us alive because the Germans weren't giving us enough to keep a kitten alive. We were getting a little package about every other week; then when the bombing became intense, and the roads were being strafed. They couldn't get to us, and so food supplies came once every month, and then once every other month. The food became very scarce and the German ration was a kind of black bread and potatoes that were overly rotten which were cut to save the best part. We also got a vegetable that looked like a turnip. This was all that we got for food, so thank goodness for the Red Cross.

To keep ourselves from going crazy, we tried to keep busy. The Red Cross and the YMCA brought in some instruments. I was a trumpet player in a band that we formed. We rehearsed every day, and we put on a show for the rest of the guys almost every week. Most of the band members were professional musicians in name bands at the time they had been drafted.

The Battle of the Bulge took place right before Christmas. The Germans made every effort they could to push the Americans out one more time, and they killed a lot of our people. That was demoralizing; that sure ruined our Christmas.

Then after Christmas, the Russians

started to move and to approach our camp from the east. We could hear the guns. We were marched away from the eastern front in the dead of winter in a snow storm with 0° F temperatures in about fifteen inches of fresh snow with the wind blowing hard. Each of us carried our personal items with us on the march. I was told I was also to carry my trumpet for signaling purposes to alert the troops to get up and move or to stop.

Here we are, a bunch of guys who had been POWs for ten months on limited food rations with no choice but to keep on marching. We walked for two days and two nights before we really stopped. A lot of people were lost through sheer exhaustion. We finally found a pottery factory with heated kilns. The dust was about a foot deep, but it was so nice and warm in there. People had frozen toes and fingers since nobody had overshoes or boots, and nobody had gloves - you just had to wrap yourself up in a blanket and keep moving or you would freeze.

We had marched sixty-two miles to reach a railroad town where we were herded into boxcars. Fifty men plus a guard were crammed into each car. If you got into a sitting position that's the way you stayed for two days. They moved us at night, in between air raids, into the town of Nurnberg. For seventeen nights, the British raided the town around us. They dropped flares over our camp because they knew where we were and didn't want to harm us. Two days after daylight raids, they said the Allies crossed the Rhine and started to approach from the west. The Germans started marching us again. It was March, wet and rainy, but it was better than the weather we marched in before. So we marched to a town called Moosburg which was near a railroad yard. It was estimated by the time we all got there that there were about 110,000 prisoners in this one great big area. We weren't there more than two or three weeks until General Patton and his forces came marching through chasing all the Germans away, and we were liberated!

We were liberated but could go nowhere because the Germans were still everyplace although they

Col. John B. Henry, commander of the 339th Fighter Group, just returning from a successful mission in May of 1944.

(Photo courtesy Tom Brown)

weren't organized. So the hungriest part of the war was after we were liberated. Nobody was feeding us then - no German food, no American food - we just suffered until the war was over; May 9th. We used to have a rule in the aviation department that your belt was only allowed to stick out of your buckle a half inch. When I was a POW, it was clear around to this loop at my side. (He designates how far around his waist the end of the belt extended.) May 10th they finally flew us out to France to a camp called Lucky Strike on the edge of the Atlantic Ocean. They gave us some clothes to wear; some of us had been wearing the same clothes for over a year. They gave us haircuts and some food and put us on a troop ship, and we sailed back. Of course, the Japanese war was still on, so we couldn't just go sailing back. We had to be in convoys and be protected by submarines and battle wagons. Anyway, the war ended for me. I was shot down April 29, 1944 and liberated April 29, 1945.

General Patton actually came to our camp because he had a son-in-law in the tank corps who had been captured, and he was hoping to find him. He rode into camp on the hood of a jeep dressed like he was going out on Fifth Avenue with his pearl-handled revolvers and shiny boots and all. You'll have to forgive my language but I'm going to quote General Patton. I was in the barracks and this kid came in and said, "He spoke to me! He spoke to me!" Somebody asked, "Who spoke to you?" The kid replied, "Why, General Patton. He spoke to me." Somebody else said, "What in the world did he say to you?" The kid's answer was, "Get off my g__ d___ foot!" Now here General Patton was signing autographs and this kid got too close and stepped on his shiny new boots.

We flew to Le Havre which is on the coast of France and were placed on a ship headed back to New York. When we got within one hundred miles of New York, we broke away from the convoy and went all the way to Trinidad. It turned out that we had 1,800 Air Force people on board who were reassigned to the South Pacific to fight the Japanese war which was still on. We were upset because we were that close to home and we had to take this diversion. Actually, it was good for us, because when the 1,800 Air Force personnel left, all the people left on board the ship were ex-POWs, and we were given ice cream twice a day and fed a rich diet and all we could handle.

The closest shave I ever had as a POW was about the notes I took in shorthand. A lot of people were abused by the Germans, but our Allied officers are the ones to know about it. I was drafted by a lieutenant colonel who interviewed these people who had been tortured. I would write their stories down in shorthand, and I kept these notes in my bag all through the war.

I went back to Germany in 1955, alone on business for two weeks, when I was working for the company which sold the Germans some railroad equipment to rebuild their railroad which had been heavily bombed during the war. The day before I was ready to come home I was having lunch in Hanover with four Germans, and we were discussing the war. I told them I was shot down in a Berlin raid of a railroad yard on April 29th. One of the Germans said, "You bombed my plant! You bombed my plant!" But then the man said, "Oh, well, it's in the Russian zone anyway." We were able to do business and to communicate because I represented the company which was helping them get their railroads built, and they needed the help. After the war, German workers worked for nothing rebuilding plants in order to have a place to work. They layed bricks, poured concrete, put in windows, and put it all back together again so they would have a place to work. They really had the work ethic.

In September 1945, Ed Powell returned to Pittsburgh. He now lives in Fox Chapel with his wife. Ed has many books and notes about the war which made my visit all the more interesting. He gave his daughter, a band director in San Antonio, the trumpet which he carried with him throughout the war.

Rudolph Pusic

447th Bomb Group
423rd Squadron
Radio Operator

by
Brian P. Young

Mr. Rudolph Pusic is a congenial, down to earth fellow whose ever-watchful eyes smile knowingly. He has held numerous occupations throughout his life. In 1942, Mr. Pusic was a shipping clerk at the Armstrong Cork Co. when he was drafted at age twenty-one. After the war, Mr. Pusic attended Penn State University and received a degree in accounting. For many years after the war he approved secondary schools for the Department of Education in Pennsylvania under the G.I. Bill. He also has his own accounting business, was Pine Township manager for a number of years, and has been proprietor of a nursing home near Butler, PA.

After Mr. Pusic had flown about ten missions in England as a Radio Operator, he was named Squadron Radio Operator, which meant that he was the chief operator for his entire squadron. He was chosen for this job because of his ability to operate the new PFF radar equipment. What this meant in practice was that he would now fly once every four missions, and when he did fly, he was always in the lead bomber. When Mr. Pusic was named Squadron Radio Operator, his crew became a replacement crew. This meant that if any member of a crew in his squadron didn't return, the corresponding member of the replacement crew would take his place. After this, Mr. Pusic flew once every four missions, and consequently he did not get a chance to complete a full twenty-five-mission tour before victory in Europe.

After the war in Europe was won, Mr. Pusic stayed in England an extra month with his commanding officer in order to wrap things up. His orders were then to go to the Pacific to fly in the B-26 Bomber. Before he got the chance to do this, his orders were changed. Instead, he went to the Drew Base in Florida to instruct new radio operators on the B-26. He realized only later that this was due in no small part to the imminent bombing of Hiroshima and Nagasaki.

Mr. Pusic vividly recalls a couple of times when he had the opportunity to observe the conduct of some of the celebrities that served in the war. Most of the celebrity soldiers, with few exceptions, were there as morale boosters, or as feature attractions on sporting teams.

There was one officer at the Drew Base in Florida who was constantly working. Surely he did his part around the base, but sometimes he worked on his backhand. That is not to say that Clark Gable didn't do his part for the war effort; it's just that his part included the game of tennis.

One scene that Mr. Pusic has fixed in his mind is the time that he went to see Joe DiMaggio play in one of the inter-base ball games that were popular. The players took their warm-up, and there was a buzz in the air. "Where's DiMaggio? Where's DiMaggio?!" was the general talk. DiMaggio was on the home team; they were to bat in the bottom half of the inning. The first half of the inning came, with no DiMaggio. The first half ended - no Joe. The game continued into the bottom half of the first. DiMaggio was batting cleanup, and as his turn approached, it looked as though a substitute batter would have to be used. Joe must have had a busy schedule on that day. Only two batters before his turn, here came Joltin' Joe rolling up in his enormous white Cadillac coupe. He stepped out of the car in uniform, stepped up to the plate, grounded out to second base, climbed back in that big white Cadillac of his, and drove off.

Nights in the barracks in England were generally late ones. The thirty odd men who inhabited these glorified tents were up half the night playing cards, music, and just having a good time in general - all except the seven or eight men who had orders to fly in the morning. For these men it was a challenge to get a good night's rest in such close quarters. There was always the night-before anxiety that resulted from not knowing their destination. The normal routine was to wake at four a.m. and go to their breakfast of powdered eggs (one of the nastiest parts, according to Mr. Pusic), and go to briefing where they would receive their flight path. This is where pre-flight nervousness reached its peak. The crew would sit in the room, facing a map of Germany, which was covered by curtains before they learned their path. As soon as the curtain was lifted, however, the crew would know if the next eight or nine hours would be a perilous run or a walk in the park.

One run that Mr. Pusic made was to the town of Kiel in Germany. Their squadron had run into some heavy flak, and their B-17 suffered a little damage from the shrapnel. It was not until they returned to England that Mr. Pusic realized just how close he came to death on that particular run. When they got in, he looked a couple of feet beside him to find a hole in the wing the size of a softball made by a piece of shrapnel.

Another frightening aspect of the air war against Germany was the German jet planes. The German jets were so much faster than the American bombers that it was virtually impossible to combat them. The only thing to do when a German jet came screaming by was to wait for it to run out of it's ten-minutes' worth of fuel.

The most important message that Mr. Pusic received as a radio operator during the war came on his first flight across the Atlantic to go to his station. His group was scheduled to fly from Labrador in Newfoundland to Iceland and then to England. As his group was heading into Iceland, they received a radio transmission which told of bad weather in Iceland. They were to turn around and land in Greenland, where they were to stay until the weather broke. Every plane but one received the fateful message. That lone plane that missed the transmission was downed somewhere off Iceland that day.

The fateful, faith-shaking tragedy that occurred that day was followed by what Mr. Pusic described as some of the most enjoyable time that he spent in the service. Their travelling group was layed up in Greenland for about three weeks after the incident. Because they were flying with a group of Canadian airmen, they played a lot of soccer and had an all-around good time. One fond memory that Mr. Pusic has from his military training was from radio school in Sioux Falls, South Dakota. In the winter, Sioux Falls gets pretty cold. It got to be roughly forty-five degrees below zero. In Sioux Falls the men lived in barracks that were no more than large tents. Instead of cooking on the pot belly stoves, the guys used to freeze a pot of water as the running joke; there was no fuel to heat them.

A radio operator on a B-17 had to do more than just run a radio. His seat was situated right next to the bomb bay, and if anything went wrong with the release, he was one of the men whose job it was to fix it. At sixty degrees below zero, sometimes the bombs would freeze to the plane. When this happened, Mr. Pusic would have to crawl out on a one-foot-wide scaffolding (from which you looked down at the ground through about twenty-eight thousand feet of open space), carrying his wits and a screwdriver to knock the bomb loose. Another one of his jobs was to watch the bombs through the open bay door and report back to base the accuracy of the run. On one occasion, Mr. Pusic could see through the cloud of bombs a small church from his perch. He remembers vividly hoping that the church would be untouched; what a strange feeling to be glad that they missed by a quarter of a mile.

Perhaps the one fact about the Eighth Air Force that Mr. Pusic is proudest of is that the Mighty Eighth was never turned back on any mission. This is a reflection of the will and strength of all the men who served in this heroic division of the United States Air Force.

B-17 one-thousand plane mission.
(Photo courtesy James Doerr)

P-38 Lightning near a bomb shelter.
(Photo courtesy Tom Brown)

James Regas
44th Bomb Group
67th Squadron
Flight Engineer

by
Steve Hornyak

A life-long military man, first in the Eighth Air Force and later working with the Navy as a civilian, James Regas led a full life. He served right out of college. He was drafted even before he could finish his studies at the Pitt Institute of Aeronautics. Later, he was awarded three Bronze Stars and an Air Medal with three Oak Leaf Clusters, signifying twenty-four total missions in a B-24 named "Cowtown Cathy".

[The military schools] were demanding, at Keisler Field they had what were called A, B, or C shifts, and they were operating their mechanics schools 'round the clock.' You had to get your work done or fail the course. The majority of us that I was with had no failures. They taught you all about a B-24 - everything you needed to know to save your life. If your job was in the turret, you had to know that turret one hundred percent. If your job was a flight engineer you had to know the duties of the flight engineer. You were questioned and tested on everything you were taught. I have to give those instructors credit.

A flight engineer, when he wasn't sitting in the top turret during actual combat time at takeoff, would stand between the pilot and copilot and observe all the instrument panel gauges and help the copilot in case there would be something go wrong with one of the engines. Not that he didn't know what to do, but I could remind him if anything was in question on his part or mine,...any type of thing that could be considered an emergency.

We only had two or three bicycles in the squadron, and everybody claimed that they were theirs, but they belonged to everybody. A lot of times I'd get a bicycle and go to the mess hall. I'd come out, and of course, it would be gone; somebody else had it. We had a ration of coal over there - a bucket full of coal a week, or so many a month. And of course, when some of the boys would use their coal unsparingly, they'd come over when we were gone and take our coal. We, in turn, would fix them up and put cartridges in their stove. What a sound that would make; nobody ever got hurt. We had a lot of funny incidents, a lot of incidents they considered funny but we didn't. Whenever we'd be at the mess hall, somebody'd come to our aircraft, and they'd take whatever parts they needed. Of course, they weren't safety or flight parts. They would just take things in that aircraft that didn't belong to them. And we'd catch them. We knew...who did it. We were forever late coming back. Sometimes, we'd be ready for a flight for the morning, and they'd tell us that there would probably be no flying tomorrow. Everybody would go to town and have a good time, and then not get back in time when an emergency was called, so we had to scramble up and get crews. A lot of the fellas were sick or have to report to the infirmary, and we'd just have to get somebody to fill their position in the aircraft. That was pretty serious at the time. They may have considered it funny, but the commanding officer didn't.

Getting acquainted with the English language was pretty difficult for some of us because of their accent. But after, I'd say four weeks, longer for some of us, they got to speak it just as fluently and with the same accent as the English folks over there. We had fun trying to interpret some of their wordings, like a "perambulator" was a "baby buggy," and an "elevator" was called a "lift", just things like that, that struck us as being funny. We got along very well with the English people. It was a mutual thing; we needed each other.

[The night before a mission] we went to bed early. Where we had to fly was an eight-hour trip. They'd wake us up for breakfast and briefing at three thirty. They'd tell you what the target was, what to do, what to look for, what the cloud cover was, and so forth. We'd go out and inspect the aircraft and be in the air by about five or five thirty.

My first battle experience was nerve-racking. It was over a town called Salzburg. We had light to moderate flak. We were all pretty nervous about the first mission. It was on February 16, 1945. We didn't get any flak hits or nothing; although there was flak in the skies. I'll say one thing about the German antiaircraft; they certainly were experts with their guns. They put it right up there. Later we were given boxes of, what they called 'chaf;' it looked like icicles from a Christmas tree. At that time I didn't understand what it was for, but after we got on the aircraft the pilot notified us that as soon as they started shooting, to start throwing that over. So a lot of times we'd start throwing the chaf over before we were even shot at, because we knew it was coming. The purpose of this chaf was to deflect the radar. It did a pretty good job, but they still got it up there."

How did you feel when you saw your own planes shot down?

Awful, I saw one go down, I saw the wing

(Photo courtesy Robert Kimball)

fold up on it. I thought he was hit from antiaircraft, but later they told me, whether its true or not I don't know, but they said it was a bomb dropped from one of our own planes. It went down with the crew in it, and I don't recall anyone bailing out. It's not nice to see one of our own go down, but it happens.

We went to...Wilhelmshaven. I was told by one of the crew my pilot was born there, and his grandmother was still living there at the time.

The missions weren't all easy missions. The ones that were easy were called "milk runs." That's when you ran a mission and didn't get shot at. They were perfect. You just went over, dropped bombs, and came back. Some of the missions were awful, as far as antiaircraft was concerned. One funny thing happened to me, I'll never forget, we went over one target;... it was the first time we saw flak. We didn't know what it was; it was just black puffs of smoke. We said "Look at that, look at all those black puffs of smoke!" They said, "That's not smoke, that's flak. You'd better hide behind your flak suit." A flak suit was just like an apron that you put on; like the police use today to protect them from bullets. We also had electric suits. At forty degrees below zero they did a fairly good job, but back there in the waist compartment it was awfully cold. Some of the problems we had after firing at enemy aircraft coming in was slipping and sliding all over the empty fifty-caliber cartridges. That was pretty hard to do; try to keep firing your gun while you're slipping and sliding.

We ran into a hydraulic problem one time, and we landed at a place called Bordeaux, France. We were treated very nicely there. They gave us good food, but it took us awhile to get the plane repaired and get back in flight. Of course we had to have one of our people stand guard by the aircraft so nobody'd come and steal any parts from it, then it was his turn to go eat.

We usually would go into town when we could, and visit the USO groups that would send the Hollywood people over to entertain the troops. We'd mingle with the English people and with the English Air Force personnel. We would go look at their aircraft and they, in turn, would come look at ours. When the war was over, they put on some high shows. After V-E Day, we flew over Germany at low level, and it was a very disturbing sight to see - nothing but destruction. I don't see how the German people survived, because every town we flew over got hit bad. There wasn't a closed roof on any of the buildings - especially Cologne, but the church was still standing there. It wasn't too long ago in 1985 my wife and I went over to Germany and looked at a lot of those towns that we had bombed; they had done a magnificent job rebuilding. We went into the church and you could see some of the pock marks from bullets. We never fired at any churches, but they would get hit one way or another.

We were very glad when V-E Day came in May of '45. We started getting prepared to come home. We flew back and had to land in a place called Reykjavik, Iceland, and it was very cold and very windy there. It was pretty hard for them to support all the incoming aircraft with what available food they had, but we made out all right. We came back, and we landed in a place called Bradley Field in Connecticut. What surprised me about all the crewmen was that they were running to a wagon. I said, "They must be feeding over there." But someone said, "No, they're not feeding; that's the 'milk wagon'." I particularly didn't like milk, and it surprised me how many of those guys were starving for a glass of cold milk.

James Regas tells a story of life-long military service and a life full of accomplishment. He is now retired and living happily in Natrona Heights, Pennsylvania.

Glenn Rojohn

100th Bomb Group
350th Squadron
Pilot

by
Emily Thomas

[Gregg Thompson's painting "The Piggy-Back Flight" featured on the cover of this book illustrates part of the following narrative.]

Mr. Glenn Rojohn had war experiences like no other. He rode piggy-back in mid-air and he tells his story with obvious emotion. It isn't somber; it's one of pride and an almost juvenile excitement.

They always woke us up at two a.m. in the morning to fly. The orderly woke me up, and I said, "Well, who am I flying with today?" "Well," he said, "you're flying your own crew today. You're going to be the pilot because we have a maximum effort. We have an important city to bomb." (The pilot was supposed to fly about five missions with another crew as a copilot to learn what's going on and how to handle things.) We awoke at two, got dressed, breakfast at three, briefing at four, and takeoff at five. That was just the normal run of everything.

In the briefing room, there was a stage where all the commanding officers were, with a big curtain. Every day we had a briefing. That's where the lead navigator gave the navigators a briefing, the lead bombardier gave the bombardiers a briefing, and the gunners got briefed, and so forth. All this time they didn't tell you what the target was.

What happened on this first mission, was they pulled back the curtain, and my target was Berlin. On this first mission, we got out over the North Sea, on our way to Berlin, and about half-way over, we were in formation and everything was going fine. I looked up ahead, and there was this big, black cloud. I radioed down to my navigator, Bob Washington, and said, "Wash, what is that?" He says, "It's flak, and we fly through it." We got through that all right, but with a few holes. Then we got to Berlin. On our way into the target, we got hit with very heavy flak again. My buddy was flyin' [his plane] on the left wing, and all of a sudden all I could see was a red flash, and he just disintegrated. He just wasn't there. The next thing I knew our plane shuddered, we got hit pretty hard. My waist gunner got hit in the head. We got our bombs dropped and got back to the base. We had a lot of holes in the airplane. When we landed the Colonel came up, and he said, "Well, how'd it go?" I said, "Sir, if they're all gonna be like this, it's gonna be a long war." That was my first mission, my indoctrination.

The last mission I flew was to Hamburg which was pretty deep into Germany. We were to be bombing I think it was submarine pens. We turned into the target from the north. I don't think at that time anyone knew too much about the Jet Stream. But we got into that target in an awful big hurry because the wind was blowing at more than a hundred miles an hour, maybe even more than that. We had a lot of flak going into the target. We got our bombs dropped, and turned around to go back, but now we're fighting a headwind, so we were only going fifty or sixty miles an hour ground speed.

That gave the German antiaircraft people a real shot at us, and it also gave the fighters a real shot. Our group got back out to the North Sea, and we were in a real fire fight. The German fighters were coming through our group; they were so close to us that I could see the faces on those German pilots. We were really into a mess.

All of a sudden I heard a crash, and my plane started to shudder. I realized I had a mid-air collision with another airplane. What happened was I was trying to fill a void in the formation, and I think the other fella was maybe trying to do the same thing. We'd lost twelve planes just like that. We crashed and pancaked one on top of one another and stuck together. There was no way I could get the two planes apart.

Now, I was the top plane, the bottom plane's engines were runnin', and one of my engines was on fire. There was a lot of fire, so my copilot and I shut down the engines of my plane to try to save from there being more fire. I was able to hold the plane in a flying attitude, simply by brute strength with the wheel.

If I were to let go of the controls, the plane would start to spin. No one would've been able to get out because centrifugal force would not have let that happen. We kept it in this position, to where my navigator, bombardier, engineer, and radio operator all bailed out, and at that point I told my - I ordered my copilot to bail out. He says, "No." He disobeyed my orders, and he said, "We're going to ride it out together." So it probably ended up he saved my life. I don't know how long I could have held this together without [him]. We kept the two planes flying together. We went into some circles, and we landed in Germany. We hit the ground, and I bounced off the bottom plane and continued for about a hundred yards. My left wing went through a German headquarters building. All of a sudden we came to a stop, and looked around. Bill and I looked at one another. We're still here. We're still all right. There was a big hole in the plane. We jumped out, and we were free.

We were captured immediately 'cause they were awful mad at us. It was up in an area where there wasn't much activity, so there weren't very many soldiers there.

Only three of the other crew survived. We think that the pilot and copilot were wounded or killed. The ball-turret gunner survived. The navigator survived and the gunner survived. The ball-turret gunner, I found out, lived in Cleveland, and we became very close friends until he passed away two years ago. I've talked to the navigator in Florida. The other fella just passed away. He was in Texas. There's really only one from that bottom plane surviving right now, and he's not in very good shape.

Of course, my ball-turret gunner didn't survive the crash because there was no way for him to get out. My tail gunner apparently bailed out too quick and possibly was drowned in the ocean because I never heard from him. I never heard from my waist gunner who did the same thing. My radio operator landed on an island which was the [German] antiaircraft battalion, and he was captured. My flight engineer landed in the water. His parachute didn't collapse, and the wind stayed in his chute and dragged him up on shore, and he survived. My navigator and bombardier landed on land. My navigator landed in a bunch of telephone wires by a railroad track, and he was just dangling (laughs), but he was captured right away.

The tail gunner that flew with me through many missions, unbeknownst to me, got frostbitten in his ears and had gone on sick call. I had a replacement tail gunner which I never saw, and he didn't survive.

The civilians, and the army that was there got us all together and put us in a schoolhouse until they decided what to do with us. They tried to interrogate us. We ended up being shipped. I was shipped out to Frankfurt, Germany to an interrogation center. What they did was throw me into solitary confinement for what was close to a week. They were trying to soften me up to see how much information they could get from me. We were only allowed to give our name, rank, and serial number. So anytime they asked me a question, I told my name, rank, and serial number. Finally they said, "Colonel Jefferies was your CO whenever you took off on your trip to Hamburg, and Colonel Sunderman took over yesterday." It shows you what kind of intelligence they had - spies and what-have-you. They told me where I went to school, I was on the school tennis team, and I worked in a bank in McKeesport. I finally said, "You know more than what I could ever tell you." And he let me go. We stayed there for a few more days and then went up to a prison camp up in the Baltic, and there's where we stayed until the war was over.

For all of his efforts, Mr. Rojohn received many honors and awards, including the Purple Heart.

The building that his left wing crashed through turned out to be some sort of German women's quarters. Fortunately, it was empty at the time of impact.

It has been said of Mr. Rojohn's experience that "There have been amazing stunts pulled in the colorful and courageous history of man's will to fly... but none more strangely heroic than the day Rojohn and Leek safely crash-landed their two planes pick-a-back on a field in North Germany."

A special note of thanks to Mr. Glenn Rojohn for granting the interview, and to Teresa K. Flatley, writer of Breeding Dragonflies, from whom I borrowed the final quote.

Flak bursts.

(Photo courtesy Robert Kimball)

Richard Smith

96th Bomb Group
338th Squadron
Copilot

by
Eric Bella

Richard Smith joined the war effort at the age of twenty-three. When Smith was just sixteen years old, he already had the skills and training to fly planes. He was a member of the 338th Squadron, and in the 96th Bomb Group. Officially, he was the co-captain and copilot of his crew. Smith's account of war life can be viewed as a microcosm of what thousands of other soldiers experienced in the 8th Air Force. Their heroic efforts should be applauded not only through our recognition, but also through our appreciation, because they helped to preserve something we all take for granted: our freedom.

Before the war, Smith worked in the gas fields, drilling gas wells - a high profile, well-paying job. It was a career that he had been involved in previous to the war, in which he continued along after the war. With the postwar prosperity, he was able to support and care for his ten children.

Smith recalled his experience on the day Pearl Harbor was attacked: "When Pearl Harbor was bombed, I remember flying that particular Sunday someplace between Greensburg and Butler. I landed at Greensburg, and when I landed they took my plane. They did not want any planes in the air because they did not know what was happening. I had to leave my plane and could not fly for awhile."

Because he was in the gas business, he was automatically deferred from the draft. However through his patriotic spirit and love of his country, he decided that the Air Force could use his skills as a pilot. Another incentive was the fact that most of his friends had already enlisted.

Before he could join the action in Europe, Smith had to undergo several long, grueling months of training and education. Since he did not have a college degree, Smith had to endure the pains of textbook and physical training at the same time. He attended the University of Tampa, where, for nine months he received a crash course in everything from advanced math to shooting a gun. He took an equivalent of two years of college during this time. To say the very least, those nine months of Smith's life were "very difficult." According to Smith, "I had to get up early in the morning, where I studied and trained most of the time, and for the rest of the day I had mili-

Nose art.
(Photo courtesy Edward Jones)

tary training."

During the war, Smith was stationed at Netherson Base, in northern England. His crew was very diverse. "The people were from all over the place. In my crew, the people were from California, Oklahoma, North Carolina, Ohio, New Jersey, and Florida." Not surprisingly, since most of the crew were in their teens, only Smith and the captain had any form of post high-school education.

Smith had a very interesting trip over to Europe. He described the people in Britain. "I couldn't believe how nice they treated us. Even though they did not have any money, goods, or even decent facilities, they were very kind and generous towards us. I remember going in to a hall to order a sandwich, expecting a big, juicy chunk of meat, and instead I only got a piece of bread with some condiments on it. That's how desperate the situation was at certain times."

During combat Smith and his crew acted in a very professional manner. He thought of the war as a job that must be done in an efficient, straightforward, and effective manner. Keeping this in mind, it was easy to see his point of view in his description of the battle conditions: "When you are flying in combat, you don't get the chance to notice things. It's just like flying cross-country. When we were on a mission, we flew around 25,000 feet. The highest we ever flew was 29,500 feet, which was over Berlin. That was very high. Before the mission, they would wake us up at maybe three-thirty or four o'clock in the morning, to go up and have breakfast. Then we'd go into the briefing, and they'd tell us about just what our mission was. Then they would assign us a plane. We didn't have any particular plane. You would fly this plane one day, another plane another day. Our squadron was made up of, maybe twenty-five crews, and we had twelve or fourteen planes. We couldn't fly every day. One interesting thing that happened was that we'd get reports on the radio from Germany on where we were going to fly that day. So sometimes the Germans knew where we were going on a particular day. That in itself was a little bit nerve-wracking. This didn't happen often. The bad thing was that we couldn't switch our mission. We had no choice. The head tells us that this "group" is going to fly to such and such point. That was their mission for the day. They would send around two, three thousand planes. It all depended on what mission it was. They would decide how many planes they were going to send over there, and assign a group to fly into that particular area. They had specific targets. The reason we could not change missions was because these missions had to be planned, and the planning that was in the works was handed down, till it finally got down to our air base.

" We only got credit for fifteen missions, because on four, we flew over them and were not able to hit the target. This was due to cloud cover, or a malfunction within the plane. But we had fifteen completed missions. I remember watching "Memphis Belle." I would have to say it was a pretty accurate portrayal of what happened. There wasn't too much out in left field, I'd say it was pretty comparable to what happened in our crew. It's pretty amazing, because of the fifteen missions we were on, there was only one mission where we didn't have a hole in us. They were shooting at us all the time. The only contact with the enemy was with the fighter planes. We got hit about two or three times with jets. Believe it or not, they had jets. We didn't. Every time we got hit with jets they would approach us from the front head on. Of course we were probably going one hundred fifty miles an hour, and they were probably going three hundred miles an hour. We really could not get a good look at them. They more or less looked like a bat coming through. They were small, and interrogation wanted to know everything they could about them. It was hard because we could not give them too much of a description on them.

"When we flew a mission, there was

something called an initial point, where we would fly to an area, going at the same speed and altitude, for a distance of about twenty miles, to where the target area was located. Then, the bombardier flew the plane, and had a bomb sight, which was like looking through a telescope-like device to help him drop the bombs. As soon as the hairs of the telescope crossed the target, the bombs dropped automatically. Since we were flying in formation, there was no plane or flak-dodging involved. They would shoot lots of flak at us. Each time they shot one, a cloud of flak would suddenly appear for an instant. You could see the flak bursting in front of you. They seemed to get closer and closer to you, but you couldn't do anything about it. You had to go straight through the cloud of flak if it was in front of you. That is how we got all of the bullet holes in our plane.

Nose art.
(Photo courtesy Edward Jones)

"We had fighter planes to escort us, but most of the time they would escort us part of the way, and then we would lose them because they did not have enough fuel. That is where we would get picked up with the fighters. There was a few trips where they had Tokyo Tanks, or tanks of fuel hanging on the wings. These tanks held in the neighborhood of one hundred gallons each. They would follow us, in a sort of flying formation, until we heard the cry 'Bandits in the area.' The fighter planes would immediately drop their wing tanks. Then, they proceeded to pursue the German planes."

When the bombs dropped, Smith did not think much about the people the bombs were going to kill. Instead, he thought of the targets he was going to hit: "Our main targets were railroad, factories, and refineries. We did not look at it as bombing people. If the people happened to be there, that was it."

Out of all the missions Smith has flown, the scariest moment occurred during his fifth mission: "A twenty millimeter hit us in the bomb bay, and some of the metal went up right behind the cockpit, and started something like a hydraulic fire. Soon, the cockpit was filled up with smoke. So everybody, like the armored gunner, pulled away from the oxygen, and passed out. It was a real disaster. It was very difficult to get everything under control. But, luckily, we survived."

"There really was not anybody I looked up to or admired. We were pretty much, as a fighting unit, by ourselves. We didn't necessarily have anybody leading or guiding us. Well, we had a commander, but they did not really give us many orders. Our crew was made up of about nine or ten men, depending on what mission we were flying and where we were going. So it wasn't like you were being told what to do.

"When we flew combat, we really didn't have a lot of time to socialize. Any time we had off, we would go to London or someplace, but the rest of the time was usually occupied with other military chores. A typical day started around three or four in the morning. We flew all day, and you would get back at around five o'clock at night.

Then, you had to go through interrogation, and this and that. By the time you got through, you were ready to hit the sack. There was not a lot of comradeship, except between you and your crew."

Smith never got to meet any enemy soldiers, because "I was always separated from them. You could understand why. We were twenty-five thousand feet high, and the enemy was on the ground. I couldn't even see who we were bombing.

"There weren't many funny or humorous things that happened. In our crew, we conducted ourselves in a manner with the attitude that we had a job to do. We were very business-like in our actions. We did it as well as we could, and came back. That was more or less it."

Sadly, not all of Smith's friends came back: "I had a friend of mine who went through school with me. He was stationed in a base adjacent to me. When I found out where he was at, I went to visit him. But the very day I went to see him, he was shot at the controls. It was very hard to lose a close friend."

Over a period of time, after several missions, Smith's journey became less and less meaningful in his eyes: "I was the oldest man in my crew. Some of the kids on the plane were only eighteen or nineteen years old. We were all young and daring. But most of all, we were tired. You get to the point where you don't give a darn what happens. I think that's what happens in the infantry also. You are pushed and pushed and pushed 'til you get to this stage of the game, and you don't care anymore.

"It was a wild party when the war was over. There was a farm community all around us, and in England the farmers would make haystacks outside. Some of the guys got flare guns, and they were shooting the guns in the air, and of course it caught the hay stacks on fire." This is probably what occurred in farms all over England during those moments.

Today Smith feels war is "a crazy thing that is never going to end. It is such a stupid thing because nothing has ever been settled. It is like a fire. You put this one out, and another comes. The people in our country have no idea what war is all about. You have to talk to the British, French, or any of the European countries - in other words, the countries that were involved in the battle area itself. I have to give the British a lot of credit for all that they put up with. The sacrifices and hardships they went through were truly remarkable. They were always jolly around us. After the war I traveled around Europe. It was devastating. All that was left were walls. It was a real problem."

In the end, the war was both "duty and adventure" to Smith. Flying was like a whole new life. He would certainly fight for America again, if the cause was just. He "wouldn't think twice" about protecting our country. Richard Smith was just one of the thousands of valiant contributors during World War II. His courage and determination were admirable. Because of people like Smith, the 8th Air Force will be remembered as a huge factor in restoring peace.

B-17 "Chaps Flying Circus" on which Rusty Pegg was the tail gunner.
(Photo courtesy Tom Brown)

Victor Troese

448th Bomb Group
92nd Squadron
Navigator

by
Jeanne Fischer

Nowadays, we tend to forget World War II and the brave men who fought in it, and we don't realize that many of the dignified older Americans that pass through our lives are World War II veterans. This fact was brought home as I entered the residence of my interviewee. I was shocked to discover that he was a familiar person to my mother. With an unbelievable memory and a quiet, yet polite demeanor, this obvious family man ushered me into his living room. His wife, Rose, sat quietly, listening with pride to her husband recounting his World War II memories. As I listened, his eyes began to dance with excitement and mischief as he reminisced about humorous incidents and desperate fighting moments.

Before the war, I was working as an apprentice plumber in my hometown, at Rimersburg Plumbing and Heating. Later, I was working at a rubber plant in Beaver when I decided to enlist in the Air Force. It was late 1942, and I figured I was going to get drafted anyhow, so I might as well volunteer for the branch I wanted. When I enlisted in the Air Force in 1943, my hope was to be a pilot. At first, I went to Miami Beach for two months of training, then I was sent to College Detachment Training (CDT) at the University of Cincinnati in Ohio. After I had completed this, I was sent to the Classification Center in San Antonio, Texas. It was at the Classification Center that it was determined whether you would be a pilot, a bombardier, or a navigator. At that point in the war many bombardiers had been killed, so there was a shortage. We were pretty much told we had to become bombardiers or get out; so I was sent to Houston, Texas to become a bombardier. But while I was in Houston, we were informed that the Air Force needed navigators, and if we chose to become navigators, we could leave Texas. I jumped at the chance to get out of Texas and was sent to the University of Miami in Coral Gables, Florida, where I attended the Pan-American Airways Navigation School.

After graduating from navigation school, I was sent to England. My base was in a place called Scething. I flew a total of thirty-four missions. At that time you were required to fly thirty-five missions to get out, so I was one short of the cutoff. My missions lasted anywhere from six to ten hours. One of our major concerns during our missions were the Ack-Ack guns. These were German anti aircraft guns that were shot at our planes. When the shots exploded, they sent bits of metal flying. The Ack-Ack were mostly concentrated over Berlin and Hamburg, so if we could get out of it, we tried not to go there.

One time I remember; it must have been a little after my twenty-fifth mission, our tail gunner was sick. So, they sent up a veteran tail gunner, who wanted to get his missions completed on a run with my crew. At that point in the war, we hadn't seen too much fighting in the air, so our crew was somewhat "complacent." It was at this time that the Germans had invented the jet airplane. The crew was talking on the intercom when the tail gunner cut in saying, "I think I see a... Bandit at nine o'clock...," and then we heard him firing his gun. The jet took a few shots at us and then decided he'd had enough. The pilot hadn't been on the intercom and wanted to know what the puffs of smoke out the window were. (They were the shots the German jet had shot at us.) If it hadn't been for that experienced tail gunner, none of us would be here today. Needless to say, after that mission my crew and I were far from "complacent."

Another desperate moment that I can recall was when our gas lines had been hit and were leaking. So the bombardier and engineer put those little oxygen tanks on their chests, and they didn't have any chutes on or anything. They walked out on the catwalk with the bomb bay doors wide open, flying up some twenty thousand feet, and they took their nylon scarves off their necks and wrapped them around those lines to try and slow down the gas leaks. At that point we were about 450 miles from home, and we still had to fly over the North Sea, so we started our flight home. Of course, we had no idea how much gas we had. I told the pilot to stay about twenty-one miles from the shore. That way, if we ran out of gas, we could glide into shore. On the other hand, twenty-one miles was far enough away that the Ack-Ack guns couldn't reach us. We flew that way for one hundred miles and then just made a moment's decision to fly the 350 miles over the North Sea. It was pretty anxious flying those last 350 miles, but luckily we made it to England where we landed at the first airport we came to.

One of the things that we always wore in the air were our oxygen masks. The reason we wore them was because flying at such high altitudes would cause you to pass out if you didn't. Most people don't realize how quickly you'll pass out. Sometimes if you're just sitting you won't pass out; but as soon as you go to do something, you're out like a light. We also wore flak suits in the air, to protect us from the flying metal of the Ack-Ack guns; and heated suits, trust me, those planes were leaky, and it was plenty cold. Well, one time I had an experience when I couldn't get the vest of my flak suit over my arm. So the nose gunner, who was

Victor Troese and crew - Kneeling, left to right - John Lyles, Charles Quirk (Pilot), Victor Troese (Navigator), Ed Rutter (Copilot), Wilczak (Bombardier). Standing, left to right - Kelly, Hoover, John E. Sharpless, Robert K. O'Connell, Kenneth Olson.

in the turret, told me he'd help me. So he pulls his mask off and he just put his hand on my arm to help me, and his hand went real heavy. He had passed out on me. So I quickly put his oxygen mask back on and revived him. But that just shows how fast you'd pass out up there.

One time, the safety of the crew depended on me. You see, we'd been flying over Germany and had gotten one of our engines shot out. We were losing altitude, but we did our best to fly with the formation. If the Germans had spotted us having trouble, they would have finished us off on the spot. Finally, though, the pilot decided he'd better break away from the formation and land in France. We were heading west toward England when all of a sudden my compass showed us flying south. The pilot had been given the coordinates of a field where he could land in France. He was trying to get there using his radio compass. Unfortunately we were in a storm, so the needle on the compass was going haywire. At this point we had no idea where we were. Then I remembered that English planes were equipped with a G-Box that gave out signals to lost planes, so they could figure out where they were. I went to turn it on, but it wouldn't work because someone had put a jackbox in front of it. So I just pulled the jackbox off the wall and then quickly figured out where we were. Then we started home. We had come to an airport and were about to land, so I had abandoned my post in the nose, because the nose always crumples during a crash landing. Wouldn't you know it, the pilot lost the airport again. I was just about to go back to the nose to find out where we were when the pilot spotted the airport and landed the plane.

When asked what he had gained from this war experience, my interviewee answered that it caused him to become very philosophical, and it gave him the opportunity to travel to foreign countries. He also noted to me his feeling that war is not a good answer. He pointed out that in World War II we fought against the Japanese, but today our country is friends with Japan. At the time he felt Hitler had to be stopped, and if war was the only way to stop him, so be it. On the other hand, he mentioned that today, the reasons for going to war are not as valid as the idea of stopping Hitler. I asked if he would have wanted his sons to have this experience, and he replied, "Yes." The thing I'll go away from this interview remembering, was his statement that he "wouldn't have missed it for the world, but he wouldn't want to do it again."

Robert A. Wiesemann

389th Bomb Group
566th Squadron
Pilot

by
Lindsey Kostelnik

Mr. Robert Wiesemann speaks very intelligently and is descriptive when he relates his memories. It is apparent that his heart is behind his stories, and it becomes easy to visualize the events he recreates in his mind. He is an extremely friendly man who gladly welcomes a high school student into the privacy of his home. He deserves recognition for his bravery, and this is an attempt to offer thanks by immortalizing him in the hearts of grateful Americans.

Wiesemann was a pilot in the 389th Bomb Group in the Eighth Air Force. He gave a brief description of each of his crew members. "My copilot was a rugged Westerner from Garfield, Kansas. His name was [Bill] McDowell but he was just "Mac" to the boys. Bill Liming, my bombardier, was from Dayton, and he was always talking about things he planned to do when he got out of the Army. My navigator, Dunford, was from Winston-Salem, North Carolina. He had a lot of sarcastic wit and a habit of chewing his fingernails. Homer Thompson, my radio operator, was a Texan, and that's all we ever heard. My engineer was from Boston. His name was Robert McManus. From just outside Boston came Robert Turcotte. He was cynical, and also he consistently talked of his girlfriend, Margo. "Porky" Prior was one of my waist gunners, and the tail gunner's name was Blair. They were both from Kentucky. Prior...always talked about his wife and the farm he wanted to own. Blair kept the whole crew laughing and was just crazy about Roy Acuff's heart songs. Marlin Morrison, or "Mike," was a big Irishman with a wonderful sense of humor. He had a wife, and from the way he talked, he was just nuts about her. We were ten men thrown together by fate and destined to face all sorts of situations together. After we got to know each other, we were more like one big, happy family. We got a reputation as being a lucky crew, and everybody wanted to fly missions when we flew.

A funny incident occurred on the way to Goose Bay, Labrador on the first leg of our flight to England. There was always a little rivalry between B-17s and B-24s. The B-24 had an optimum altitude for bombing missions of twenty to twenty-five thousand feet. The B-17 would fly maybe twenty-eight to thirty thousand feet. But the B-24 could carry more; they carried four 2000 pound bombs. Anyway, there was always this rivalry, and while we were still in the United States getting ready for takeoff, my tail gunner was being razzed by the crew chief on the B-17 that was parked next to us. I said, "Don't worry about that." But he was so upset. Anyway, we took off. In fact, the B-17s did not fly as fast as the B-24s. So they let the B-17s take off first so that we would all be arriving at about the same time. We caught up to the B-17, and I told my tail gunner, "Watch this!" We climbed about five thousand feet above them and put the airplane into a dive. We feathered the props on all four engines, so that the propellers were all standing still. We came from five thousand feet, and we hit the red-line flying speed for a B-24. We flew right by him without any engines running. (Laughs.) Then we started up the engines again later. Anyway, we landed in Goose Bay way ahead of them; and by the time they got there, the protective coverings were on the engines. My tail gunner, needless to say, had a lot of fun. (Laughs.)

Robert Weisemann
(Photo courtesy Robert Weisemann)

The second leg of our flight to England took us to Meeks Field in Iceland, and they had to do some work because we had a problem with the oil cooler on the engine. The fellow who was doing the work on it, noticed that I was standing around watching what he was doing. He said, "Hey, aren't you ever going to bed? It's one o'clock in the morning." I said, "Gee, it's still daylight." He says, "Yeah, you might as well stay up for fifteen more minutes and watch the sun go down and come right back up again." (Laughs.) And it really did. It went down and came back up again. It never really got dark.

On my first mission, I flew as an observer. It was to become familiar with various procedures. You had to form up into squadrons, then from squadrons into groups, and from groups into the bomber stream. There was a procedure for that, and you had to become acquainted with it and also the procedures for a bomb run and so forth. So I was always one mission ahead of my crew. What happened to many crews was, their pilots finished first, [because of their first mission as an observer] and they had no pilot. To get their one last mission, they had to wait around until they can get a chance to fly with someone else. So when I got my thirty-fifth mission, my crew came to me and asked me to fly with them on their last mission.

On the sixteenth of August in 1944, we flew a mission to Dessau, Germany. That was probably, from a psychological standpoint, the worst mission that I was ever on. There were some other missions that were pretty tough, but that was the worst one. We took off and flew up over, sort of northeast, across Denmark and down between Denmark and Berlin. As we were flying on the southern leg, we looked up to the east, and we saw that the sky was filled with flak. We said, "Boy, someone over there is really getting it." So we flew on south and turned east, then the flare went off, and we turned north. That block of flak-filled sky was right in front of us. We were flying into that, and right at our altitude was where the twelve-gun battery was firing. You get to recognize these things because you see twelve bursts of flak go off at one time; that means it is a twelve-gun battery firing. As we're flying in, there's twelve bursts, twelve bursts, twelve bursts; and just as we approached that area it stopped. They have to stop firing and let the gun barrels cool. Otherwise, the barrels would warp, and they'd lose their accuracy. I told my crew that they had stopped, and they were happy about that. (Smiles.) Just as we went through, my tail gunner said, "There they go again." And they shot down the plane that was flying right behind us. There were many airplanes going down. In fact, the one thing I remember most vividly is seeing a whole wing just fluttering down. You see people in parachutes, you know, and airplanes going down all around us. That was the worst mission from a psychological standpoint.

One of the later missions to Hamburg, we had over one hundred holes in our plane when we got back. That was the one where I thought I had my arm shot off. The bomb bay doors were open, and a shell went off very, very close to the airplane and hit me on my crazy bone. My hand was on the throttle when the flak hit me, and it felt like my arm was gone, but it was still there. (Laughs.)

On November 9, 1944, we flew a mission to the forts at Metz in France. The French had built these forts as a defense against the Germans, but the Germans were occupying them. General Patton was probably one of the heaviest users of air support in this campaign, and he had us come in and drop two thousand pound bombs on the forts. Now there's no way you can destroy them, but the concussion of the bombs made it easy for them to move in and take over the forts, because it knocked the people silly.

There was one mission we didn't fly. We briefed for a mission in support of Patton, and just as we were completing the briefing and getting ready to go up in the airplanes, the officers came running in and told us it was cancelled because Patton had taken the target. (Laughs.) He moved pretty fast, and he reached a situation where he didn't have any maps so he was actually using road maps. (Laughs.)

It was January 5, 1945, I was over the target [Neustadt, Germany], on a bomb run, and we had a shell go right through our wing. It went right through the number four engine. My waist gunner, he was a big guy, he said; -(laughs)- it was funny because he was stammering and we used to call him "Porky", "The, the, there's a hole" -(laughs)- just like Porky Pig, "There's a hole big enough for me to crawl through." We couldn't see the hole, but we could see jagged pieces of metal sticking up. So we went ahead and dropped our bombs, and then we left the formation and went down to a lower altitude. Fuel was being sucked out because the tank had been ruptured, so I had the flight engineer close off the line. Later, we were told that the people who got back from the mission reported that we had gone down in flames 'cause they thought that the fuel that was coming out of the hole was smoke. And then we disappeared in the clouds, so they couldn't tell. Anyway, we looked down and were going to try to get back to England. We had enough fuel that we could make it on three engines. But then we let down to a lower altitude because you can get a better performance. When we got about five miles off the Belgian coast, we lost another engine. It was also damaged when we got hit. And so we decided that we had better turn back to the continent. So we did and began looking for a place to put the plane down. We saw a highway and thought, "Oh , we can land on a highway." Then we got closer and realized that there was a tree line right down the middle of it; -(laughs)- it was a divided highway. My nose gunner spotted a field and said, "I see a field with a B-17 sitting on it." I said, "Boy if there's a B-17 on it, we can get in there." See a B-17 needs a longer runway to land, so I knew that our B-24 could make it. Just as we got close to the field, power lines popped up over the horizon. So we had to climb over those, but that was no problem. We put the plane down; it stopped after about eight hundred feet - which was extremely short. And when we got out, my flight engineer climbed out on the wing, and I said, "What are you doing?" He said, "I want to find out how much gas we have left." (Laughs.) He had this big, long stick that he stuck in the hole. He said, - "Well, -(laughs)- it just wets the very tip of the stick." And he said, I remember him saying, this, "We can probably clean a pair of gloves." (Laughs.) But we were happy to be down. And we didn't know this at that time, but that B-17, incidentally, had not made it. It was off the end of the field and had its landing gear wiped out. It had tried to make it but hadn't made it. We used almost all of the runway, but we made it. Anyway, the people that were manning this [British] base came running out with cups, and I said, "Oh boy! I wonder what it is. It's probably rum!" (Laughs.) It was tea. So we stayed one night in that little town right by Brussels, then they took us into Brussels. We went into a schoolhouse that had been occupied by the Germans. It was interesting because they had painted the whole inside of the school with murals. We were there for a couple of weeks. We must have looked pretty scraggly because we had no clothes to wear other than our flying suits. So we were walking around Brussels in our flying suits and our beards. We were low priority, so we had to wait to get a flight back to England. When we did get back, we had to go all over the base to get our stuff back because everyone had supposed that we were not coming back. In fact, they told us that if we had gotten back to the base one day later our parents and closest relatives would have received "Missing in Action" notices. But as it was, they didn't get them.

We completed our missions, but my copilot and I didn't want to go back to the States at that time because they were sending B-24 pilots over to the South Pacific. We really didn't care for that, so we went to a lot of different bases looking for a job. We actually went from base to base. We finally got a job, and the job was to go over to France into some place where a B-24 had crash landed, and they had patched it up and fueled it up. We'd go and fly it out of the field and bring it back to the base. Then they would fix it up and do a little bit of additional work, and then we'd fly it across the Channel to a depot in England. Then they'd fly us back and we'd do it again. On V-E Day, we were over in France getting ready to fly an airplane back, and we knew that they were going to announce it while we were over the Channel. We had flare pistols with us, but we were over the Channel and figured that no one would see them, so we waited to fire them. We got to England, and we stayed at a lower altitude. The hospitals in England had a long veranda on each floor. When we came by the first one, we could see there were all these patients, some of them in wheelchairs, some of them on crutches, and some of them just standing there, on these verandas. So we flew between the verandas of two levels. We stuck our wing in right over top of these guys. (Laughs.) There were no posts or anything; these things were just sticking out. We started shooting flares. We stopped later and wondered how many fires we started. (Laughs.)

Robert Wiesemann and his copilot, Bill McDowell received a promotion to first lieutenant extremely early in their careers for the techniques they used in formation flying. Weisemann also received a Distinguished Flying Cross, and six Air Medals. An Air Medal was given for every six missions that were completed, but the pilot actually received one Air Medal and the rest were Oak Leaf Clusters which were pinned to the ribbon of the Air Medal. No one on his crew was seriously injured during their missions. The "lucky crew" was split up for the trip back to the United States. Unfortunately, the bombardier, Bill Liming was killed on his way home.

GROUND CREW AND SUPPORT PERSONNEL

© John Gumpper

"Allied air power was the chief factor in Germany's defeat."
Hugo Sperrle
Luftwaffe Field Marshal

Cleon Barber

392nd Bomb Group
578th Bomb Squadron
Crew Chief

by
David N. Snyder

Cleon Barber was a crew chief in the 392nd Bomb Group. This is the story of his involvement in the 392nd Bomb Group and how he got there.

As Cleon Barber and his friends drove into his Uncle Wally's barn to get out of the pounding rain, the lives of millions of people were beginning to change. In his uncle's farmhouse, the family was gathered around the radio listening to the news bulletin alerting everybody in the United States to the tragedy of Pearl Harbor. In order to avoid having his draft notice sent, he and his buddy decided to join the Army Air Corps immediately. He was sent to many different bases while still stationed in the U.S., basically to train him to be a member of the Ground Crew Maintenance. Cleon met his life-long friend Ernie Barber on a train ride from Chanute Field to the Willow Run Ford Motor Company Plant in Michigan, where they were building B-24s. From there, he and the rest of his twenty-five member class were sent to Salt Lake City, Utah. This was almost like a waiting room. They waited here until the Air Force decided where they were to go next. The next stop was Davis Manthon Air Base in Tucson, Arizona. It was in Tuscon that he and another air mechanic, Elmer Goff, completed one of the fastest engine changes ever. The two men were scheduled for night duty, and orders were issued at eight P.M. that the number-three engine needed replaced. Well, Cleon and Elmer got to work, pulling the prop, then the engine. They took the old engine to the storage hanger, retrieved a new one, and had it on and running in time for a test run when the instructors showed up at seven a.m. the next morning. It had been taking civilian employees at the base three days to do the same engine change. Cleon and Elmer did it in eleven hours. As one would imagine, they were the talk of the base for some time. Unfortunately for Cleon, they put him on K.P. duty for thirty consecutive days, which was how the authorities did it at Davis Manthon. On the up side, he never had to pull K.P. the rest of his military career.

When the Air Force called upon his squadron to form the 578th Bomb Squadron of the 392nd Bomb Group, Cleon was left off the list, and Ernie was left on. He questioned the executive officer why he had

Cleon Barber in his service days.
(Photo courtesy Cleon Barber)

been held back. The executive officer told him not to worry, that they usually had other plans for those who were held back. In his case, he was to be line chief on the next cadre to be formed in a couple weeks. But Cleon did not want to be separated from his best friend, Ernie. The officer said that he knew that he and Ernie were such good friends, and since Cleon had made quite a name for himself on an engine change, he would respect his wishes, and make the necessary changes to allow him to remain with his group. This group was now being sent to Alamogordo, New Mexico. After going on a flight to get some bomb racks, they were issued orders to go overseas. They took a train across the country, then a ship to Scotland. From there, another train took them almost down the entire length of England to Wendling, a Royal Air Force base, which had been made available to the United States Air Force. Shortly after, he was assigned to a plane as crew chief, and given five men to work under him. The pilot and his crew asked him if it were all right if the plane took the name of "Miss Diversion." Cleon agreed, and within a few days the squadron artist came out and painted a pretty lady in a bathing suit on the side of the plane.

Few people actually know what the men on the ground crew did. Sure, the pilots and the bombardiers get all the press, but no one actually knows what all goes on on the ground. Most of the crew lived in the barracks, but Cleon lived in a line shack, a little shack on the line, that enabled him to be closer to the planes. Cleon explains it pretty well. A little maintenance, a little fun, and a lot of worrying.

"The incendiary and fragmentation bombs came in tin-lined boxes. Bill Ankoviak [one of his mechanics] was quite handy with a saw and a hammer. I don't know where he came up with a hammer and a saw, but we did have a hammer and nails. We straightened a lot of nails that we took out of the boxes. We scabbed the boards and made 'em long enough. He built a twelve-by-twelve foot shack. We flattened the tin liners out and made shingles that gave us a water tight building. It was large enough for two cots and a stove. I practically lived on the line after the shack was completed, and one of my mechanics stayed with me. They rotated a week at a time, and the two of us could handle a mission take-off...

"When they got ready for a mission, we would be called out between three and three-thirty a.m. and have to get dressed and go ... to our planes. We had to do a pre-flight before the crew came out. They'd give us the bomb load, the fuel load, and the take-off time. Then we'd go out and start pulling props through and takin' the covers off the cockpit glass, if we had 'em, and we usually didn't. We'd just wipe them off. Sometimes we'd have frost, and we'd have to get up on those wings and get all the frost off so that it wouldn't interfere with their air foil. Then we would run them up, check out their manifold pressure, check the right mag, left mag, then change the pitch a little bit on the props. We always checked the oil screens and level. We had to make sure everything was working before the crew came out.

"The group took off, and then waiting began. Ground crews always worried about the combat crews. [We] wondered what shape the plane would be in when it returned - if it returned. We had binoculars, 7 mm x 35 mm, and when they returned, we would pick out our ship when they were on their approach and try to tell if all four engines were turning over.

"It was always interesting when one of my crew was on K.P. I didn't know how they did it, but they were real good at so-called 'midnight requisitioning'. I think that they tried to out-do each other, as we always had butter, jam, crackers, and canned milk...

"One night Bill Ankoviak came in with a whole beef loin over his shoulder. It was late. I was beginning to give up on him. He had to wait 'til it got dark before picking up his contribution from its hiding place. [There were] long days in England. We put it up overhead in the little engineering tent that we had right next [to the line shack], that kept all of our parts and junk in...

"At that time Lieutenant Joe Walker was the pilot of the crew that was assigned to my plane, so we invited him and his crew out for supper. We had steaks, bread and butter, and coffee."

By the end of the war Cleon had only two men for mechanics, and they were responsible for two planes. Most crews were still restricted to one. He was allowed to return to the States after D-Day. After returning home, he resumed the job he left when he enlisted, working for Talon, a tool and die manufacturer in Meadville, Pennsylvania. He also worked for the U.S. Postal Service for many years after the war. Cleon is very strong in his faith and beliefs. He told me, "You had your job to do; and as long as you done it, you were okay." Many of the crew chiefs received Bronze Stars for their service, yet Cleon was overlooked. He was the only man in his squadron who was good enough to get two airplanes to crew. He fulfilled his obligations and responsibilities, but still - no Bronze Star. History doesn't remember medals and awards. It remembers the people, their memories, and what they did for us.

Cleon Barber at home in 1996

(Photo courtesy David Snyder)

Charles Besser

453rd Bomb Group
732nd Squadron
Ground Crew

by
Brooke Swidzinski

Mr. Charles Besser was on ground crew during the war. His experiences have made an unmistakable impact on his spirit. Mr. Besser has an enthusiastic outlook on life. He related his encounters, even the unfortunate ones, with a great deal of laughter.

I was being trained in Boise, Idaho. We were on the night shift. They put us on B-24s. This one had a plexiglass front on it. The instructor said a...part of the fuselage needed air. You needed a high-powered compressor to pump it up. We had these...what they called cleotracks. They were like a tank, pretty much, but they had an air compressor on them that was high powered...lot of psi. [The instructor asked those of us in the] student group, "Who knows how to drive the cleotrack?" I don't remember...[there were] twenty-five of us there. No one was putting up their hand, so I put my hand up. "I can drive them!" So he goes down to the hangar and gets it. So I went down, and I got to start it and came on up about a quarter mile to the airplane with it. [There was] no steering wheel, just two [braking] levers. That's all you have your hands on...two levers, and you want to go [left], you pull the left side back. If you wanted to go to the right, you held [the right lever] back.

Well, I'm coming up, bringing that [cleotrack] right into the nose of that plane, which is all plexiglass. And as I'm coming up to it I thought, "Where in the world's the brakes? There's no brakes. I can't stop it." (Laughs.) I tell you I got so paralyzed I just let go of both levers, and the thing came to a stop. Everyone thought that was great, but I was sweating like mad because...if you [did] any damage you had to...sign a statement and stay in the Army until you paid for it. And I'm looking at this couple-million-dollar plane, and I thought, "I'm running in towards [the plane]...I'm going to have to pay for this...and I'll never get out of here." (Laughs.)

But, anyhow, the next day I asked the cleotrack operator, who was my friend,..."How do you stop that when you want to stop?" He said, "You pull both levers back! You brake both sides!" Simple thing. Simple until you're panicky, and you know you can't [think of the right thing to do.]

Right now I have a snowblower down there with the same gizmo on it, and now I know how to work it. (Laughs.)

But anyhow, we went over on the Queen Elizabeth. There was, I think, twelve thousand troops on the Queen Elizabeth. You only got a bunk every other night. The other nights you had to sleep out in the hallway on the floor. You only got two meals a day.

[One day] I thought, "It's the first time I've been on ship like this. I might as well enjoy it." It was a beautiful day. [There were] all these hundreds of thousands of men running around on the deck. "I might as will enjoy this like some luxury." You could hear loudspeakers, but there was so much commotion you couldn't hear what the loudspeakers were saying. Something shook the ship, and I thought we were hit. I'm not a swimmer, but I [had] already jumped overboard. I figured I'd be better off jumping overboard, getting in the water, than on that ship that's being hit! As it turns out, it wasn't hit. They were dropping depth-charges on the German submarines. The [depth-charges] are huge garbage can-like fifty-five gallon drum-like things that they have on the deck, and they push them overboard. They blow up submarines. So there [were] submarines pursuing us.

The Queen Elizabeth was faster than any of the convoys. So...what it did to avoid submarines was it zigzagged the whole way across the ocean. They'd take a different direction every seven minutes because it takes a submarine nine minutes to line up her sights. By the time they'd get their sights lined up we'd be going a different direction. That's why it took us five days and four nights to get over there, even though it was fast.

That ship was huge. I forget the dimensions of it. The reason I remember [it held] eleven or twelve thousand troops was because our population in Ellwood City [where I lived] at that time was about that same number. I couldn't imagine all of Ellwood City being on that ship. It [moved] so much. We'd be sleeping in the hallways at night. They were three or four feet wide hallways with rubber tile on the floor-always waxed. You would actually slide to either wall every time they'd switch [directions].

Mr. Besser now lives with his wife, Rose, in Western Pennsylvania. They have several pets and enjoy traveling the United States. Both agree that they don't plan on growing old soon. Because of his positive attitude, he is pleasant and entertaining man.

P-51 Mustang being refueled.

(Photo courtesy Tom Brown)

William Bowers

305th Bomb Group
364th Bomb Squadron
Head Mechanic

by
Nicole Beblo

I met her at Kennywood [amusement park.] I worked there. She came out with one of her girlfriends. She told her girlfriend, "There's the guy I'm going to marry." From then on, I didn't have a chance. We've been married now fifty-one years - eight kids all raised and gone.

These are the proud words of Mr. William Bowers. Mr. Bowers has lived a prosperous life. He refers to his days in the military as some of his best. A twinkle comes to his eye every time he looks back and reflects upon one of his distant but fond memories.

I took care of all the mechanical stuff on the airplane. Except for special stuff: propellers, radio, gunnery, and that. We did repair work like patching holes and changing engines. I had seven airplanes in one year, and I never lost one over enemy territory. They all made it back to England. Crippled or what, they came back.

One time one of my planes was flying in practice formation and the pilot told me, "I'll be flying in the number-two position," which is over in the right-hand side. Well, when he went over the field, he was over in the left-hand side, and him and this other plane were trying to get over where they belonged. When they got above each other, they hit an air pocket; and the two planes went down, and burned.

One night, they told me, "Go with your airplane. You're going over to the next field fourteen miles away." It was a Pathfinder airplane, which instead of a ball turret had a radar dome. It would fly lead in the group. So I had to go with the airplane over to this other field. Well, you've never seen fog like they have in England - never. I ran into a street sign, in the night, on account of the fog. [I] couldn't see.

We got over to this other field, and I stayed there all night with the plane, got it ready, and they started taking off the next morning. Somebody forgot to take the Pitot tube cover off, which is a cover with a little arm sticking out with a hole in it. It gives you your air speed. When he got halfway down the runway he didn't have any air speed, so he put his breaks on. [It was] foggier than heck. He called the control tower, and they shot off flares. Nobody could see them. Here comes another airplane. Boom - into him. Two more airplanes. Boom. Boom. Four airplanes blew up.

A plane took off from our place. There was a string of them waiting. He didn't have enough air speed, and he crashed. The next plane that came down, when he got off the ground, saw the first one and went the wrong way, and lost his lift; and he went down. The next one that came down saw those two; and he lost his lift, and went down. I was in the barracks sleeping. At dinner time I was waking up, and they were talking about bombs going off. I asked them what they were talking about. They asked me if I heard the bombs. "You didn't sleep through that?" they said. I said, " The heck I didn't."

[A] plane came back. The pilot told me he was losing oil pressure in the number-three engine. So I preflighted the engine and found out that oil was getting into the two bottom cylinders. I couldn't pull the prop through when I first started. You have to pull the prop through nine times to clear all the cylinders of oil, then you can start it up. When I took the spark plug out of the bottom cylinder, I got oil. I told the engineering officer, and he said, "Get the engine loose, ready to drop in the morning." We took it all loose, ready to drop. Line chief comes out in the morning and says, "You're supposed to change cylinders not engines." I said, "Get me the engineering officer." The day before we had a meeting with a group engineering officers, and he told us that a crew chief knew his plane. He should have the last word on whether its going to be a cylinder change or an engine change. The engineering officer came down. I said, "What did he [the Line Chief] tell you was wrong with this?" He said, "Couldn't keep the oil pressure up." I said, "He said nothing about oil in the bottom cylinder?" "No." He told me to change the engine. I wasn't going to send someone up in a plane with an engine I knew was going to conk out on them.

One time a plane came back to our field, and everybody said that a bomb had dropped through the front end. So we all went over to take a look at it, and the whole front was gone. The bomb from our own plane above it [had] dropped. It went through there, and it knocked the bombardier and navigator out with it. So some yo-ho major was standing in front of the airplane and he hears, "Shhhhhhh," [from an] oxygen leak. He said, "Somebody get up there and shut the oxygen off." How can you shut the oxygen off when its pipe is hanging loose? (Laughs)

When we first went over [to England] they did not have bullet-proof windshields. The Germans found out about it. They also found out that a 17 can't shoot in the front because there is a dead space. The ball turret couldn't come up far enough, and the top turret couldn't come down low enough. So they'd come in on a head-on attack. That's what killed [our squadron CO]. A bullet went through the windshield, through him, and hit the armor plate behind him which was just a quarter-inch thick. It put a big bow in it and just fell on the floor.

It only snowed one time all the time I was over in England, and we had nothing to remove snow - no snow plows, nothing, because it never snowed over there. We wound up going out on the runway with shovels. Shoveling it in a truck. You wouldn't imagine six hundred feet by sixty feet wide [of runway].

This son-of-a-gun dog, in the morning, he knew we got up, and got on the truck, and went out to the line to work. He was the first one on the truck. He knew we'd come back at eleven thirty AM to eat dinner. He was on the truck waiting. He'd run around the field all by himself. But when it was time for dinner he was on the truck.

We got a brand new airplane. They said, "Get it ready for combat." I got it ready the next day. It went on a mission. Pilot came back. He said, "That son-of-a-b." I said, "What's the matter?" He says, "You can't trim it." Each B-17 has a trim on them. There are wheels in the cockpit that you turn to get the plane to fly level and straight. I thought he was cranky, and didn't like his mission. So I let it go the

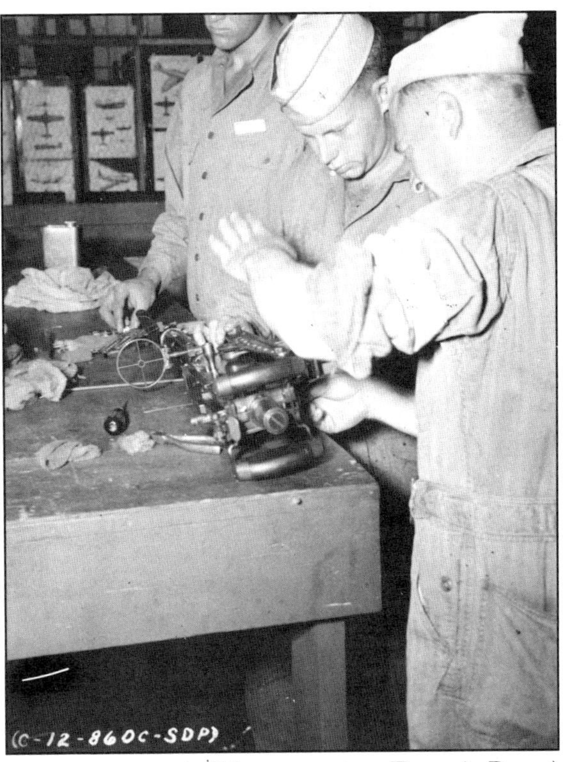

(Photo courtesy Francis Dugo)

first day. The second day he came back and said the same thing. So I went down to the main hangar to get a tensiometer which checks tension on the control cables. I got up in the wing and checked everything. Perfect. I went up in the other wing and saw the cables were not safety wired at the factory. They were hanging down three inches. I tightened them up with a turn level and safety wired it. The next day the pilot went on a mission. When he stopped the plane he came running at me like he was going to kill me. He kissed me. He said, "What did you do to that airplane?" I said, "Nothing, why?" He said, "It flies like a dream." Then I explained what happened.

Mr. Bowers experienced the war through different eyes. Even though he did not actually fly in combat, he saw death and many other elements of war. He even received a soldier's medal for bravery for taxiing a plane containing ammunition away from a burning plane.

Currently, he and his wife, Clara, live comfortably in a cozy home in West Mifflin, PA. Completing their family circle are eight children, seventeen grandchildren and one great-grandchild.

Repairing a .50 caliber machine gun from a P-51's wing.
(Photo courtesy Tom Brown)

Thomas A. Brown

339th Fighter Squadron Photographer

by
Jenn Geibel

Talking with Mr. Thomas A. Brown, I noticed a kind of serenity in his face as he gazed nostalgically into the past. Perhaps, he, more than others, found benefits in the war, especially since it was during his stay in the European Theater that he met and married his present-day wife, over fifty years ago. However, it is likely that even without the initiation of his happy marriage, Thomas Brown would have appreciated his service, for he was doing something he loved to do - photography.

I was working in a steel mill, Pittsburgh Steel, and I was working then making tubing, [when] I was inducted into the service. I was twenty years old. A lot of my friends were being inducted at the same time, but my family, especially my father, was very worried. I guess my mother was, too, but she didn't show it as much as my father did.

First, I went to what they call boot training. It was in a hotel in St. Petersburg, Florida. They'd stripped all the rooms and put six bunks in a room for soldiers and personnel. We were in the hotel, and that's where we learned how to march, basic stuff, handling guns and so forth. After we left there, we took an IQ test to see what we were qualified for, and I ended up as a photographer. I'd done a little bit of it in civilian life so they kinda picked out my vocation for me. I went to a field in Colorado near Denver and that's where I spent three months in photography training. I was trained as an aerial photographer, to go in bombers. At that time they were putting cameras in the planes to take pictures of places as they bombed them, but by the time I got overseas this was all eliminated and electrically controlled, by a switch, which anybody could put on.

Well, I was a base photographer. That's how I got most of my pictures. Probably got a lot more than other people because film was scarce. Of course, being on the base as a photographer, I had access to a lot. I took pictures of all the crashes near the base. There were lots of automobile crashes. The Americans drove on the right-hand side of the road and the English drove on the left, so there were a lot of head-on collisions. I drove on the left side, and I got pretty good at it. I also took pictures of plane crashes and damage to planes. We lost a lot of pilots. Sometimes they didn't all die over enemy territory. Some of them made it back to the base and crashed near the base, and I'd take pictures of the wreckage.

I took pictures for publicity purposes, too. Kids in Hackinsack New Jersey High School got enough money to buy a plane, and they called it "The Comet." They sent it over to our group. What happened was, I was all morning taking publicity pictures for this high school, showing them the plane, and the pilot and his crew, and the last picture I took was it taking off on the field. I went and got my mess kit to go down for dinner, and I got to the top of the hill... I saw him come down and pull out. When he pulled out of the dive, the wing came off and started floating down like a feather. Then the plane started a flat spin. I kept saying, "Jump out. Jump out." Finally I saw his chute. He jumped out, and the plane came down and crashed. Now I went back - I didn't eat dinner - got my camera again, got a jeep, and went off base to take pictures of the crash. So I spent all day long

Thomas Brown ready for action.
(Photo courtesy Tom Brown)

taking pictures. I took publicity and then the crash afterwards. What they did was name another plane "The Comet," so the kids wouldn't be disappointed.

There was always people coming over entertaining. I took pictures of three - Mitzi Mayfair, Kay Frances, and Martha Ray. High brass officials came sometimes, too. I got a picture of General Doolittle. He was the first pilot to bomb Tokyo. We also had to make fake identification papers for pilots, in case they got shot down over in Germany, so they'd have some means of escape if they could get out of there. . . So we took their pictures in civilian clothing and made them fake papers. But sometimes this didn't work because the Germans would see the same clothes on different pilots. They were pretty smart in tracing us down.

I never really got depressed during the war. Some of the fellows I think got very disappointed, but I don't think I ever did. When I was younger I was used to going and camping out away from home, going on fishing trips, hunting in areas that I camped. So I was sort of prepared for it - more so than some of the people. Probably some of the fellows that came from big cities and had never done this before, had only seen home or work, whatever. There was never too much that went on over there as far as bombing and stuff goes. We did see what they call buzz bombs. They were bombs that the Germans had rigged up; they had wings on 'em, and a tail, and they had a little engine on them and they would putt-putt along. And they'd put so much fuel in 'em that when the fuel ran out the bomb would fall down. We'd hear these things. They'd fly about five-hundred feet above the ground. When they cut out we'd have about thirty seconds to find a hole to get into before they went off. But none of them hit real close to us. The closest one was about, let's say, three hundred yards off the base. During the invasion time, they'd send them over quite often. I seen so many of them go over that when the first ones came, well, we used to go into an air-raid shelter, but after a while you sort of get used to them. We'd just sort of stand and watch them go by and figure as long as they went past, we was all right.

When I was getting out of the service they asked if you wanted to reenlist, but since I had a wife and a child at that time, I thought it was best I get out. But they offered me. . . an advance in rank when I got out. The highest I had got was a corporal because once the quota was filled in a group you couldn't advance anymore. A couple of times they had me up for sergeant cause I did a lot of the picture-taking and had more experience than some of the others taking pictures. The major in charge of the photography group at that time wanted to know why I was still a corporal. I think the oddest picture I took, which nobody else could get a picture, of was one of the flights come back [and] there was a hole [in the plane]. Part of the flak went through the wing and out through the top, and they wanted to see if there was any structural damage in between the wings. Nobody knew how to get into the wing to take that picture, so here they took the guns out, and, well, when I went over and looked at it, I looked around and looked inside there. I had a flashlight with me and I shined it inside to see where it was at and found out where the area was. In the holes where the guns jut out, the muzzle-loading guns, I put the flash in one hole and the camera in the other and took the picture that way. It turned out real well, showed them what they wanted to see.

It was an experience, a good experience really, because it's something that you'll always remember. I got the chance to go to the Art Institute in Pittsburgh on the GI Bill, and I graduated from there. I worked three different photography studios. I did work for years afterward until it changed to color photography. I did a little photography before the war but it was my service during the war that helped me get training in it.

Thomas Brown can still thumb through his huge album of pictures from the war, and recall the scenes, events, and circumstances concerning each picture. His album contains photos of everything from bombers, to accidents, to the photographers' dog, Hypo.

After a great deal of adjusting, Mr. Brown and his wife settled down. They had three children, one of which survived a trip from England after being born in the midst of World War II.

Mr. Brown still does photography work today for the church and his own enjoyment.

Lt. Evan Johnson and Capt. Bova standing by "The Comet." See Tom Brown's account in this article for the real story.

(Photo courtesy Tom Brown)

Robert Damico

399th Bomb Group
Crew Chief

by
Kerri Nicastro

Mr. Robert Damico and his wife, Dorothy live in a housing plan just off of Main Street, Saxonburg. When I visited their pleasant house, I did not notice much evidence of World War II, but my assumption that the war had not deeply affected the couple was wrong.

Before he got out of high school, Mr. Damico was working for a company that installed chain-link fences. "I had two brothers older than myself, and they were both in the Navy. The oldest one was drafted. He had two children when he left. My youngest brother enlisted. He wasn't married when he left. When it became time for me to get drafted I got my notice that my foreman wanted to get me a deferment for six months. I told him 'Well, all my buddies are gone, and both my brothers are gone already, I may as well go now that they're calling me.' I was drafted in November, and I left for camp in December. That was in 1942."

His first assignment was to go to Mississippi to Airplane Mechanic's School. After three months, he transferred to Yipsilani, Michigan where he attended a special B-24 school. Next, he was sent to a port of embarkation in Salt Lake City, Utah, where he was supposed to go overseas. "When it came time for the ship out, I was sent to another air base in California. I spent a lot of time at the March Air Force Base in Riverside, California. While I was there, the B-29 became a popular bomber for the US Air Force, and they sent me to Seattle to school where they built the B-29 Bombers.

"When I got (back) to California, I was all hep on going overseas, and I did everything I could to go. I thought I wanted to go, but in the end, I guess I'm glad I didn't have to go, from what I see of people who did. So I spent the last three years of my service in California.

"I was a crew chief on B-24 Bombers, but when they became sort of obsolete, they put me on other kinds of aircraft's, such as P-38s, P-51s. Finally the jet came out, the P-80, and I was crew chief on one of them for my last three months in the service. And then I shipped back home to Indian Town Gap, which was where I was inducted into the service, and I got discharged from there in March of 1945."

As a crew chief in California, Mr. Damico performed the daily inspections on the aircraft: (service them, fill them with fuel and oil, give them a general check-over). "The food we thought was lousy, but it kept us alive, anyway. I got so tired of chicken and eggs, I didn't want to see either one for the rest of my life. But now I like them again. The training that I got was more than what a lot of the fellows got, because of the fact that I stayed in the States, and they kept sending me to school. When I became a staff sergeant, I was able to save up days [off] to work four days in a row at Lockheed Aircraft. The pay wasn't too great, but they did pay us, and it was a good experience to work in a factory where they made fighters since I was always on bombers. I enjoyed it a lot."

Working this extra job, Mr. Damico was able to earn his Airplane and Engine License, but it did not leave him very much free time. "There were three of us that usually went [to Lockheed] together. Me and two of my closest buddies. One was a Jewish fellow, from New York City; one of the best buddies I had. His name was Leon

Bernstein. And my other buddy was from Chicago. His name was Carnavelli, and we kinda stuck together pretty good in the service.

"When we left Salt Lake City, Utah and went to California on a troop train, it took us a couple of days. We were pretty rugged and worn out when we got there. It was just pouring down rain. It rained all that night, and for three days and three nights. It never quit raining. By that time I said, 'Take me back to Utah!' Then after that dried up a little bit; we got a sandstorm, and we couldn't even go out of the barracks for two days! All we could do was cover our faces with handkerchiefs or something and run to the mess hall for our lunches. We couldn't do any work or anything. Two different times we were alerted that we were to go overseas. We packed up all of our gear and did all we had to do to go overseas, and our orders were always canceled."

"Our test pilot, he was a real Joe, he was just an everyday person. He came out one morning to my plane. We had just replaced one of the engines in it; and he said, 'Get a 'chute, we're going for a ride!' I said, 'I don't want to go today.' He said, 'Well, you might as well. Go get a parachute.' So I went in the hanger; they had a place in there where you had to check out a parachute, even if you didn't use one. It was January first, and the Rose Bowl was on. It was just him, the copilot, and myself on what they called a test flight. They would shut down one engine at a time and check them out. He had all four running pretty good. I was standing with my head up in the cockpit watching out ahead. He said, 'Look down there!' I said, 'What's that?' He said, 'That's the Rose Bowl! They're playing football down there!' I couldn't believe it. So we made one pass over the Rose Bowl, then we dropped down and made another. Then, he said, 'Well, we'd better get out of here now. They probably can see the numbers on our plane.' That was really a great experience - flying over the Rose Bowl when they were playing a ball game.

"After being [in California] for two-and a-half years, I finally got used to it. I said, 'Well, I really like it.' I really wanted to go back after the war, but it didn't work out that way.

"Actually, [I met my wife] during the war."

"Before the war," corrected Mrs. Damico.

"Yeah, before the war. I used to attend the church that Dorothy went to. After I left, they put out a newsletter-"

"When you left," chimed Dorothy.

"When I left what?" replied Robert. "Anyway, they put out a newsletter, which she started sending me. That's how we really became better acquainted. We wrote to each other every day.

"[When I left,] Dorothy was quite a bit younger then me. I kissed all the other girls good-bye, but when I came to her I shook her hand. I said to her 'Now you grow up, and when I come home I'll take you out.' So what did I do? When I came home, I married her. (Laughs.)

"Whenever I came home, there were no jobs; no automobiles to be bought. Things were really in a turmoil. Finally, I took a job working at the American Bantam Car Company Plant in Butler, which at the time was making tractor trailers. I worked there for about six months, and then I transferred down to Pullman Standard in Butler, where they made railroad cars. I worked there for three years. I left there and went to work in a coal mine. Later on, I became an electrician. I worked in construction the rest of my working days.

"I think that being in the service is a great thing. I don't regret it one bit now. I think [the other wars are] just a loss of life. It's not necessary. If the people would negotiate more and fight less, everybody would be better off. They're costly, and they're deadly. I had a lot of buddies who went to Europe and fought, which I didn't have to do. I didn't go overseas. Some of them didn't get back."

Francis Dugo

452nd Bomb Group
730th Squadron
Ground Armorer

by
Charlotte Kelly

Imagine saying good-bye and saying it for good. Picture a sky colored in with aircrafts rather than blue. Experience the emotion of helping an entire country that was in need. A nineteen-year-old ground personnel stationed at Deopham Green, England, did not have to imagine, picture, or experience any of these things because he lived them every day of his life from 1944 to 1945. His name was Francis Dugo.

Mr. Dugo joined the war effort in 1944. He was assigned to ground personnel and was in charge of armament. This job included the duty of putting the bombs in place and loading the machine guns with ammunition. Mr. Dugo never met face to face with the enemy, but he encountered a whole different aspect of the war.

He remembers befriending a bombardier for only a short period of time, the "awesome sight" of two thousand airplanes flying above him, and attempting to end starvation in Holland.

Mr. Dugo left for England in January

"Top Hatters" from left to right Francis Dugo, Henry Castel, and Byron Solt on leave in Norwich, England.
(Photo courtesy Francis Dugo)

Francis Dugo on leave with English girl, Rena Dovoni in Trafalgar Square.
(Photo courtesy Franics Dugo)

of 1944. Only a few months after his arrival he was assigned his first plane. It was a B-17G, which was the latest model at that time. One day Mr. Dugo took on the task of cleaning the chin guns. An officer from below yelled to him, encouraging him to do a good job. When Mr. Dugo came down from the ladder he saluted the officer. The officer did not feel that this was necessary. He informed him that the war was a joint effort and that they were all working together towards a common goal. He was surprised and happy the officer felt this way. They soon became friends. The officer was a bombardier. This same officer came into his barracks on the night of March 19, 1944. Mr. Dugo immediately stood up to salute him, and the officer told him once again not to do that. Mr. Dugo recalls, "He was a regular good GI man." He then asked Mr.

Dugo if he would check and clean his .45 automatic, which each officer had in his possession. He offered to do it right away, but the man informed him that it was an extra, and that he must be prepared for tomorrow's mission. Mr. Dugo continued with his regular duties that night - loading the planes with the bombs for the next day's mission. The following morning the crews of the planes had their briefings and then went to their assigned planes. Before the planes left Mr. Dugo spoke to his friend and told him that his .45 would be ready when he returned. The planes then took off. Mr. Dugo returned to his regular day. When Mr. Dugo was about to fall asleep a sergeant by the name of Goldberg came in and informed him that he had some bad news. The sergeant said, "Your plane is o.k., but they had a mishap over the target. The plane above released the bombs, the bombs then went down through the middle of the plane below and killed the bombardier." Mr. Dugo remembers he was very upset about the incident. That evening the plane did return from the mission and there was a burial for the man, but Mr. Dugo was just too upset to attend. His response to the incident- "Those boys that fly - they say the enemy was coming at them, but we didn't but we had a different way of fighting the war we saw our guys go and never come back."

His memories of this incident during the war were brought back to life when Mr. Dugo returned to England to visit his son, who is part of the United States Air Force stationed there. It was during this visit that he attended the grave of the bombar-

Francis Dugo (middle), Gordon Christensen (left), and Robert Gaither (right) load the first napalm bombs ever to be used by the 8th Air Force at Deopham Green, Norfolk, England on April 15, 1945. The plane shown here ("The E-rat-icator") was a veteran of 125 missions. It was destined to be the only original B-17 of the 452nd Bomb Group to survive the war and return to the U.S.A.

(Photo courtesy Francis Dugo)

dier, Lieutenant Lawrence Anderson. The grave was located at the American Cemetery near Cambridge, England. Although over four decades had come and gone, Mr. Dugo continued his friendship with a man who had died so heroically.

There were sad times during the war, but there were also good times for the nineteen-year-old fulfilling his duty for his country. One of these was spent being part of a band. He played bass fiddle. He performed three or four nights a week at different officer's clubs and different fields. He really enjoyed this, and it kept his mind and time occupied. This was important because the country of England was very "blah" during this period. It had been hit pretty hard since 1939, and not much was left there.

There were also things that Mr. Dugo experienced, which were almost unexplainable. One of these was the sight of over two thousand planes flying in the air above him. This was an incredible and unbelievable sight. He could not understand how that number of planes ever got that much fuel to fly. They can fly up to fifteen or sixteen hours on one flight. According to Mr. Dugo, the amount of fuel needed to fly the missions had to be incredible. Another thing that amazed Mr. Dugo was that the men in the planes would return from their missions suffering either from heat exhaustion or frostbite. He recalls, "They really took a beating up there."

Just before the end of the war Mr. Dugo remembers a call informing the United States that Holland was in desperate need of food. This was before 1945. The United States made a special deal with Germany shortly after to fly food into Holland and aid the people of that country. These missions of aid were to be called the "Manna Chowhound Missions." Mr. Dugo was excited when he heard the news about these missions because they were not going to be dropping bombs, but they were now going to be dropping food. They would be using their aircraft to do something good. He recalls modifying the bomb bays to put the platforms in to load up the food. After they had loaded the food there was a request that one person from armament go on these missions. Mr. Dugo volunteered to be that one person. He remembers the bomb bay opening and watching the food leave. "The first time we dropped food was in Rotterdam, Holland. When the food first left the bomb bay I could see the people running trying to catch what was falling. There were no parachutes. The food was just kicked out of the plane." Instead of actually catching the food, the people were getting hit by it. Mr. Dugo tried to tell them to wait till the food was dropped, but it was impossible for the people to hear him. After the food was dropped he would motion to the radio operator to close the bomb bay doors. He had to motion him because he did not have a headset to wear. On the last mission the operator told him to look down. He looked down, but could only see fields. He soon saw, written in tulips, "Thank-you Boys."

Mr. Dugo visited Holland in 1992. He stopped at a place called the Cheese Factory, which is a tourist attraction in Holland. It was there that Mr. Dugo encountered his past again. While waiting for his tour bus he began talking to a man named Charlie that was selling postcards. Charlie spoke English very well, so communication was not a barrier. During his conversation, he kept glancing towards a field in the distance. Charlie asked Mr. Dugo what he was looking at. Mr. Dugo recounted his missions to Holland. Charlie jumped three feet up in the air and said, "Oh my God! I was two years old, with my mother. I saw you!" Charlie then began to cry. After this he asked Mr. Dugo to thank the boys that had helped in the missions.

The "Manna Chowhound Missions" were something good that happened during the war. Mr. Dugo is very disappointed that today these missions were never recognized in any films or documentaries about the war. This bothers him, because there were some good things that happened during the war, and this was one of them.

The war was full of several different emotions for Mr. Dugo. He experienced sadness and at the same time happiness. Although he had seen planes take off and never come back he continued to live his life and aid his country in it's quest for freedom. It is hard to imagine a nineteen-year-old confronted with such a task of not only defending the rights of others, but being mature enough to handle himself in a foreign nation surrounded by strangers. The idea of going into a completely different country and seeing firsthand the destruction and devastation that the war produced would be a hard sight to handle. Mr. Dugo recalls that "It hits you." looking at the ruins of the war, but that he continually tried to keep his mind occupied with other things.

After being discharged from the service, Mr. Dugo returned home to his parents. He was not the only person in his family to go to war. He had two brothers that participated in the war too. Both of his brothers continued to stay in the service after the war, so Mr. Dugo felt it was his responsibility to return home to help his parents. He then continued going to school, eventually married, and had children of his own. One of his sons has followed in his footsteps and now serves in the United States Air Force stationed in England. Although Mr. Dugo is now almost seventy-two years old, he says that he would fight for his country again if given the opportunity, but he is happy to know that his son and other young people today have taken an interest in the military. He feels that he is too old to do it all over again, but if he had to, he would.

Although it has been a little over fifty years since the war has ended, the memories and emotions of this man will live on forever in him.

Planes drop food over Holland during the Manna/Chowhound Missions in May of 1945.
(Photo courtesy Francis Dugo)

Rita M. Strobel Geibel

325th Photographic Wing Reconnaissant Base Laboratory Photographic Technician

by
Julie Croft

Many people do not realize the number of women that were involved in World War II. Mrs. Rita M Strobel Geibel is one of these women who are so often forgotten. Her story will remind Americans that women played an important role in the war, and that they endured many of the same hardships as the men.

The women were criticized, and ya know a lot of it was nothing but garbage. There was a lot of conflict between the men. There were seventeen thousand [women] that served overseas, and I was in one of the first battalions to go. What was unusual with mine was the fact that I was in photography. I knew nothing about photography. I graduated from Butler High in 1941...I went to defense school in Pittsburgh for the government and studied sheet metal.... They sent me to Baltimore where I studied blueprinting for two months, and then they gave me a job. I was making real good money, but I wasn't content, I wanted to go into the service. So I came home and told my mother, and she didn't want me to go...but I convinced her, and finally I went. She told me afterwards she says, "Ya know...when you were about seven years old you told me...that there was gonna be a women's army someday and you were gonna be in it." ...I was twenty-two [when I went over].

[My] basic training...[was in] Georgia. ...We went through the same basics anybody else did. We had to climb obstacles. We had to lay down in the mud. We abandoned ship at New York...in case we sunk when we were going overseas. We did everything just like them [the men], 'cause we had to in case anything were to happen to us.

In fact, when we were crossing, we had a fifty-ship convoy...and to the right of us was a U-boat, and the U-boat fired at us, and so we sunk it. I saw the debris. Not only that, then we had to change course.... When you were in the boats going over and coming back...there were a lot of mines the Germans had, and you were always afraid you were gonna hit one of those, especially at night. You wouldn't be able to see them....

When we got overseas it was just such a thing that I had never seen. I have pictures of everything. This is why I have this collection. I took a wooden box and put these pictures in.... I have a whole room of stuff that is just unbelievable.

We printed over two million prints in a month, and you know...it was history on a multi-printer. We had never seen these machines. They just put us on it, and we learned to use them. There were seven of these machines all together, and we put out seventy-seven percent of the pictures in these machines. That's how fast they were at getting them out. Sometimes we worked twenty-four hours, around the clock, with three shifts.

One of those big rolls of film that they had we put on the machine in complete dark. After it went through the chemicals and into the hypo you could turn a yellow light on. One time one of the splices got loose and it started a fire.... They got it out in a hurry though, but we could have been burnt to death because there...was no place to go.

The photographic work that we had was so complicated you wouldn't believe. [When] we did the developing of the film we were among the V-1 and V-2 Rockets the whole time, night and day, from '43 to '45. The V-1 was like an outdoor motorboat, and when it shut off you knew it was gonna land near you; and if it kept going, you knew you didn't have to worry about it. Everthing was so serious...you never knew what was gonna happen to ya. You were worried about your family and vice versa.

At our photographic lab...they had twenty-four hour guard all the time, all around the lab. The guys told us after the war they had no ammunition for their guns. If we'd of ever known that, we'd of been hysterical. The guys weren't allowed to tell; and when you keep a secret you have to keep a secret.

We used to be afraid when we'd walk up and down the lab at night, 'cause it was pitch dark. ...You never knew when the enemy, or somebody may come in and grab you. At the... entrance, coming into our base one morning they found an English woman dead. She was stripped of all her clothes. Whatever happened to her we never found out, but it was enough to frighten you.

[When] we'd come off a shift at eleven o'clock at night, we had to walk two miles up a hill from the lab in complete dark. We would just get settled down and all of a sudden those sirens would go off.... You were so tired from working, and you wanted to sleep. When those sirens would go off we had to go out and stand in those foxholes until they called clear. We used to always say, "I'd rather be in the hut and hit with them than be out in the open and hit with them."

We had two blankets, wool blankets. We gave one to the boys in France 'cause they were short. That only left us one blanket. We had a mattress, - a three-piece mattress, the hardest thing you'd ever laid on. And we had pillows, Chinese pillows, they were hard as a rock.

We had an unheated building, no heat whatsoever, very damp. Sometimes we wore our woolen overcoat, a long horrible looking overcoat. ...We had high top shoes, brown shoes that we wore. They were above the ankle. When you polished them up, they were nice.

We were the first women to make history in sports. We came in second place in this [basketball], and first place in volleyball. We made history in all the sports. We got two medals. I played softball, basketball, and volleyball in England, Germany, and Belgium. I even shot rifles, but...it was so loud it started to bother my ears, and I quit it.

We were also the first women to wear slacks, but they were ugly. They weren't

(Photo courtesy Rita M. Strobel Geibel)

The Queen visiting yesterday U.S. 8th Army Air Force H.Q. at High Wycombe, inspects a smart parade of United States W.A.C.s. She was received by General Doolittle.

(Photo courtesy Rita M. Strobel Geibel)

nice like the ones they have now.

We had a real nice thing at Christmas time. It probably was in '44. It had to be in '44. We decorated all our huts with anything we could get. We went down the hill and got pine trees. We tied for first place, and we got two bottles of champagne...dated 1929 for a prize.

We had this open house. We had one hundred orphans who had no home - orphans of the war. We had them for a turkey dinner. They came to our huts, and we made popcorn, and put it in our helmets, and passed it around to the kids. It was very touching.... They were just beautiful children.

[When we went to Germany] a German boy set our hotel on fire. He was working for us. We were clear up on the top floor. They had to send up three times to get us out. By the time we came down, smoke was coming [up].

So here they had to hold all the personnel, and they had to search them, and take all their clothes off. You should've seen the jewelry they stole. So they put it out on the table and had us come down and identify it....

[In] Germany one of the W.A.C. officers and the girl from Dayton, Ohio, and myself were able to get a jeep. We wanted to see Hitler's home at Berchtesgaden. We got lost and ran out of gas. We ran into a black infantry cab, and they filled our jeep up. They advised us not to go up to Berchtesgaden because there was snipers in the woods, and they said there was snow in the mountains. They said, " Why don't you go see Dachau." We said, "What's Dachau?" And they said, "It's where they put thirty thousand people to death, mostly Jews, some gypsies, and there were some Germans...."

I had no idea, but when I got there you just wouldn't believe...they were still cleaning the camp up. And the smell, five miles before you even got there, you just couldn't believe. A Polish fella took us in, and he took us over to these dog pens, and the dogs were dead.... He said that if a prisoner would not tell what he [a German officer] wanted, then they'd feed him to those dogs.

We came back, and we went into a room which was a gas chamber. ...They say there was no gas chamber in Dachau. There was, I was in that room. They had two hundred bodies in the room piled one upon another. The bodies were taken out, but there was blood stains, and it was just horrible in there. It looked like they had maybe scratched with their nails or something.... They took everything from them, all their clothes and everything and just laid them in there, men, women, and children. From there we went down to another room where the remains was still there. They had the bones of these bodies ground up into fine pulverizer, just like fertilizer.

We came back from there...and there was a place where they had a very big stone. There was a brown rope hanging down...and on that they either hung or shot them. There was blood stains all over the ground there...tremendous blood all over. And ya know, another thing they had from every one of the prison camps, they had over one hundred box cars of women's hair....

Well, ya know when I first came home... nobody wanted to see them [pictures of the prison camps]. They said they didn't believe it.

Just about three years ago...we were waiting for a trip. A man with several children came, real tall fella, and his wife. He had to wait too. I said, "I'm gonna go talk to him." I said, "Sir, you're from England." He said, "Yes... High Wycombe, why?" I said, "I was stationed at High Wycombe." He said, "You were? You were really one of those girls up there?" I said, "Yeah." He put his arms around me and hugged me. He said, "Ya know what, I never had an opportunity to thank you for what you people did for us."

Mrs. Rita Strobel Geibel received many awards, including the Pallas Athens Medal (W.A.C.), the American Theater of Operation Medal, the Victory Medal, the Good Conduct Medal, and various others.

History books do not teach of the women's part in the war, and so children grow up thinking that only men carried important roles. Women also served their country, though, only in a different way. From Mrs. Geibel's story, Americans are reminded of their efforts. Just like the man who thanked Mrs. Geibel, the world also needs to give all the women a big "Thank You" for their help.

Bridge damage on the Rhine River at Bonn
(Photo courtesy Gene Hinchberger)

Arthur D. Gerson

390th Bomb Group
571st Squadron
Ordnance

by
Kris Toft (Gibbs)

Mr. Arthur D. Gerson is an extremely polite man, who also has an extreme enthusiasm to share his life experiences. One corner of a room is devoted exclusively to the collection of various photographs and articles on his bomb group. It is plain to see that he has experienced various things which can only be imagined by the current generation.

I live in Pittsburgh, and I'm seventy-five years of age. I went into the service in January of 1943, and was discharged August/September, 1945. I was with the 390th Bomb Group, 571st Squadron, stationed in England. I was in ordnance, so my job was handling bombs and ammunition. At some point I spent a couple of weeks in an English bomb disposal school to identify any bombs that were dropped around the field by the German forces.

It was a B-17 bomb group and we had participated in 301 bombing missions. The group was given two Presidential Citations for participating in some massive bombing raids on Regensburg.

There is a hilarious story, and I wasn't aware that this had happened until about a month ago. The 390th Bomb Group had a reunion at Cherry Hill, New Jersey, and I had been in contact with one of the fellows that had been in ordnance with me during those years. He had asked me to try to make the Cherry Hill, New Jersey meeting, because most of the ones that they had had in the past were out in the West, or in the deep West, and I was unable to attend those reunions. But this one was east of Pennsylvania, of course, and quite close to Pittsburgh. I decided, at the age of seventy-five, that this might be a good time for me to see some of the fellows that I had been with. Consequently, I went there and met up with five of them.

Now, we originally had twenty-eight people in the ordnance. A number of them passed away through the years, and some of them had not been able to attend. But, in any case, I got to the hotel, and I checked the room numbers where these people were going to be. I was given their numbers and went up and knocked on the door of one person that I had been contacting in California. It's a good thing that I had an opportunity to see these faces by going to their rooms, because had I walked by them in the hallway, I would not have recognized them, or they me. The years had taken their toll, and consequently we all had changed quite a bit.

Meeting with these people was a very emotional, and a happy experience, for me. But, in any case, at dinner one night, two of the men who were there started laughing about the time when we were at the port of embarkation in New York, just the night before going overseas. I had been issuing carbines to a number of people and registering serial numbers, and I was quite busy. Everybody else was packing up their bags. One of the guys told me that he would be glad to do mine for me. I was unaware of it, but they started laughing and wanted to know if I had ever discovered the fact that somebody had put a couple of big rocks in my barracks' bag. I really had not because they had packed the bags, put these rocks in, and watched me struggle, carrying these bags when we boarded ship. When we unloaded in Liverpool, England eleven days later, I was still dragging these bags. I thought it was quite funny, so I laughed.

One of the wives asked them how they could have done this to me, but the guys thought it was a big joke, and I did too.

One of the loads that we were putting in were five-hundred-pound bombs, with what we called an anti-withdrawal fuse, and it also had a time delay in it. Now, there was just another man and myself loading the plane that night. The purpose of this type of fuse in a bomb was that whenever the target was going to be an industrial site, they didn't want the German bomb disposal crews to be able to get into the areas that had been bombed and set on fire. They used this type of fuse because some of the fires had started by bombs that did go off, but ones that did not go off would go off at differently timed periods. This was to keep the German bomb disposal crews from going in and putting out the fires because they had no idea when these bombs would go off. If, later on, any of the bombs had not gone off on time-delay, when the fires had subsided, I suppose they went in and attempted to dig out bombs where they would find holes of entry. This type of fuse had an anti-withdrawal end to it. There was a locking-ball device at the very tip of the fuse, so that once they tried to unscrew the fuse the bomb would go off.

Placing an arming wire through a fuse.
(Photo courtesy Tom Brown)

I had twelve five-hundred-pound bombs in the bomb bay, and finally worked my way down. You start at the top and work your way down, and my very last fuse - the last bomb that I had to put this fuse in became cross-threaded just as I was putting it into the fuse well. The very end of the fuse looks like the type of fuse that you would put into a fuse box in a home, and I could see the locking-ball had caught. As I tried to turn it counter-clockwise, those two sections were opening up. I turned it twice, and I could not loosen it, so I tightened it up again. I was quite concerned, because I guess it was about five o'clock in the morning. I could hear the other planes cranking up around the perimeter of the field. I looked out of the bomb bay doors and could see the crew for this plane coming up the roadway. I walked out through the bomb bay and down the road to meet them. I told them that they had better wait there, and I would let them know when they could come to get into their plane. I went back to the plane. It was hold-your-breath time because I really had visions of a problem. But it was my responsibility, and I had to take care of it. Thank goodness I was able to get that fuse out of there, reset it, and put the arming wire into it. I closed up the bomb bay doors and went out to these guys. I told them OK, that it was all theirs. They had enough problems on their hands once they went out on a mission. They didn't need any more before they ever left the field. That problem has haunted me all through the years, and I think about it quite often.

The bulk of the work was at night, and the weather generally in England was horrible. It rained constantly, and we had deep fogs, snow; and we were cold. Some of the little Nissen huts that we slept in were only heated by a very small English unit - you can't really call it a furnace - but it was about the size of a good-sized stove pipe, and that was it. We got English coke to heat this Nissen hut. There were fifteen or eighteen guys that slept in this contraption, and it was very cold. The coke didn't hold up very well, and consequently we also used to burn these big heavy cardboard rings that would come in on new shipments of bombs. We'd take them off the bombs and use those for fuel to heat our barracks.

Well, the weather was miserable, but it was worse for the guys that had to go flying all the time. One of my most distressing times came when, later on in the war, I had hurt my back quite badly, and I was put on light duty. I became in charge of quarters at night. One of the duties was to answer the phone in the orderly room and to go and awaken the crews that were to fly the next morning. When a call would come in at 3:30 or 4:00 in the morning, I would have to go out through the perimeter with a little flashlight into some of these Nissen huts where the crews slept, and wake up these poor guys. It was difficult. It was heart-breaking. The worst part for me was to watch them struggle getting out of their bunks, knowing what they were faced with. Worst of all was seeing the empty bunks where maybe the day before, or two days before, other young people had been sleeping; and they were no longer around.

There were three thousand people in our bomb group, and we had trained, with exception of the flight crews, pretty much all together. All the people who were on the planes and people who had other jobs on the ordnance knew everybody else. Once the crews started flying, they had a difficult time because they had very little fighter cover at the beginning- in early '43 and towards the end of '43. Once they left England and started across the Channel, our fighters couldn't give them a lot of coverage, so they were pretty much on their own. The minute they hit the French coast and started heading toward a target they met up with German fighters and all kinds of flak. We suffered a lot of casualties.

When the replacements for these guys started coming in from the States, we knew the first batch of guys that we had trained, and we got to know some of the first batch of replacements. We became a little friendly with them, and they with us. When they started disappearing, we got more replacements. But I, for one, did not make it a point to become too friendly with them any more. Over the two years guys came and went; it was just horrible. There were three thousand casualties. The bulk of them were made up of KIAs and MIAs. There were any number of POWs, guys that bailed out. Ten percent of the casualties that were suffered in the war came from the Air Force.

Mr. Gerson went on to say that he, for one, would not have changed his experience for the world. He said that he was glad that he was a tiny bit of it all, and that he was grateful that he had been given the chance to do something.

When Mr. Gerson came back from the war, he continued in the furniture business. He is now retired, and living in a nice home in the suburbs of Pittsburgh.

Samuel Goldberg

96th Bomb Group
Base Air Depot #2
Airplane Mechanic

by
Laura S. Majersky

Samuel Goldberg is an older Jewish man with a full head of hair, thick glasses and a goatee. He is probably one of the few World War II veterans that can still fit into his uniform. He and his second wife, Phyllis, live in a large residential neighborhood in Monroeville.

Samuel Goldberg had tried to enlist in the services at an early age, but was not accepted due to his bad eyesight. This handicap was easily overlooked by the government as Congress began to draft young men in December 1942. In February 1943, at the age of nineteen, Goldberg received his "invitation from Uncle Sam" and by March he was enlisted in the Army-Airforce on limited service. "Before the war, I had never traveled more than twenty miles outside the city [of Pittsburgh], but Uncle Sam took me all over."

Basic training was in Miami Beach, Florida, and it only lasted two to three months. From here, Goldberg was sent to Civilian Engine Mechanics School in Flint, Michigan. The school was sponsored by Buick. They were paid as well as sergeants even though they were only privates.

"They must not have had any work at the time for engine mechanics, because we were shipped off to Piote, Texas, a B-17 training base, to work in the supply base. After two months in supplies we finally got to work on the B-17s."

"The base in Piote was nicknamed the 'Rattlesnake Airbase' because of all the snakes and tarantulas around. We used to have to slam the latrine doors in the mornings just to scare them away."

"We went to the bombing ranges and would fly around in circles dropping bombs that were filled with flour to practice accuracy. It was here that I had my first ride in a plane—I have never been so sick in my life."

"I remember one day when a trainload of parachutes had come in and the officer in charge said that as soon as they were unloaded we could take off. We worked like crazy. We even built an igloo with the parachutes so we could go in the hole and sleep for a while. As soon as we were done, I went to tell the officer that I was going; and he said, 'No, no, you're not going anywhere. You're staying right here.' Well, we got to arguing and I just left. The C.O. called me in and said, 'Goldberg, you have a choice—either you get a court-martial or you get an Article 104.' A 104 was a duty given in lieu of doing something else. Well, I wasn't stupid. I took the 104 which turned out to be a week of kitchen patrol. The first thing they made me do was clean out the grease trap in the sink. Talk about odor - that was horrible! It was right after the argument that I was shipped overseas."

"I didn't know what had happened. I was still on limited service and not supposed to be going overseas. Just recently, I sent to St. Louis for a copy of my records, and I saw that the words 'limited service' were scratched out. So somebody had to do that. Whether it was the officer in Piote or not, I don't know."

On February 3, 1944 Goldberg and fifteen thousand other men were shipped across the Atlantic on Britain's Queen Elizabeth. He and eight others slept in a room designed for two people, while some soldiers slept outside on the deck. The trip lasted five days. They landed in northern Scotland because it was one of the few places with a large enough harbor. From there, he was taken to his station at Base Air Depot number two, located in northwest England in a small town.

The depot was "like a big factory. For every guy that participated in combat he had to have ten people behind him working the supply, equipment maintenance or repair-and that's what I did." Planes would be delivered to the base from the United States and would need to be prepared for combat or modified battle. "Replacement planes came to the base to be checked for everything: engines, guns, etc. We did modifications, like on the P-47 Thunderbolt. They decided it needed a little more power, so we installed water injection systems that helped them make it the whole way to the continent." The base also assembled the gliders that were used for D-Day. "We all knew something was going to happen because our base was full of airplanes. They filled up every available space with them. It's a good thing we had control of the skies or Germany could have gotten through and destroyed us all."

Goldberg remembered one day, in particular, at the base. "Unfortunately there was a very bad accident that occurred there. That probably was the closest I came to getting killed during the war. A B-24 was coming into the base. It was raining, and somehow he overshot the runway. He was coming down, so he must have thought he was on the right approach. He went over the top of a school and he took the top floor of the school off. In the top floor was the kindergarten class - forty children were killed. Across the street was a cafe where we used to go and buy meat pies. The plane went straight into that cafe. Fortunately I didn't go in that morning. He killed everyone in the cafe, everyone in the plane, and the forty children. That was a bad accident."

On V-E Day, everyone was celebrating the announcement of victory. "We spent a lot of time in town drinking. I really don't know how I got back to the base, but when I got there, the guys were shooting flare pistols that we used for signaling. The base we were on, was in the middle of a farm, and the farmer had a lot of haystacks around. The flares set all of the stacks on fire, smoke was everywhere. The government, of course, had to pay for all the damages."

Mr. Goldberg remained in Europe until the end of the war. For a short while he was stationed at a bomber base in southeast England, where he was the crew chief for an aircraft. He was to go to Germany for occupation, but at the last minute, orders were changed and he was to go to the Pacific. Before the group departed the bomb was dropped.

In the two-and-a-half years he spent overseas, Sam was fortunate to visit much of England. Bus trips, train rides, and sight-seeing tours were a common way he spent his free time. He traveled to Scotland, Wales, and London, to name a few. It was on one such train ride, that he met his future wife, Lillian Flemming. "A friend and I were going to the seashore on the east coast to visit some girls we had met earlier. We were all standing in the back on account of there were no seats. Lillian and I started talking. One thing led to another and I got her address. I started visiting her which turned out to be much closer than going up to the east coast."

In 1945, at the end of the war, Goldberg and Lillian were planning to marry. He could not leave right away, because he lacked enough points to be sent home. He volunteered to stay another three months, earning him the title of corporal. During this three-month period he was able to complete all of the necessary paperwork for the marriage license. The two were married in May of 1946. They planned to honeymoon on the Isle of Man, but orders were changed and Goldberg was shipped home.

"I remember getting on the ship in South Hampton. I was bringing home the top of the wedding cake in my duffel bag, and a line of us were walking down to the dock when a sergeant yelled 'Halt!' The bag came over my shoulder and landed at my feet. I heard a loud noise like a gun had

Nose art on a P-47 Thunderbolt fighter (Photo courtesy Tom Brown)

gone off. We all jumped. That noise was actually the icing shattering. In England, when they make a wedding cake they use royal icing which gets hard like cement. It was quite a startling bang for a wedding cake."

Lillian was brought to the United States by the Army the following August.

Upon his return to the States, Goldberg initially inquired for work as an airplane mechanic at the major airlines. He was told that he would have to go to school and qualify for the job through testing. "I had worked on every plane ever owned by the US; if I had to go to school, I was going to college." Through the GI Bill, he received a Bachelor of Science degree in chemistry at the University of Pittsburgh. He was hired by Hall Chemical but left this job to pursue a career in research. There was a time lag of well over a year before another opportunity in chemistry appeared. Goldberg supported his wife and three children during this time by taking work in machine shops until he was offered a position in combustion research in the Bureau of Mines. In 1971, he was placed in charge of running an analytical lab at the Bureau, which eventually became a division of OSHA. He remained there until his retirement in December of 1985. The only time he used the abilities he acquired as a skilled W.W.II mechanic was when he popped the hood of his car.

Mrs. Lillian (Flemming) Goldberg passed away in 1982. In May of 1984 Samuel and his second wife, Phyllis, were married. Phyllis' deceased husband was a W.W.II paratrooper. The retired chemist is now involved in a real estate development in Cranberry Township. The couple actively participated with the organization Volunteers For Israel and have offered their services in 1986 and 1996. The organization recruits people of any religious affiliation to live and work with the Israeli forces and aid them in improving the nation. Being of Hebrew lineage, Goldberg feels it is especially important for him to assist the country. Working with this organization has also provided a prime opportunity for the couple to tour Israel and its neighbors. To them volunteering has been "a fantastic experience all around." They are hoping to travel to Israel again before the end of 1996.

Leroy Harriger

479th Fighter Group
435th Fighter Squadron
Ground Crew

by
Amanda Johns

As one views Mr. Leroy Harriger for the first time, he strikes one as quite colorful. He is tall and slim, and his manner of dress, consisting of a flannel shirt underneath red suspenders and brown tweed trousers, coincides with his farm-orientated residence located in a rural area of New Castle, Pennsylvania. Mr. Harriger's disposition is generally calm and quiet, until he speaks of a subject of personal significance. Then he exhibits strong emotions and sincere concerns. For this patriotic jack-of-all-trades, the experiences of WWII have provided a lifelong treasury of memories.

Before the outbreak of World War II, Mr. Leroy Harriger was employed as a DHIA milk tester in Lawrence, Mercer, and Beaver counties. This task "involved taking milk samples, testing them for butterfat and keeping records on each farmer's animals. You would go in the evening and take samples, stay overnight, take samples in the morning, then do the book work and move on to the next farm. It was like a continuous cycle that revolved every month." It was a method for farmers to pinpoint the cows that were not producing properly. This vocation still exists today, although the technology involved has improved one hundred percent.

Mr. Harriger was drafted into the service early in the year of 1943, although he had previously signed up to join in 1941. "When things began to get hot, and Japan and Germany opened up, then they [the U.S.] were desperate for bodies, live bodies," and the number of men enlisted dramatically rose. "It was a case of Pearl Harbor being such a catastrophe, and everybody was so mad, that anybody that was able to was going to join the service. You would try to join up before they drafted you, and that way, you thought you had a better chance of a choice [of service]. Patriotism ran so high at that time, and it was just the way Hitler had invaded Belgium and Poland, that when we entered the war people just felt that this is my country and I'll live or die for it."

Mr. Harriger was incorporated into the organization of ground crew for fighter planes, but prior to departing from the United States, much training was necessary. In order to acquire this instruction, Harriger attended four different schools in less than three months. He traveled from Wisconsin to Illinois, then to Colorado, and finally California where he studied topics ranging from radio school to communications. The skills that Harriger acquired at this time such as; cleaning the guns and checking the head space so that they would fire properly, keeping ammunition boxes constantly loaded, and refueling the gas tanks were later put to an invaluable use for the care and maintenance of P-38 fighter planes. When Harriger first arrived for war duty, his work was strictly on P-38s, but then "the British came out with the P-51 which was a terrific plane. It would go up to five hundred mph, and was so maneuverable that it just ran rings around the German fighters." These newer planes were used for long-range, bomber escort missions and played a key role in the American victory in WWII.

Leroy Harriger went overseas as a member of a hundred-ship convoy, which was the last group to arrive in Europe intact. After this, everyone was strictly replacements. The nearest town to the airfield that Harriger was stationed at was named Ipswich, England, and the veteran had several fond memories of the time spent there. One particularly amusing story was, "Two or three of us put a tent up on the airplane line, because we were down there most of the time. We ate there and would go to the mess hall and bring food back. Well, some of the other guys seemed to think that we were supplying them food, and they would come in while we were still in bed and eat our grub. So one evening, we caught a stray cat that was running around, cleaned it, cooked it, and left it sitting where they could find it. When they came in the next morning, we pretended that we were asleep and one of the boys said, 'Oh! Rabbit!', and boy, they tore into it. We said, 'Hey, how do you like that rabbit?' 'Yeah, this is good.' 'Have you seen that cat that's been running around out there lately?' 'No, where is it?' We said, 'You're tasting it!', and boy, they headed for the tent door. We weren't bothered with anybody stealing our food after that."

"The worst scare that a person would have was fear of the German buzz bombs. The Germans would send these over every night, one right after the other, and they were more of a psychological thing, attempting to deteriorate the enemy's morale. These buzz bombs were radio controlled; the Germans would set the mileage on them and did not even know themselves where they were going to land. The bombs had an odd motor on them that could be heard from below making a sort of 'putt, putt' sound. You would hear one of those coming and all you could do was just stand there and say, 'Keep moving baby, Keep moving baby.' A hit from one of these bombs would have been disastrous to the entire airfield. Fortunately, the air base was never hit."

While at Ipswich, Leroy witnessed the demise of many fighters and bombers. Planes that were going down would often

Checking .50 caliber ammunition in a wing

(Photo courtesy Tom Brown)

"belly in," come in on one wheel, or flip over. One aircraft crashed into the engineering department, located at the base, while another that had been shot in the rear caught on fire and "went down in a blaze of glory" on one particular invasion day. Members of the ground crew were assigned to a particular fighter until it did not return, and then they would simply move on to the next one released from the "Reppodeppo," the storage place for replacement planes. In between long-range missions, members of the ground crew usually slept, played cards or wrote letters to loved ones. Harriger and his fellow ground crew members truly formed a melting pot. People from all walks of life came together to support a cause and they learned to work together.

Leroy Harriger first heard the glorious news that the war had ended over the radio. His response to Victory in Europe Day was to "go to London and dance in the street." After the war in Europe had ended, Harriger was shipped into Germany to work at a health center that the Eighth Air Force had taken over. He spent six months there in police duty, and at the end of this service, he and a friend arranged airplane reservations on an Army flight back to London. They arrived at the airport at nine o'clock on Saturday morning to get on board, but sat waiting until one-thirty or two o'clock in the afternoon until they were told that they had been scratched from the flight because there was too much luggage on board. So, the pair made arrangements to leave the next morning. When they arrived at the airport on Sunday, they were told that their plane from Saturday had crashed in France and killed everyone on board. " We felt very fortunate that they scratched us," Harriger stated.

Mr. Harriger believes that the younger generation of today does not fully comprehend or appreciate what went on during the war and what was sacrificed. "Patriotism has sunk so low right now, that I shudder to think what would happen if we got into another conflict. People felt before that 'This is my country and I'll live or die for it.' I hate to say this, but I really don't think that would happen today." Mr. Harriger would definitely fight for his country again. "I don't think there is a better country in the world. If there is one, show it to me."

Leroy Harriger had spent three years abroad without ever coming home or seeing his family. When he first returned, he reentered the milk-testing business for a time. He then attended college for one year at Westminster, with a part-time job at a steel mill. A variety of occupations followed: he drove a school bus, pedaled milk, worked in a brick yard, and drove a semi-truck for seventeen years, and then retired. Fifteen years ago, he bought a franchise in window coating, and among others, he has coated the windows of both Burger Huts in Butler. Leroy leads an active lifestyle. He enjoys fishing, hunting, bowling, and is a crucial member of a two-time boccie champion team. He and his wife are former scuba divers, and right now what Mr. Harriger would most like to do is to parachute from an airplane.

Mr. Leroy Harriger is certainly an amiable and interesting man. His contributions to the WWII effort can be measured in both quality and quantity, and he will always be remembered as a vital member of the American cause.

Richard V. Helsing

339th Fighter Group
504th Squadron
Radio Transmitter

by
Emilly Swartz

Richard Helsing is full of energy and enjoys life. He sees the best in everything he does, has an easy-going nature, and is easy to talk to. He recalls the events in his life fondly.

I was twenty-two when I was drafted. When you were drafted you got on a revolving belt and just moved along. We went to Camp Meade in Virginia, and were taken through our classifications. They gave us classes, and put earphones on us. We were supposed to mark if it was a dash, or a dot, or two dashes and a dot. This let them know if we were good with codes, and I passed fairly high, much to my regret later on. A portion of the questions they had were about weather and different cloud formations, and I rated high as a weather observer as well. After being there for about four days, we took trains down to Miami Beach. When we got there we realized we were in the Air Force. By that time Miami Beach was taken over by the government, so we were put up in hotels, but instead of two beds to a room, they put two extra cots in. There we had our basic training, learned how to march, and drill, and all that stuff. I talked to them of the knowledge that I had before I went into the service. I was in the mail room at the American Bridge. We listed three different choices: to stay down there and work in the mail room was my first choice, weather observer was my second choice, and my last choice was radio. Well, they don't need as many weathermen as they do radiomen, so I was sent to radio school.

Radio school was in Scottsfield, and after about two weeks they sent me up near Madison, Wisconsin to Truax Field. There we learned radio mechanics. I graduated from that, and we went to Tomah, Wisconsin and learned advanced radio. They taught us what they called the Control Net System. It consisted of three direction finder stations and radar. Radar would pick up the enemy and the direction finder stations would pinpoint where their friendly aircraft was by voice transmissions. Three direction finder stations would give the bearings to the control center. There their location would be plotted on a grid, and then the fighters were steered toward the enemy. I was given a ten-day en-route pass and I went home and got married. After I got back, we were shipped to an Air Force base in Long Island, called Mitchell Field. From

Richard Helsing in front of "Old O'Boe"
(Photo courtesy Richard Helsing)

there we went to Bradley Field in Connecticut. I was there with nothing to do, so a guy asked, "How would you like to have a three day pass?" I said. "Yeah sure. What do I have to do?" "You'll work with the M.P.s for two weeks. You'll be on guard duty for them." I was on night turn at the supply duct. After my two weeks were up, I went home to Ambridge and got my wife. We found a room in a house that we shared with three other G.I.s and their wives. This lasted about a week, and then I got a notice that I was going to ship out. I went back to town, got my wife, and got her to the Pennsylvania Station where she took a train home. I got back to town around six in the morning, and I was running down the street to the barracks as the guys were coming out of the barracks for roll call, so I wasn't missing. We were then shipped down to Tampa, Florida. There was a Pullman car full of us. When we got there, we were given our overseas' shots. A couple of days later, about eighteen of us were put on a Pullman car to California. We got into Needles, California and had a two-hour wait there until some trucks came and took us to Rice Air Force Base. We spent two weeks at Rice and were then sent to New York to Camp Shanks. We had twenty-four free hours and then got on a boat headed for England, the Sterling Castle.

It took us fourteen days to get to England. We ended up in Fowlmere, outside of Cambridge. When we got there three of us went to the transmitter site, three went to the control tower, and three went to what they called the "homing station." The ones at the transmitter site monitored the main transmitter and receiver, which went by phone lines to the control tower. The ones in the control tower were the ones who monitored all transmissions during a mission. They knew who was calling whom, and what was going on. So they had a complete record. Over in the "homing station," whenever pilots come back from a mission, they would give them the steer back to the base. The first ten months I spent at the control tower recording transmissions. Some of the more memorable events at the control tower were:

- the chilling effect at the end of a mission when the control tower officer would give the call signs of the planes that had not returned - and the silence when there was no response;

- the transmissions of a pilot who was checking on a group of bombers who's plane was being hit, and the surprise and dismay in his voice (he was advised to switch to Channel Four and call "May Day" - no further recording as we didn't monitor Channel Four);

- while over half the group was still on the ground, the excited transmissions of a 339th pilot who had already taken off, asking for permission to land but being told to circle, trying several times to land but having to wait until all planes had taken off, then coming in and crashing near the black and white signal truck (He was badly burned, and I believe several of the men working at the signal truck received Soldier Medals for their part in the rescue);

- the excitement when a P-51 came back from a mission with a bomb hanging under the wing by only the front support, and the tension until a smooth landing was completed without dropping the bomb;

-watching a P-51 belly in on the field next to the mess hall while on my way to the E.M. mess and pedaling my bike across the field, arriving just as the pilot got out, unhurt;

- the day a British glider landed at the base after its tow cable broke.

The last eight months I spent at the homer station. The most impressive sight I remember was the group's fly-by on the last day of operation at the base when the whole group passed over the field.

We were over there for eighteen

Loading a bomb under a P-51 wing.

(Photo courtesy Tom Brown)

months, which gave us three of what they call "gold bars" to put on our uniforms; you get one every six months being over seas. When we were leaving the guys checking us on the boat were the ones to have six of them on their uniforms. You were supposed to leave in the order you came. The first one in would be the first one out. We were getting ready to get shipped to the South Pacific when the H-Bomb was dropped, and that stopped everything because the war was over. Because we were on the list for shipping already, they said, "Go ahead and go." So we got out of England before the old-timers did.

I went home and found that my job was waiting for me. After my wife and I went on a belated honeymoon, I returned to work at the American Bridge until my unit closed down. I have been retired ever since.

Paul R. Meeder

34th Bomb Group
7th Squadron
Mechanic

by
Jason R. McCormick

The hills around Butler, PA are the home of Paul R. Meeder. Mr. Meeder has lived in Butler County for his entire life, working as a printer at the Butler Eagle. Mr. Meeder was in the U.S. 8th Air Force from June 1943 to October 1945. These are some of the remembrances that Mr. Meeder had from his days in World War II.

I graduated in June 1942 from Butler High School. I was seventeen when I graduated, and I got a job as a printer with the Butler Eagle. Spirits were high in Butler regarding the war. I was kinda looking forward to getting into it [the war]. [I] guess I thought that Germany needed to be stopped at what they were doing. We thought we should get into it. I was kinda anxious; a lot of my friends were already into it. I was just looking forward to it. I think that people were pulling together to get the fighting done and stop the Germans, and the Japanese too for that matter.

First, we had basic training for about seventeen weeks, and that was the training if you had to do any combat fighting. Then, when that was done, they sent us to mechanics' school, in Gulf Port, Mississippi. That was about a seventeen-week course. When I went down there it was a school for C-47s, which is a two-engine cargo plane. I was about a week from graduation when they pulled a whole bunch of us out to Greensburg, North Carolina, and then they prepared us for going overseas. At the time we didn't know what we were going to do. So we landed in England on March 21, 1944 in Liverpool. They marched us off the ship and into the railroad station. That was quite an experience seeing the English cities where everybody drove on the left-hand side of the road. Then we got on the train and ended up at a British Air Force base that was flying Spitfires. The one thing that I'll remember after getting off the train was all the aircraft flying over. I've never seen so many aircraft in all my life. I was stationed at a little town called Mendlesham. I was in the 34th Bomb Group. The group went overseas with B-24s and the group flew B-24s from May 23, 1944 into August. Then they switched the whole group over to B-17s because the 3rd Division was flying mostly B-17s, and the group's B-24s were flying too fast for the rest of the group. We flew the rest of our missions into April, 1945 with them. We [the mechanics] were responsible for changing engines, refueling the planes, and any other repair work needed. We also had to conduct twenty-five-hour inspections and fifty-hour inspections. I was always in England, the group never transferred to France.

I have some stories. I could tell you some things that had happened to us. After they pre-flighted their airplanes, the pilots would all taxi to the runways, and the guys would walk down to the end of the runway, and watch them take off. Of course they liked to make smart remarks about each ones aircraft on takeoff. We were watching these planes come down and everybody was standing around there talking. All of a sudden this one plane pulled its wheels up from under it, and it sat back down on the runway. You could see the flames shooting out the back, and of course there was eight or nine of us there, and we all took off running. Everybody hit the ground expecting a big explosion, but it never happened. The plane went off the end of the pavement into the dirt, split right in two; one piece went one way, and one went another. I got up and turned around. All the guys that were in the airplane were coming out.

Another time when I was scared, [a plane] had started to take off. I don't know what he did, whether he blew a tire, whether the shear-pin on the tail wheel had broke or whether he forgot to lock the tail, but he started to go like this [Mr. Meeder begins waving his hands in a fishtail motion] and I happened to be standing up where our airplane was parked. It was heading right towards me, and I thought for sure he was going to hit me. But he veered off the other way, and he ended up in a ditch. I got a picture of that one.

They had little villages around there. We used to go to a little place about seven miles from there called Stowmarket. We would ride our bicycles down there. They had dances and stuff for soldiers around there. The whole area was just full of air bases. One thing we never had was a famous singer. The Red Cross would come around with doughnuts sometimes. They had movies they would show at night. They were mostly English films. The best time I had, I suppose, was after the Germans had really surrendered. We didn't really have much to do, so I had a little time on furlough and went up to Edinburgh with some fellows for a week. I was in London a couple times during the war too. I had some exciting times down there. The Germans would send up these V-2 Rockets, and you had no idea when they were coming, and all of a sudden there would be a big explo-

B-17 Flying Fortress at Fowlmere Field.

(Photo courtesy Tom Brown)

sion somewhere and you knew a rocket had hit. We saw the buzz bombs come over down there. The buzz bombs came over our bases too, but they never hit us. They flew so low I thought they'd hit the water tank on the base. It sounded like a powerful outboard motor. Our base was bombed once right after the group had got there in April, 1944. On June 7, two days after D-Day, the group was coming back from a mission, and the B-24s were circling to land. The German planes had slipped into the group and shot down four airplanes right over the field. One of them crashed in the equipment building and put us out of commission for four days until we could get resupplied. They killed twelve men out of the thirty-six crewmen on those planes.

Some of the guys that were fliers that had bailed out told me this one. When they landed on the ground [in Germany], some of the farmers started after them with pitch forks. They got rescued by some of the German Army. One fella told a story about being marched into a town, and some of the people wanted to kill the crew. Then they herded them into a boxcar and some of the people came after it to burn the boxcar. The Germany Army saved them that time, too.

Just before the war ended in the first part of May, the Germans had opened up the dikes in Holland and flooded the people out pretty good. They were starving. They had what was called the "chow-haul run." They loaded boxes of rations into the bomb bays and took a lot of us ground crews out and flew low, about 350 ft. over an airfield, and they'd push the whole lot of it out.

The biggest thrill was when they flew us back home. They took all the airplanes and added ten ground crew to the flying crew. They put us all on the airplane and flew us home. We flew from our air base to Wales and from Wales to Iceland. Got into Iceland at midnight, but it was still daylight in June. Then we stayed overnight and flew on to Newfoundland - then from Newfoundland to Connecticut. I don't know what happened to the plane after that. Probably flew it out to Arizona and parked it there.

We had a thirty-day furlough in June 1944. But they told us that our group was slated to go back overseas to work in B-29 squadrons. I was at Fort Dix, and they shipped us out to Sioux Falls. They shipped us around from there to get time on B-29s. We were still there when we dropped the atomic bomb on Japan. We were slated to go to Okinawa, and I'd only had three months on B-29s. We dropped the bomb, and the war ended. I think it [the bomb] was a good idea. A lot of people talk now about how they didn't think so, but I think it was. It would have been a lot worse if we hadn't dropped it. If we hadn't dropped that bomb, we'd been marching right over there. They already had plans to march into Japan.

After the war I went back to the Butler Eagle and worked there as printer for forty-eight years. I'd sometimes thought about going down to Pittsburgh and getting a job as a mechanic with one of the airlines down there, but I didn't. I had a job offer to go back to work at the Eagle, so I went back to work as a printer. I think the Army Air Force had an excellent school for mechanics. They gave me a very thorough training on fixing aircraft, and the experience came in handy. I've never been back [to England]. I'd like to have gone back. Some of the fellas have gone back, and they tell me the concrete is still there where our plane was parked. The engineering building has a hole in the roof, but is still there. The runway is all gone. They have (at the end of the runway) a memorial on a big plaque, and the British take care of that.

Mr. Meeder is one of millions of Americans that helped defend this country against the evil forces of the world during World War II. I thank him for his time.

Robert E. O'Brien

339th Fighter Group
503rd Squadron
Aircraft Painter

by
Jeremy J. Reeder

For a man who claims he does not have a lot to say, Robert O'Brien certainly can relate tales about his experiences during World War II. As with most other veterans, Mr. O'Brien is (and should be) proud of the work he did. A native of Butler, Pennsylvania, Mr. O'Brien is definitely willing to give up his precious time to talk to anyone interested in the Second World War. When he was just twenty-six years old, Robert O'Brien began a journey that would take him into the center of the greatest armed conflict ever known to man.

You'll find that we had a pretty valuable outfit. There were three groups: the 503rd, the 504th, and the 505th. I belonged to the 503rd. We started out in Savannah, Georgia and then we went from there to Tampa, Florida. That's where the 339th really got started. The 8th Air Force started in Savannah, and then we moved to Drew Field for extensive training - that's in Tampa, Florida. And after being there for about three months, then we moved out to the desert-out to the California/Arizona borderline. That's Rice, California, that's down south. And we had extensive training there, wartime training. That was in 1943. Before that I was shipped off to Scottfield, Illinois. That was one of the top schools in the Air Force. I came out of there a radio mechanic. Then I was transferred from the school in Illinois to the outfit out in California. I joined up with the 339th there. When I went out there and started, we were training on P-39 aircraft.

After being there for awhile, they needed a painter to paint the aircraft and the insignias. Due to the fact that I had painting training before I went in the service, I said, "Boy I'd like that job." So they gave it to me. I was an aircraft painter from then on 'til the end of the war.

We reached England from New York in March of 1943. We crossed the ocean in an English boat, and there was about four thousand troops on the boat. We had about a fourteen or fifteen day journey across the ocean in real high seas. We landed in northern England. What an experience that was. There were sunken boats all over the place. Old Hitler had been in there and just tore that place all to the devil with his bombing. It was all new to us. We had to march through the city, and the buildings were all bombed. We boarded the train, and we took off for a day . . . and reached a village. We boarded trucks and went from there to a place called Foulmere, a little village. We took that over. That's where our airstrip was at.

Then come the P-51s, the Mustangs. That's when my job came in - putting the stars and stripes and all the numbers on the planes. That was quite a busy job.

The first part of April we really got started with our missions. We got down to business then. Then the fun started. We started losing planes. We started losing pilots, we started getting into trouble. Lots of excitement.

[Two men designed the 503rd insignia] and gave me the drawing of it out there in California, and I painted the picture of it for them on a box just so they could see what it looked like. They liked that. They thought that was great so . . . they brought the doors off the P-51s over. I painted this insignia on almost all the plane doors out there. Boy, did they look nice. They didn't want anything too serious, but something that was in vogue at the time, like a Disney drawing.

New planes came and you had to get them ready for the next mission. A lot of work. I took care of all the painting on the planes. The crew chief would come to me [and give me my assignment]. At times I'd have to get help because I couldn't do it all myself. You got your orders from headquarters.

D-Day came along. We got the word at six o'clock the night before and all the airplanes had to be conditioned, ready to go at three o'clock in the morning. Everything was real secret. All the planes had to be marked. The wings had to have white and the black stripes on them. At first, we started out with two white stripes on each wing. So I had eighteen planes that had to be marked. I got a couple good brushes and I got the paint, and it's fast-drying paint. I said, "If we can get (the planes) dry and we can get them painted, they'll be ready to go, rain or shine." So we started out and it just kept raining - just enough to make it awful miserable. Everybody pitched in. Once the paint was on there, the rain didn't hurt it because it was real fast-drying. It was some kind of an English fast-drying chalky paint. At one o'clock [in the morning], we had 'em finished. We had started at about seven o'clock. It was really a good feeling. The crew chiefs were happy. Everybody was happy. Then they took off, and that was a day I'll tell you - a day of excitement. We escorted B-17s and we also did a lot of strafing. That was a long, long day.

So as time went on, we lost some men. Then the Germans invented the buzz bomb. We had them to contend with. They were hitting all around, and that was a menace. On Christmas Day of '44, there was just a steady stream of them. So we had all that to contend with through all of this fog.

We got the planes airborne and got some help over to the people on the other shore in France. After that things went our way. After many hours of hard work and a lot of sadness from losing our men here and there, we finally got the thing settled.

Nose art. (Photo courtesy Fielder Newton)

Nose art. (Photo courtesy Fielder Newton)

I just hope and pray we never have another war like we had there because if we do have another World War, everybody's going to be involved. This country's going to be involved as far as damage is concerned.

We had one of the greatest fighter groups in all of the 8th Air Force. I'm sure we have the best records of any in the European Theater.

I was always proud of my work.

During the third month of his training, Mr. O'Brien received a ten-day furlough so that he could come back to Butler and be married. He and his wife, Della, are still married and live in Meridian. Ever since returning to the States, Mr. O'Brien has lived and worked in Butler, Pennsylvania. Mr. O'Brien usually has the opportunity to reunite with some of his old buddies from the Second World War at least once a year.

Kal Shonthaler

34th Bomb Group
7th Squadron
Ground Crew Mechanic

by
Rachel Hinterlang

During World War II, Kal Shonthaler worked on ground crew as a mechanic for B-17s and B-24s. He worked in the Seventh Squadron of the Thirty-Fourth Bomb Group. The plane he worked on most of the war was the "Misbehavin' Raven," which flew sixty-five successful missions. Although he was not in the direct line of fire, Mr. Shonthaler certainly had his share of war experiences. When I met Mr. Kal Shonthaler, he wasn't prepping an airplane; he was watching the Steeler game.

I was a mechanic for the airplanes. We got the planes ready for the crew's missions, and we repaired ships that were hit pretty badly by the Germans. When the crews were off on their missions, we would sometimes repair the ships if there was one that could be repaired. Most of the time, we would hang around the barracks, and some of the boys would have a cigarette. I never got into that. Sometimes we would go down to the pub. Anyway, it was mostly just waiting for the crews to return. Too many times, the crews never returned. Other times, the plane ran through so much flak, the boys were cut up pretty bad. So, my job was mostly to fix the planes and prepare them for their missions. I didn't choose this. We took a test, and this is what they gave me. It's quite different from what I had first hoped to do in the service, which was to be a cook and never leave the United States.

When the planes would come back in for a landing, as a rule, they should keep their lights off and keep their guns in their position and everything, but like everyone else, as soon as they got over the English Channel, they would pull in their guns and get ready to jump outta the plane. Well, one night when a plane came in for a landing and turned its lights on, the Germans were right behind 'em, and just blew 'em up to hell. They came in for a landing and knocked a building over. They hit a supply building that all the supplies were in and blew that all up. Then they were announcing that the Germans were dropping paratroops over our area and so forth. Well, then everybody was shootin', and we couldn't see nothin', and didn't know what was going on. Here, there were no paratroops; they were our own because they were jumpin' outta the planes that were shot up. Here, we were shootin' at our own men. That's what happened. They left their lights on as they came in for a landing, and the German fighter that was up in the sky... followed 'em right back and ran right in with 'em. The fellows [the gunners] were pulling their guns out, and everybody was in a hurry to get outta there, and they couldn't shoot back... The Germans were real tough that way and real smart. They [the American fighters] chased this one plane [the German fighter] all over hell, and couldn't get him, and finally he got going over the English Channel again. I guess they said they finally got him over the Channel. That was a hairy night, but they learned not to do that again. So, there were a lot of big problems that night.

We took our bikes every night and drove down to the pub, and it was all blacked out. You couldn't see nothin'. . . and of course coming home was tougher because, by then, after a few beers, why. . . they [the English] would drink their beer, and sit with one all night, and play their darts. We'd be drinking the stuff up like water. (Laughs.) If you wanted ice in your beer or whiskey or something, they thought you were nuts. So, yeah,

(Photo courtesy Kal Shonthaler)

we had a good time. We had a lot of fun incidents coming back from the pub every night. You wondered who was gonna end up in the ditch. Then we had to come back and service the airplane. Many nights we set those engines on fire, you know, giving it too much gas or something, and they had propellers in those days. So, we had to prep the engines and get everything ready for 'em [the crew]. We did all that before the crews took off in the morning. So that was kind of hairy, you know, after we'd been drinking all night, come back and start working on these airplanes. (Laughs.) They [the crew] were kind of worried. "Boy! Good luck guys!" but they were doing the same thing. That was just something everybody did because there wasn't anything else you could do. There was just a little village and a little pub, and that was it. That was where your social life was. When you went out that's where you went. It was fun, but you always had to worry about coming home. Believe me, it was pitch black. You had to wheel your bicycle, and someone was always in the ditch. (Laughs.) Like I said before, we'd get back and start up the airplanes and get them ready for their mission. We think it's funny now, but someone was actually basing their life on us. . . We won anyway, so think how bad the Germans were!

I remember D-Day pretty clearly. It was my birthday, and I was sitting on the wing of an airplane. I was repairing it. It had been hit up pretty bad from a mission a few days earlier. I can remember hearing the noise first. It wasn't the "putt-putt" of a buzz bomb. I looked up, and I couldn't even see the sky because of all the fighters and bombers. I knew then we were going to win. We were all pretty tired, and I knew the Germans wouldn't have been able to handle it. What a sight!

We knew the war was over when they closed up the pub and wouldn't let us in. I don't remember when I heard it first, but I do remember that. We must have heard it at the base and gone down to the pub to celebrate. They probably thought we were going to tear up the place. So, they took a barrel of beer, and rolled it out in the field for us. We just laid in the field and drank the beer. We were content enough. We had beer, and we were going home.

I flew home with my own ship. . . and

almost went into the ocean. Yeah, we really did. We ran outta gas, and I forget where we were at, but they had us all lined up on the side ready to bail out. We figured we were going to have to go into the water. We turned around instead, and I think we went to Greenland or Iceland. We just stayed there, got fueled up, and got outta there. It turned daylight, and it turned dark, and it turned daylight again all the time we were up in the air. I can still recall when I went up to look at the fuel tanks. They were completely empty. We wouldn't have been able to stay up much longer. It was a long trip home. So, when it was mostly all over with, we almost got killed.

I think a lot of wars are just a waste of a lot of good people. I don't think they accomplish a lot. When they're all over with and everything's said and done, we wonder what did we get out of this, but a lot of dead people? I don't think you'd be able to draft our kids today. The government couldn't say, "Well we're gonna take you in tomorrow." There'd be quite a protest. "I have something better to do." All the boys in the neighborhood were drafted. Everybody went. Yet, World War II was something the United States was forced into. They attacked us. We didn't have a choice.

These old guys [soldiers] they remember everything, and I don't remember nothin', and I could care less. They tell me about this and that; and I say, "Hell! I don't remember!" Hey, I just want to forget all that. I'm home, and that's all over with. I save nothin'. I didn't bring home any war souvenirs. The only thing I brought home was a pin cushion from Ireland for my mother. I played on the basketball team for my base, and we made it to the championship. My captain told us if we won it, he would take us to Ireland. Well, we lost, but he took us over anyway. We took a bomber during the middle of the war and flew over to Ireland. Over there, I bought the pin cushion for my mother. . . She doesn't even sew.

Mr. Shonthaler held several jobs when he returned from the war, until he finally got into sales. He has many nice memories of the war, however, he does not dwell on them. The war was a part of his past he wishes to keep there, although he does think about it. He did get the opportunity to visit his base in England with his wife, Evelyn. He and his wife were overwhelmed by the kindness of the English people. They were even allowed in the pubs.

Dec. 1944

(Photo Kal Shonthaler)

William Simmers

Transportation Divisions 590 and 595 Transportation

by
Douglas Bender

William Simmers remembers vividly his time spent during World War II. Whether it be exciting, sad, or humorous, all of his moments over in Europe are embedded deeply into his mind, but more importantly into his heart. He is currently seventy-four years old and retired, living in Grapeville, Pennsylvania.

They were all messed up after Pearl Harbor. They didn't know what was going on. I made arrangements to go for a physical. I came home and...there were three brothers and sisters in my family and...I told my brother, who was eighteen at the time, that I was up to enlist. So he said, "If you're goin' then I'm goin'." So he went up the next day to enlist, and the sergeant up at the recruiting office said to "Tell your brother if he wants to go in the Air Corps he could go." My IQ was high enough that I didn't have to worry about high school.

They sent us down to Cumberland. We stayed down there until after New Years. My brother went with the Army Engineers, but they kept me up there until about a week after New Years. Finally they sent me to truck driving training, and that's all I ever did until I went in. I took my basic training down there, and then they sent me to New Orleans, Louisiana to Lake Pontchatrain. I stayed there for two months, and then they sent me to the south of Florida outside Tampa. I stayed there 'til about October when they sent us to Mississippi. That was the training base. I stayed there until Christmas Day. We then went to New Jersey. We stayed up there 'til after New Years.

Then we went to Stone, England. I'll never forget what happened. We got there at night, and we had full field packs: rifles, gas masks...and everything. We pulled into this station...and we're waiting to get on these trucks. I said to this one truck driver, who was a GI., "Do we have to pitch our pup tents?"

"Nah!" he said, "Where you're goin' there's two men in a room."

I said, "Ah, you smart ass!" and walked away from him. I thought he was some wise guy. We get up there, and it was like that. It was an ammunition factory that the limeys had built to make ammunition, and something happened. They took it over (the American government), and we had two men in a room, and each man had a dresser and a place to hang his clothes up. Anyway, we stayed there for two weeks, and they sent us to an R.A.F. base [Huntingdon]. We took over from the limeys and set up a motor pool... and we got trucks and everything. We started operating out of there and set up a depot. It was an 8th Air Force depot which was controlled by the 8th Air Force Service Command. We hauled all the bombs, rations and airplane parts and all that. We also set up a Station Transportation Office. We took over... everything.

They had a big ceremony. I remember we tried to march to the limey band. The cadence was different than what the American cadence was and we had a rough time. We were all out of step. They apologized later, and said that they didn't realize that they had a different cadence. I guess we looked like a bunch of damn rookies.

We stayed there until August, and then they moved us out of there. They moved us to another R.A.F. station. It was about forty miles away. We were there for about a month and they said, "Hey boys, we're gonna have to move you to the other side of the field." There was gonna be an operational base on the side where we were. They had a bunch of English Mosquitoes which were used for mapping. Roosevelt's son was the commanding officer on that side of the base. We were on the other side in tents. We were waiting for them to get our barracks done. We had no heat! All we had was cold water.

Back when I was in Huntingdon, the first sergeant said to me, "Hey Simmers, do you want to be a dispatcher?"

I said, '"I don't know what to do."

He said, "All you do is answer the phone and write trip tickets."

So I said, "I'll try it." and that's how I got into the dispatch office. When we went to Watton, we set up a B-24 depot. They made our CO. the Station Transportation Officer. Any transportation off the base had to be handled through this office. Eventually we had four truck companies.

I stayed in that transportation office, for about six months. This old colonel came in and took over this transportation office from our CO. Our CO. said, "These are my men and I'm taking them back to my outfit." This new colonel said, "No way! If they're willing to work for me, I'll keep them in this office."

Then he said, "Stay with me and I'll give you each a promotion of one rank." At the time I was a corporal, so I got promoted to sergeant.

Our CO. said, "Simmers, don't put your stripes on. I would have promoted you myself, but we're at full strength." So, we didn't sew our stripes on.

That colonel came in and said, "Boy, you guys aren't very damn grateful! I get you all promoted, and you don't even sew your stripes on." I told him what our CO. said and he went through the roof. He was furious. He said, "You sew them on; I'll take care of that!"

I worked in the office with him [the colonel] and I got to be pretty good friends with him. I told him that I was getting tired of this job. I would like to get back into driving trucks. As a sergeant, I had to take care of what they call a section. I had fifteen trucks and fifteen to twenty men. I ran convoys. I got a food run. We had to go to a depot and pick up the food and run it around. We hauled bombs 'til about a year before the war was over. Then we started hauling airplane parts.

The day after the war was over, they put us on a 17, and they flew us over Germany to show the damage we had done there. It was really something. We were airborne for over eight hours. That was the highlight when the war was over. He flew about one thousand feet off the ground. You could see all those airplane pieces all over the place, and some of those ten and twelve story buildings...you could see all the way to the cellar. It was really something.

About a week after the war was over, the first sergeant said, "Simmers, Colonel Harris wants to see you."

I thought, "What the hell did I do now?'"
I went off to see him, and he said, "You've been over here a long time (I was overseas for over two-and-a-half years) and I know that you'd probably like to get home. I have to send one truck company back to the States for thirty days, and then they're going to Okinawa. If you wanna go, I can send ya. If you go with this outfit, you'll be go-

Shower Room of the 301st Fighter Wing.
(Photo courtesy Merle Keister)

(Photo courtesy Edward Jones)

ing in a week." So I took a chance on that. I came home, and I landed back in New York on July 19,1945. The war ended in August. Also, when I got home, I got married.

Other than this brief history, three major stories still stick in Mr. Simmers mind, and he was kind enough to share them. They are very humorous and somewhat touching.

Colonel Harris called me into the office one day and said, "Simmers, they've sent about nine or ten guys to this rocket-launching school." These guys, they were all coming back and they were flunking it. So he said, "How about you going up there and seein' if you can do it." I think I was there for a week. I had to wear my uniform up there. When I went in there, this old sergeant came up to me and said, "Hey! I see you're a quartermaster. I don't like those damn Air Corps guys! If you listen to what I tell ya, you'll come out of here with a good grade. I got 100%. All the guys flunked it. There was nothing to it. He just didn't like them and he flunked them all. (Laughs.)

When I was in England, my brother got sent over there. I tried to find out where he was, but I couldn't find out nohow. My brother, he was smart. He met a limey girl. This limey girl sent me a letter and told me where he was at. So I told old Colonel Harris that my brother was here, and that I wanted to go see him. He gave me a pass, and said, "Go tomorrow!" I had no idea why he said that. Here, he knew that the invasion was coming off. I went down. We were in the northern part of England, and he was in the southern part down where they were ready to go across the Channel. I got to see my brother, and I stayed there overnight. I went back to London the next day, and then took a train back to the base. It was already restricted... we weren't allowed off the base. I remember the day of the invasion, because it was on my day off. We went six days on and then one day off. When we had a day off, we slept all that we could. Anyway, I was sleeping, and the first thing I heard was this bang. Two bombers had come together. As I looked out the barracks door, I saw a tail section come down. They must have exploded up in the air. The engines windmilled down and made a funny noise. Everybody got killed that was in the two planes.

England's a foggy place. When we were driving, we weren't allowed to use headlights. All we had were two little "cat eyes" to follow. I don't know how many limeys we ever ran over. The bobbies would always be out at our base checking all the time - looking for paint or anything on our trucks that looked like we ran over somebody. Again, all we had were two little "cat eyes" to follow. If he went off into the ocean, we would have all followed him in. This was one of the things of being in a strange country. You're off, driving on the wrong side of the road. I remember one time when I was dispatching we got two new drivers. I said to one guy, "You realize, you're in England and you drive on the wrong side of the road."

'Oh, no problem!' He didn't go down the road but a mile and hit some limey head on.

The other guy, I sent him to Manchester. I said to him, " Now don't forget, if something happens and that truck won't move, check the transfer case. Make sure that it's in gear." The transfer case transferred the power to the front wheels. It had to be in gear, or it was just like being in neutral in your car. He goes over there and then starts back and calls to say it won't move.

I said, "Did you check the transfer case? Make sure it's in gear."

He said, 'Oh yeah!"

So I sent one of those big four-ton wreckers over there. First thing you know, this wrecker comes back and he doesn't have a truck on the back. I said, "Where's that truck?"

He said, "He's coming."

I said, "You mean he's driving?"

He said, "Yeah"

I said, "Well, what was wrong with it?"

He said, "The transfer case was out of gear!"

That's the kind of experiences I had!!!!!!! (Laughs.)

I'd like to take this opportunity to thank Mr. Simmers and his wife, Larue, for their wonderful hospitality. I also want to congratulate them on fifty happy years of marriage, which has brought them five children and eighteen grandchildren. Best wishes in the future.

Coke and refreshment bar at Fowlmere. (Photo courtesy Tom Brown)

Joseph Volpatti

305th Bomb Group
422nd Squadron
Crew Chief

by
Brianne Stellfox

Mr. Volpatti was the boy next door that cared about everybody in the neighborhood and found every opportunity in life to laugh. Perhaps it was his devotion to friends and his ability to cope that made him the happy, successful man he is today.

It was a Sunday afternoon and we were sitting down to dinner. Our family always had dinner at two o'clock in the afternoon. I was fifteen years old. We went down to the corner where we all hung out, and all the guys talked about was what we were going to do, and what we were going to enlist in. I couldn't wait 'til I was seventeen. That was the age you could enlist in the Navy and the Marine Corps. When I was seventeen every Saturday a couple of us guys would go into Pittsburgh and get enlistment papers, bring them home, and our parents wouldn't sign. So at one point another friend and I went up to enlist in the Navy.

There was a Navy cadet training program. You enlisted at seventeen, and they called you at eighteen. We went up there, and the quota was full. So the Navy man there said, "The Air Force isn't full downstairs." We went down and enlisted in the Air Force. Then, when we were eighteen, they called us in. So that's how I picked it, because the other one was full. (Laughs.)

[We left] kinda quick! I mean everybody that was leaving during that period of time left at night, and everybody had an opportunity to go to the train station and weep and wave goodbye. Anyway, we went down to get our instructions, and the officer standing up there says when this period of time is over we're going right to the train station, and we'll leave. (Laughs.) I was sitting there without a piece of clothing, a toothbrush, or anything. My Dad called home, and they ran down with everything. Before I knew it, I was on the train. I didn't have time to realize. It took days for that to set in - that, oh, this is it ! All our friends were calling that night. You'd have ten, fifteen, twenty people, family and everybody waving. I was gone before they even got out of school, or my sister even got out of work.

We went to Indiantown Gap first, and that was the induction center, and then I went to Biloxi, Mississippi for basic training. We went into what was called a cadet training program. We were supposedly like you people, we were gifted - special - which was just a ruse so we would enlist. (Laughs.) Then you went to AM school, which I did, and radio school. That was, like I said, just a trick. You went down and enlisted, and when they got you there, they just failed you. We were supposed to go on and study and be pilots, navigators, copilots, and things of that nature, and be commissioned officers. Well that was a joke . We never got near the school.

I went to school down in Mississippi after basic training. I went to AM school, that's "Airplane" and "Engine Mechanic." Then from there we went up to Georgefield, Illinois. We were training on C-46s. That was a troop carrier command. That was where they took the airborn infantry. Pilots would come up and get training on twin-engine ships, 'cause when they got their wings and their commission they learned on single engines. Then they had to learn to fly twin-engines. We were the flying crew and the ground crew for them. We fixed the planes, and we would get up and fly with them. I was a crew chief with four guys, and we took care of one particular plane all the time... kept it flying, kept it repaired; and then we'd fly with them. What you did was stand behind the pilot and copilot and check all the dials and the gauges and make sure everything was working properly. We used to kid them -(laughs)- that we'd do all the work and knew all about it, and all they did was steer. I'm sure some of them took offense to that.

The time I was in, I only had one fifteen-day furlough in a couple of years. You're supposed to get a fifteen-day furlough every six months. (Laughs.) I laugh because this all seems so ridiculous to me now. You were supposed to, but we didn't.

We were going to the South Pacific as a support group for the attack on Japan. Well, when they heard I was coming they quit - (Laughs) - they surrendered. That's what we were doing, we were in that process, because the war in Germany was over, and we were fighting the Japanese. They were going to bomb Japan and launch an attack on the mainland, the same as they did in Europe. We were going to be support. Then when the war ended, they shipped us to France. From there we went across France in what they call "forty and eight," [meaning] forty men or eight horses [could fit into] boxcars. In the dead of winter you just got in with no heat and traveled across France and into Germany. We were stationed in a base in Germany. That's where I was when I was assigned to that bomb group that we belong to in the 8th Air Force. I know it sounds ridiculous to you, but I was a baby. Most of the fellows in this are in their mid to late seventies. I just turned seventy this year, so actually I was really young.

It was scary all the time. Seriously, I didn't have the experience that some of the combat men had, particularly on the ground. My experience like that was rather limited. There were moments in the air,

Loading .50 caliber ammunition in clips.

(Photo courtesy Tom Brown)

training pilots. It's like when your parents taught you how to drive. It was the same thing when they were teaching those officers to fly those twin-engine ships. I mean it was just like somebody getting out of a car after they got their driver's license and getting into a tractor trailer. There were times I wouldn't even look out the hatch, 'cause nobody knew where they were. They were just all over the place, and we had some near collisions. But when you're eighteen you figure you're coming home anyhow. I don't think at that age they went into the service thinking they weren't coming back again no matter what.

I never had a problem with that, [keeping morale up]. There were some fellows that had a difficult time with that. There was a little group of us (smiles) kinda not too tight up here (points to his head). I mean we had guys that in basic training were sent home because they couldn't handle it. They were sick all the time. The one fellow, when we left Indiantown Gap, sat there. We were on the train. He sat there in his seat by the window with his mother and dad's picture on one knee and his girlfriend's on the other. He cried all the time, and he wouldn't eat. When we got down to Mississippi, and were assigned quarters, he was in our barracks. After a month he was called to headquarters and one day came back, and he was packing his bags. I said, "What are you doing?" He said, "I'm going home. They're discharging me." We all started crying then. (Laughs.) We thought, Hey, we'd get out. It was sad to watch some people, but there was a group of us that just made a game out of it, which sounds silly. That's the way you handled things. You can't take that stuff too serious. You would get homesick. There were no two ways about it. If you came in the barracks and there was a guy laying on the bunk just looking at the bunk above him, you never said a word to him 'cause you knew what his problem was. It would come on you all of a sudden. For maybe a day you'd be kinda crushed and feeling bad. After that it would pass, and then your buddies would start all over again. I mean all kinds of tricks they played on each other.

He's dead now, a friend of mine, but once, I went downstairs to take a shower, I came up and my bunk was empty. When you got into a camp they gave you a mattress, pillow, mattress covers and blankets. Everything was gone. What he had done was taken all my equipment and turned it back in to the quartermaster. I had to go back over and try and explain to him what happened. (Laughs.) You know those army cots - they had little springs all the way around. What they did to another guy while he was showering, was take all the springs off and tie string to hold the whole thing up. He would come up and run across the barracks and dive in his bed. The whole thing was tied up with string, so you can imagine what happened when he came from the shower. There were other things that I won't tell you that those guys did. (Laughs.) We were all the bottom of the alphabet, down at the end of the barracks, and we got in trouble for cutting up too. One man, his name was Wanamaker, we called him Murphy, 'cause the sergeant couldn't pronounce his name. He said, "From now on you're Murphy." We were in formation messing around, and the officer got mad. They were giving us shots, and he came by and said, "Get the names of these last four guys. They're going on K.P." The next day there was an induction at Indiantown Gap, we woke up, and the four of us were in the barracks. Nobody else was there. All day long we didn't see anybody. You know what we determined - they took our four names, and left us off, and turned the rest of the barracks in to the K.P. When those guys came back they were ready to kill us. We were supposed to be on K.P., and whoever took the names thought he meant that we weren't supposed to, but the rest of the barracks was. (Laughs.) So we were fearing for our lives. They went out at four o'clock in the morning to go on K.P. and came back after dinner.

[The war] did change my life, and my attitude a little bit too. I had four sisters,

Nose art.

(Photo courtesy Frank De Cola)

and I was in camp, and I got a letter one day from my oldest sister. I'm reading it, and it says, "Mother had a baby boy." I folded it up and put it back in the envelope. I thought I had someone else's mail. Here my mother was expecting, and my mother was little and round. She was always little and round. My brother is eighteen years younger than me. I didn't know him 'til I came home, and he was several years old. Even when I came home with the G.I. Bill of Rights, I was supposed to go to the University of Pittsburgh to study engineering. I was twenty-two, and I went out to the campus, and I'm standing there, and I see all these kids running around acting goofy and giggling. I mean, you went away eighteen and came back older, but I don't mean in years. So, I came back home and said, "I'm not going to school." Now if I would have come out of high school and went right into college, it might have been different today.

When you're eighteen years old, wars look pretty neat, and they look pretty stupid when you're seventy. We're fortunate! We have five sons, we have a bunch of grandkids (smiles), and everything's wonderful. But I feel for those guys that never made it, never got back to have that opportunity. The way I see people acting today - they don't care. They don't appreciate it. They did an awful lot so that you kids can do what you want. People laid their lives down for that. I feel bad for them, I really do.

Joseph Volpatti is a modest veteran who doesn't think his time served needs to be mentioned because his combat time was limited. However, his time served has changed his life significantly and has made him an even more fanatically patriotic American. He cares even more about everybody in his family and neighborhood and still finds all the right reasons to laugh. He's everyone's favorite dad, grandpa, neighbor, and friend.

Robert Walters Sr.

556th Service Group Ground Crew

by
Angela Edwards

Mr. Robert Walters Sr. is a warm, optimistic man with a very friendly smile. He has a rather soft, comforting way about him. He is a very family-oriented man, quiet and reserved, but yet personable and enthusiastic about detailing his career and past experiences. He had a vivid picture of the past and was able to recount it well. Most importantly, Mr. Walters understood the value and worth of every individual involved in the war, regardless of their position. Mr. Walters knew these planes inside and out. As he showed me every corner, crevice and cramped space that was occupied by the crew, he rattled off names of engines, parts, problems and their solutions while I listened in awe. His collection of WWII model planes can only be described as perfectly complete. His wife, Lillian described him as "everybody's handyman", and I must agree, and also conclude that Mr. Walters certainly should have the utmost pride in his accomplishments.

I worked as an automobile service manager for an Oldsmobile and Cadillac agency in Brackenridge. I had worked there since I was sixteen, and I worked there until I went into the service. I graduated from high school in '39. I enlisted when I was twenty-one. I joined and met Murry, oh I can't think of his first name... from Springdale; and we went into Pittsburgh and enlisted, and then we were sent to Cumberland to the induction center. At that time I was in pretty good shape. (Laughs). I didn't have any trouble. I wanted to get in as a pilot, and I had this knuckle that was broken before; and they said that at high altitude it would affect my trigger finger. So I didn't make that. Well, I went right into Cumberland. They put us on a train, a troop train; and we ended up in Biloxi, Mississippi. I went to the Air Force school there. I was a specialist on the Rolls-Royce engine, and the English Spitfire. They called it the Merlin, but it was the same engine. The schools we went to were fantastic. When you went into the service they questioned what you did and well. That's where you would go to. I really liked it... I could never replace it - the experience - what I've been through. The twenty-seventh of October [1941] I graduated. I went through that school for all the engines, not just one type. It was all kinds. Some that never were in combat. Some that were experimental. This was down in Keisler Field [Mississippi]. It was really wonderful for me, because I was mechanically inclined.

That was my training there; and when I had graduated, they sent me to Detroit, and I went to the Packard-Loder Company. The P-51 and the English Spitfire, I was a specialist on them. After Detroit I was sent to Groton, Connecticut, and a new airfield just opened up. It was for fighter squadrons to train, and they had the P-47. They looked at my service record and knew that I had rode a tow truck and worked in a garage as a service man, so they put me down in the motor pool. They sent me up to Bradley Field to learn how to run a big snowplow because of the snow up there, and we didn't have equipment. Then I was called and transferred to Long Island, to an air base. They sent me on trips to Springfield, Illinois, and we rode big tank trucks for the Air Force. We had the big gasoline tankers, and we would take them though the [turnpike] tunnels five at a time. I liked it all, I mean, I loved to drive! I love airplanes, too. I've loved airplanes all my life - cars and airplanes. Then I was in Northern Ireland, and our colonel went to the CBI (China Burning India theory). He wanted our squadron to get in preparation to go there. Then this field opened up in France - this emergency field. We were all equipped and ready to go; so we flew over [to England] instead.

I was only in England maybe a week at the most, but I did like the people. The Irish people I was with quite a bit, and I really liked them, too. I met a couple of Irishmen who had their own taxis, and we used to get them all the time and go into town from the base. As a matter of fact, a lot of the guys would call me because I knew them the best, to get the taxi to take them into town and bring them home. And the few times that I was in England, the buzz bombs, you'd hear them coming. They'd land off a bit from you. But we were lucky. Some people weren't.

[After arriving at the emergency field in France], we did anything there was to be done to a plane: sheet metal work, engines changed, props changed, battle damage. We patched it to get it back to England. We didn't do a perfect job or anything like that, but we did an emergency to get it back 'cause we were on this field for emergency purposes. After their first bombing, they [the fighter planes] had a long ways to go back to England. Maybe they couldn't make it. Some would be captured. We were there, and in case they did go down someplace else, we were notified. We sent people out to check the plane, and see if it could be salvaged, and get it back in the air. We worked on anything and everything. We worked on B-17s, B-24s, P-51s, P-47s, B-26s, and A-20s. There was a P-51 that went off the end of the runway, and where its wheels were, there were deep holes in the ground. The ground was soft. It would be frozen,

P-51 being towed for a repair. (Photo courtesy Frank De Cola)

and by eight o'clock in the morning the planes would start to sink if you got off the concrete. I never saw ground like it. (That was in France). This one B-17 came in, and they had been flying in formation. They hit an air pocket. One plane went down, and one went up. It took the tail gunner right out. He was the only one that was killed. When we got it back [the plane] the tail fell off shortly after. It's just, things like that, though, you wonder how it didn't collapse while they were flying. What held it there? It was cracked the whole way up. We always had something to work on, something to patch up. Sometimes we'd be out there all night. If a plane went down in the field, why, we would send out a crew to patch it up there; change the engine if it was burnt up; change the oil, filter, lines, wheels, anything we had to do to get that plane back. We didn't work by hours; we worked by days. We were on call all the time. You'd go out there, and you might be there all day and all night. Sometimes we would just sleep in the plane out in the field. We had an A-20 come in. It crashed its landing gear when it hit the dirt, but there was nothing we could do about it. He was out of fuel.

I know one time we needed a supercharger duct for this Pathfinder. The Pathfinder was the one that led the flights. So there was this 17 bellied in, over in Belgium, and they got word to us. They thought we could get the part for the Pathfinder. It was supposed to have been in our allied territory. When we went over the plane had been stripped. All the guns were gone, and nobody was there. Ed and I cut down into the wing. We cut a hole. This was a 24, and we took that duct out. We spent a day and a half. Coming back we ran into the British Army. They hadn't taken over that area yet! (Laughs). We saw this group of people coming up at a distance and thought, Oh Geez! I had a .45 and a Tommy gun, and Ed had a rifle and a pistol. They came up, and talked English, and wanted to know what we were doing. The underground had got the [the crew] out. Ed asked them, "Have you seen any Germans?" They said, "This morning? Yeah." The British were supposed to have taken over this area, but they hadn't got there yet. That's the way communications was, you know. We ran into them when we were leaving town. They were just coming in. When you're driving a jeep and you make a turn and all you see is that barrel of that cannon coming out of that tank - (laughs) - you think a little bit.

The way some of those pilots could fly those things! And the way some of these planes came in, it was unbelievable!. But they still got them in and got out of them... Like they said, a wing and a prayer. Some of the flights were, maybe eight or ten hours. It was long because at that time you didn't have the speed that you got now. We didn't have a lot of supplies. We couldn't keep all the engines because you didn't know what you would need. All the scrap was just left there after the war. If a guy would have bought that field and dug up all that, he would have been a millionaire. Sometimes I would like to go back.

The German fighters came in and strafed us. It was New Years' Eve, right at midnight, and we were living in Meruille, France, in a seminary building with a courtyard in the middle. My bedroom was right in the middle of the building on the top floor. Only one guy got hit in the leg. Some of the rooms were shot up pretty good, and some of the beds. One guy said he was going to be good from then on. (Laughs). Then, at the time of the Bulge, we were stationed at a dance hall in Danier, France and we had to be moved because of it.

[After the war] I went back to the garage and worked there for a couple of years, and then I went into the steel mill and worked in there as a repairman. My brother-in-law and I went to school for bricklaying, and my wife and I were able to get our first house [on the GI Bill].

Too many people were connected [to WWII], but a lot of good stuff went on, and everybody worked at their best.

George Wolfe

466th Bomb Group
784th Squadron
Crew Chief

by
Andrew Otterson

Mr. George Wolfe is a sharp and energetic man who was raised in Altoona. He has an enthusiastic wife, whom he named his plane after, and a family of nine children. He is involved in various clubs and still rides his motorcycle around on the weekends. Mr. Wolfe was a crew chief in the war and tells his story with both seriousness and humor.

Well, I went in on October 10, 1942, I enlisted rather than be drafted 'cause I figured if I enlisted I could get in the Army Air Corps rather than the infantry or artillery or something like that, and I already liked airplanes. I worked in Baltimore as a sheet metal man and machinist. I left there and went up to Middletown, and they sent me to a school where I went into the engine overhaul department. I was there awhile working as a mechanic. However, I decided I better go enlist before they drafted me, and put me where I didn't want to go. So I went and enlisted.

The Air Force sent me to basic training out in California, and I went from there to Airplane Department and Mechanic School for a whole year and then to B-24 school down in San Diego. They assigned you a serial number of a plane that wasn't even built yet. You stayed with that airplane from the time they built it to the time it was finished. When it was completed, you would go up on the first flight with it - which I did. On that first flight we went up, and flew up over the Salton Sea which is a sort of salty lake there northeast of San Diego. We flew around over there, and the one instrument was bad, so we came back in, and landed. The crew came out and put a new one in, and we went up on another short flight just to check it out. Then the Air Force checked and signed the airplane off as their property. After that they sent us, of all things, to gunnery school up in Utah. That had nothing to do with airplanes! We were going back to basics which we had already been through.

They assigned me to a B-24 outfit in Salina, Kansas, as a mechanic. I was only there six or eight weeks, and they deactivated that outfit for reasons I didn't understand then, but I know now what happened. The outfit had to drop practice bombs on targets, and be at certain places at certain times. Depending on how they do on that determines whether the outfit is certified as good or not so good. Well, as it turned out the outfit wasn't as good as they should have been, so they were deactivated.

I was then sent out to Alamogordo, New Mexico. I went out there and was on Production Line Maintenance, where each crew did a certain thing, and that was all you did. I was on an engine crew working on the engines there. We did that for a couple of months; then they started moving some of us to the west side of the base to a new outfit which was the 466th Bomb Group. We got our airplanes in, and they were mostly training planes then, not the latest stuff. They would fly and fly, practice bombing, practice flying, and navigation. When the airplane came back, of course we had to work on it, put fuel in it, check the oil in the engines, and any minor troubles. Then the next or maybe even the same day they would go back out again and would keep doing that. They did it for months. Eventually they passed the Preparation for Overseas Movement Test, which my former outfit failed. They sent us in groups east, I went up to a place outside New York City about twenty miles. Then they sent the pilots back to San Diego for all new airplanes. They flew the planes across the country down to Brazil, over to Africa, and up to England.

We met the pilots over in England at the base. I was at Station 120, and the village was called Attlebridge. While the war was going on they used numbers for base names so the enemy supposedly couldn't find them. I got there in February of 1944 and started operations just a few weeks later. The base life wasn't bad, we had a little hut that was a wooden building. The building was about forty feet long and eighteen feet wide or something like that. They had bunks inside, but there was no water or bathrooms in the huts. They had bathrooms in certain areas that you had to walk to. You would go there in the morning to wash and shave, and the water was always cold unless you could beat the crowd. The airplanes were about a mile away from this area. It's funny, because when I was back in England I lived about fifteen miles from the base, and the base had been converted into a turkey farm. They had built a turkey hanger right where my airplane used to be!

I was at Station 120 from February, 1944 to June, 1945 before it was over and all that. In fact, when the war was over, I was sitting out in the plane. I knew everything was over, and I was sitting out in the plane listening to command radio. I heard Churchill say that everything was over. (When asked how he felt when he heard that, he smiled, nodded, and said, "Pretty good.")

Our outfit was one of the lucky ones, I guess. We didn't lose that many planes, but we did lose some. We had some crash on take off. A couple that had been shot up crashed on landing. The worst one we ever had, that I know of, happened on take off. One of the other squadrons was taking off one morning; and when you get new pilots, they didn't realize that the runway came uphill a little then leveled off. Sometimes when they would go up there, their plane would be going about ninety to one-hundred miles per hour, and the plane would actually lift off the ground a little. Well the old pilots knew better and would let their planes settle down on the runway again and get up enough speed. This guy apparently pulled up too soon and did what they call a "stall." I don't mean the engines stopped. The engines were still beating away, but the airplane didn't have flying speed. They went off onto one wing and went into the ground, blowing up with nearly all of their bomb load also exploding. So there was nearly nothing left. There were ten guys that were killed. That was the worst one we had. Then we had another one. A plane was taking off, and they didn't get high enough - ending up flying through the tree tops. This was in early spring, so there weren't many leaves on the trees, but it caused an incendiary bomb to fall off on the bomb bay and begin to burn. The flight engineer tried to get it out, but he couldn't, and the plane went into a field about a mile or so away. In England open fields had telephone poles placed in them so gliders couldn't land, but of course when the plane went down he was knocking over the poles like they were picket fences. The plane caught fire and burned up, with only one or two of the crew getting out.

I was what you call a crew chief on the airplane. I was in charge of the airplane with one or two other guys working with me. After we were there about eight to ten months, they got rid of our regular bomber, and we got what they called a "Pathfinder." It was one with a lot of radar on it, carrying a little less bomb load. This plane would go ahead of everything about half a mile, and they would look at the target with radar. When they dropped their bombs, everyone else would drop their own. That's what they called "pattern bombing". There could be about four hundred to five hundred airplanes up there each having about eight to twelve bombs, and they could really make a mess of things.

I stayed until June, 1945, then we flew back from England, over to Iceland, to Labrador, and then to Connecticut. When we were flying back from Iceland the navigator had a bet that we would get there at a certain time. If we did, we would all buy him a drink; and if he was wrong, he'd buy us all drinks! I got out of that plane and haven't seen it since, but I still remember that plane so well that I could get in it and do a preflight, just like I was there yesterday. A preflight was just a simple check of the propellers, filling the gas tank and wiring the cap shut. Then, when they came back, I had to look it over to see if it got shot up, refuel it, and clean it out inside especially the .50 caliber shells from the gunners. Also if anything was broke, we had to repair it. The crew would take a test flight to make sure it was all right, and I would usually go with them. So I got to fly quite a bit.

One of only two that came home from the Schweinfurt mission of Thursday, October 14, 1943.

(Photo courtesy Tom Miller)

I always wanted to fly a mission, but the crews had superstitions and so on. One time I even got out there one morning with my flight suit on and ready to go, but the pilot said, " Hey you're not going with us. " So I didn't go. Some of the crew chiefs in the air were pretty bad and messed things up every once in awhile. One time my airplane came back, and they had to land at another field. They said it was out of fuel, and I said, "Baloney, it was full when they left, and nobody else ran out." So they took me in the jeep with my boss, and we took the dipstick. It turned out that the guy didn't transfer the fuel right. So when we flew home, I took over the fuel transfer because I wasn't much of a swimmer and the North Atlantic wasn't very warm.

Shortly before the armistice was signed, they began taking us on milk runs over Germany. About ten or twelve of us would get on a plane. We would fly down the Rhine River, go around Munich and up to Berlin, and back over the country right over windmills and everything. The cities were rubble. It is amazing how they could ever rebuild it. When the whole city is bombed, there was not a complete building standing. There was nothing. We hammered them with our B-24s. and B-17s. One of the stupid things the Germans did was not having any big bombers. Instead they used fighters, dive bombers, V-2 missiles, and buzz bombs.

We (my wife and I) were living at the Alamogordo base when they set off the first atomic bomb. We were about thirty miles away, but there was just a long boom at about 5:00 in the morning. Everyone thought that an ammunition dump blew up, or that was the story.

After the war in Japan was over, I was discharged from El Paso, Texas. They closed everything. People were running around going crazy flipping streetcars over and everything. Boy did they celebrate! Every town all over the country had celebrations.

Lt. Col. Clark speaks at V-E Day ceremony. (Photo courtesy Tom Brown)

M.P.s fold the flag during a V-E Day ceremony. (Photo courtesy Tom Brown)

OTHER CREWS
UNTOLD STORIES

O Wind of heaven, by Thy might
Save all who dare the eagle's flight; And keep them
by Thy watchful care From every peril in the air.

"Eternal Father's, Strong to Save"
Lyrics by Robert Nelson Spencer

OTHER CREWS - UNTOLD STORIES

The only unfortunate part of "Operation Immortality" was that there were some veterans who were unable to be interviewed because of various factors including; distance, schedule availability, health, the number of students involved, and the fact that time simply ran out. The photos in this section and in other places throughout the book indicate that there are still many untold stories out there. We only wish we could have gathered them all.

Frank De Cola and crew at Topeka, Kansas. Eight of these ten stayed together for 35 missions over Europe. Top row, left to right - Duke Matteas, Tom Miller, A. Muntean, Martin Richards. Bottom row, left to right - E. Patagine, Vince Haley, Frank De Cola, O.S. Kaplan, Bud Combs.

(Photo courtesy Frank De Cola)

Elliott Klein and crew at King's Cliffe 18th Weather Det. - Top row, left to right - Dunn, Mason, Powers, Stern. Bottom row, left to right - Klein, Kadzielsky, Oliver.

(Photo courtesy Elliott Klein)

Lacy Lackey and crew of 390th Bomb Group. This photo was taken at the conclusion of this crew's last mission November 12, 1944. Top row, left to right - Lt. Col. Joe Walters (Wing and Group Command Pilot), First Lt. Richard Willits (Group Bombardier), First Lt. Gougas (Squadron Bombardier), Capt. Lacy Lackey (Lead Pilot), First Corp. Rosen (Group Navigator), First Lt. Mike Heaton "Mickey" Operator. Bottom row, left to right - First Sgt. Leonard Coglietta, S/Sgt. George Shioaker, T/Sgt. John Grznar, T/Sgt. George Walters (Flight Engineer/Top Gunner).

(Photo courtesy Lacy Lackey)

Robert Lloyd and crew. Mr. Lloyd flew thirty-four missions. His crew was stationed at Seething, England. Top row, left to right - Harry Harris, Carl Eggert, Hosie, Adamodis, Cone, Harley Plante. Bottom row, left to right - Ed Sichtell, Bob Lloyd, John Sexton, Don Mach.

(Photo courtesy Robert Lloyd)

Charles Swjantek and crew. Top row, left to right - Galloway (Navigator), Beatty (Bombardier), Litz (Copilot), Marchbank (Pilot). Bottom row, left to right - Doran (Ball-Turret Gunner), Swjantek (Waist Gunner), Buck (Tail Gunner), Tracy (Engineer/Gunner), Gardipee (Nose Gunner), Williams (Radio Operator).

(Photo courtesy Charles Swjantek)

Robert Yowan and crew. Those indicated with an "" were killed in action over Leige, Belgium, on December 24, 1944. Top row, left to right - Sgt. James Weber (Flight Engineer/Top-Turret Gunner), * Sgt. Donald Huck (Radioman/Waist Gunner), * Sgt. Donald Kausrud (Waist Gunner), Sgt. Robert Yowan (Ball-Turret Gunner), Sgt. Donald Boland (Waist Gunner), Sgt. Charles Haskett (Tail Gunner). Bottom row, left to right - * Lt. Kenneth Lang (Pilot), * Lt. Howard Miller (Copilot), W. O. Samuel Alvine (Navigator), Lt. Kenneth Cox (Bombardier).*

(Photo courtesy Robert Yowan)

(Photo courtesy Stephen Kinzler)

"Bud" Knecht's jacket after 50 mission - sixteen in the 8th Air Force and thirty-four in the 15th Air Force.

(Photo courtesy "Bud" Knecht)

This plane flew 110 missions. (Photo courtesy Frank De Cola)

Writers

© John Gumpper

To you from failing hands we throw
the torch; be yours to hold it high...

"In Flander's Fields"
John McCrae

Student writers ***1995-1996***
Front row - Eric Bella, Doug Bender, Nikki Watterson, January Sta. Romana. Back row - Charlotte Kelly, Suzanne Kile, Jeanne Fischer, Jason McCormick, Nathan Tagg, Kevin Snyder.

Student writers ***1995-1996***
Front row - Emily Thomas, Amanda Johns, Laura Majersky, Amanda Ross, Emilly Swartz. Back row - Brian P. Young, Joshua Ray, Kerri Pakutz, Amy Stewart, Chris Wolfe.

Student writers 1996-1997

Front row (seated and kneeling) left to right - Lindsey Kostelnik, Heather Perkins, Stacy Geibel, Julie Croft, Kevin Tritch. Back row, left to right - Sara Giallombardo, Jennifer Nelson, Rachel Hinterlang, Amanda Holmes, Jolene McConnell, Andrew Otterson, Lori Robinson, Janice Whalen.

Student writers 1996-1997

Front row, left to right - John Hanratty, Angela Edwards, Nicole Beblo, Rachelle Olenic, Michele Van Duesen, Randy Krampert, Leann Whitesell. Back row, left to right - Brooke Swidzinski, Emily Johnson, Kristen Newell, Beth Rutowski, Brianne Stellfox, Joseph Sobieralski, Tina Snyder, Kris Toft, Nicole Webster.

Student writers 1996-1997
Front row, left to right - Jeremy Reeder, Steve Hornyak, Rachel Crider, Erin Brady. Back row, left to right - Erin Hoehn, Tara Washko, David Hoovler, Todd Ellis, Patricia Thalhofer, Jennifer Geibel, Steve Wasko.

From left to right - John Gumpper (Illustrator), Stephen Heasley (A.P. European History Instructor), William Ellis (Computer Coordinator), James Clements (Editor, Advisor).

STUDENT THOUGHTS ON "OPERATION IMMORTALITY"

When all their interviews and write-ups were done, those who participated were asked to respond to the following question: What insight have you gained, and what are your feelings now that you have completed this project? The responses were almost completely positive. The following are excerpts from approximately a third of the replies. Each paragraph represents one individual student's thoughts and feelings.

His stories of the war proved to be very insightful and fascinating. The two and a half hours spent at his home seemed to fly by as if it was only a few minutes. At times I was totally mesmerized by his personal testimony on World War II. It was well worth the effort, and I think the experience will stay with me indefinitely.

I was not thrilled about this project when it was first mentioned. Now, I'm glad I did it. I took my younger sister along, and Mr. _____ was pleased to have an audience to share history with us; things that you can't find in textbooks. He was very easy to listen to, and we could have stayed all day. It made me happy when he told us how glad he was that we were interested, because his own children had never asked him about his years in the war. In that moment, the whole project seemed worthwhile, and I understood why we were doing this.

I have gained a new appreciation for the veterans of WWII and all wars... the amount of patriotism and bravery that existed.. My interviewee had so much pride for the United States, that he easily would have done it all again. Overall, I feel that I have learned much valuable and memorable information from this experience that could never be found in any history book.

The knowledge I gained is priceless and is different from anything I could ever get from a book. I also got more than just facts; his stories contained a tiny piece of him, of his personality. I expected to have some difficulty in writing the paper because I was not sure if I would have enough information. I soon discovered that I had too much. Some of the stories had to be cut out. That is honestly the only negative thing I have to say; it broke my heart to leave things out, a part of his personality was lost in doing so. I feel that my interviewee and I gained from this experience. He was given the chance to tell his story to someone who was eager to hear. I was mentally transported into a different time and given a piece of history. I was able to share his memories and now they have become a part of mine.

Talking to Mr. _____ was quite enjoyable. He was very nice and had a lot to say. I felt badly that he did not feel that he was a hero. Everyone from any war is a hero in my eyes.

I thought that the project was very worthwhile. There's a gap between the generations, and I think that it's growing. Personally, I was filled with a terrific respect for the men and women that fought in the war... I don't think that I could ever give as selflessly as they did.

I learned that there are a lot of people alive and well who have helped create America's history, and we rarely show our appreciation. I learned you can discover a lot about our history when you just ask someone who was there.

After I talked to Mr. _____ , I went to work and told my friends about the project. I said that my interviewee was the nicest guy that I had ever met. Mr._____ spoke not only about bombers and missions, but about people. There was one thing in particular that struck me about his stories. Over and over again, he said that he did not hate the Germans. He was only doing a job. This is probably the most profound thing that I learned from the project. The human side of war is something that I had never thought about. It is possible that this aspect of war is gone forever as a result of high-tech weapons... Regardless of this, I have learned that there is a human aspect to war, and that it lives on in the memories of the men who fought.

I would recommend a project like this to anyone who would like to bridge the generation gap between those they believe they have nothing in common with. It turns out that people of the Eighth Air Force and today's youth have a lot more in common than they may think,

My feelings about this project are all positive. It gave me the chance to meet a very special and knowledgeable man. The project made me feel as if I were preserving something very special. Personally, I feel that I am very fortunate to have met a person who embodies many of the qualities one should have when it comes to defending peace and liberty.

Numerous people, including my parents, have commented to me that this research project was a wonderful idea, and I now completely agree. This was a unique experience, that I will remember for the rest of my life.

I was touched that someone who had never met me before could open his heart to me and just tell me anything that came to mind. I could not help being a little awestruck. I was sitting beside a man, who when he was younger than I, was willing to sacrifice his life for this country. I am not sure I could be that noble. Listening to him talk, I realized I was gaining pieces of history that I would never learn in a classroom from a textbook. It was raw, the kind of stuff they do not like to teach in school. I felt like I was actually taken back into time and seeing everything he had seen.

These people that we interviewed are all heroes in my mind. Whether they were pilots or cooks, gunners, or nurses, they all did what they had to do in order to help our people survive. I believe Mr. _____ said it best when he said, "The war made me patriotic...I still am." Doing this project has been one of the most memorable times of my senior year... an experience that will remain etched in my mind for a very long time. I'd like to thank Mr. ____ for taking time...to sit and talk with me, but more importantly, for adding new perspective to my life

It's so amazing to think what those young men did for our country - they gave up their lives at home with family and friends to go to a foreign land and try to make this world a better place for everyone to live in. All of them are true heroes, and I learned from him that we can't take life for granted. I'm really happy that I was given the opportunity to meet such a man and share these experiences with an older generation.

Mr. _____ taught me more than just stories about World War II, he taught me to appreciate life. My interview with him gave me a totally different view. Life is something that most people seem to take for granted, at least I did. But after spending an hour with Mr. _____ my appreciation of life expanded. I came to the realization that life is too short to focus on the negatives. It is a time to experience, learn, and meet many people.

At times this interview made me a little sad when I realized what these guys had done.

When this project was first assigned, I was reluctant... I was nervous about entering a stranger's home to dig up old memories. I thought it would be a dry, dead-end subject. Then I met Mr. ____ . Mr. ____ is one of the most interesting people I have ever met. He told so many wonderful stories that it was difficult to choose just a few for my paper. He made me understand how it felt to be in WWII, not just the statistics of the battle. I have only the highest respect for him. As I talked to Mr. ____ , I began to realize the fortune of my generation. We are sent to college for thousands of dollars, not sent overseas to defend our country's honor. At 21 we are completing a junior year of college, not a series of 28 bomb missions. Mr. ____ helped me to realize how lucky I am to be living in this time.

I had heard a lot of war stories and had seen many pictures and movies, but for the first time they actually became a reality to me... I felt guilty when I thought about the fact that I sometimes feel so stressed and pressured because of things like picking a college, keeping may grades up, or winning a softball game. Meanwhile, these young men, who were the same age as I am now, were faced everyday with the fact that they might not come back from that day's mission.

He told me that I know more about his experiences in the war than his children and grandchildren know. I feel very fortunate having had the opportunity to meet Mr.____ and produce a piece of work that would show how he feels about the time he served.

After sitting and contemplating the whole project, I really think it was a good thing. A sort of bridge, or bond between generations was formed.

I am so glad I went to the interview. I learned much more about the war from Mr. ____ than I could have from a textbook. I only wish that we had more time with the project.

I've gained so much by doing this project, both knowledge and compassion. While I listened to the tape of my interview, a lump formed in my throat and tears formed in my eyes. Never before had I realized what these men actually did for us. I've come to know a little bit about what they went through. I've gained so much compassion for the men that fought for our country. All we can do now is recognize what they did. We wouldn't be where we are today without them.

Butler Area Senior High School
Butler, Pennsylvania